FROM 1860 TO THE PRESENT DAY
THE WORLD'S GREAT
MACHINE GUNS

THE WORLD'S GREAT
MACHINE GUNS

ROGER FORD

CHARTWELL
BOOKS, INC.

This edition published in 2005 by

CHARTWELL BOOKS, INC.
A Division of
BOOK SALES, INC.
114 Northfield Avenue
Edison, New Jersey 08837

Copyright © 1999 Amber Books Ltd

ISBN-13: 978-0-7858-1986-8
ISBN-10: 0-7858-1986-X

Editorial and design by
Amber Books Ltd
Bradley's Close
74–77 White Lion Street
London N1 9PF
United Kingdom
www.amberbooks.co.uk

PICTURE CREDITS:
Robert Hunt Library: 21 (both), 26, 29, 30, 41, 47, 58-59, 67, 68, 72, 93
Salamander Picture Library: 17, 87 (bottom), 89, 91, 92, 104, 136 (top), 137
TRH Pictures: 6-7, 10, 12, 16, 18-19, 24, 32, 34, 38, 43, 46, 48-49, 51 (both),
53, 57, 60-61, 63, 64-65, 69, 70, 71, 75, 76, 79 (both), 80, 81, 83, 84, 87 (top),
96-97, 99, 100, 103, 105, 110, 112, 115, 119, 121, 122, 125, 126, 129, 130, 134,
136 (bottom), 138, 140, 142, 145 (both), 146-147, 148, 150, 151, 153, 154,
157 (both), 160-161, 162, 164, 166, 168, 169, 171, 173, 174

Artwork Credits
John Batchelor: 8, 9, 10, 11, 13, 14, 15, 20, 22, 23, 24-25, 26-27, 27, 28, 31,
34-35, 36, 36-37, 37, 38-39, 40-41, 42-43, 44-45, 45, 48-49, 50-51, 54-55 (both),
58-59, 66-67, 68, 69, 72, 73, 74-75, 76-77, 78-79, 82, 84-85, 86, 88-89, 90-91,
94-95, 98, 101, 102-103, 104, 106, 107, 109, 110-111, 114-115, 116-117, 117,
118-119, 120, 121, 122-123, 124-125, 125, 126, 127, 128-129, 130-131, 132, 133,
134, 137, 138-139, 140-141, 141, 142-143, 143, 144, 150-151, 152, 155, 156,
158-159, 160-161, 162-163, 164-165, 167, 170, 171, 172
De Agostini: 135, 148-149

Printed in Singapore

CONTENTS

CHAPTER 1
MANUALLY OPERATED MACHINE GUNS

The third quarter of the eighteenth century saw dramatic changes in the way firearms worked, yet in a sense, the technology was actually falling over itself in its haste to embody new inventions. Not a few wrong turns were taken as a result – not least among them the mechanical, hand-cranked machine guns.

Even before the gun had become a truly effective weapon of war, men had begun to look for ways to increase its potential for destruction. The most obvious means, it seemed, was to combine the essential parts of many guns – their barrels and the chambers which held projectile and charge – into one weapon. The result became known as battery guns and volley guns – since all the barrels were to be fired together – or organ guns, after their resemblance to the wind-powered musical instrument. Such guns were normally mounted on carriages, like miniature artillery pieces, though there were multi-barrelled muskets, too, notably the model produced for the Royal Navy by the innovative London gunsmith Henry Nock in the 1780s, and ultimately rejected as being both too expensive and too hard on the men expected to fire it, the recoil from seven barrels discharged simultaneously being fearsome.

The volley guns were slow to load, naturally, being charged from the muzzle one barrel at a time, and were thus only marginally effective after their first volley had been expended. They were normally employed from static defensive positions. Rather better, in fact, were

■LEFT: The Gatling Gun (Model 1886), in use by US Marines in Samoa in 1899, was to change the nature of warfare and become a symbol of devastating concentrated firepower.

ordinary field artillery pieces loaded with canister (nothing more sophisticated than cylindrical tin cans filled with musket balls, which were blown apart on firing); grape-shot (balls about the size of the fruit, loaded into a wooden framework which also disintegrated) or an exploding Shrapnel shell (named after the British Army officer Lieutenant-General Henry Shrapnel who came up with the idea), the fragments of which turned themselves into lethal projectiles; it could be recharged relatively speedily but achieved very much the same effect as the organ guns – at least in theory – and had the added advantage of being able to fire ordinary solid shot too.

BREECH-LOADING
Roughly halfway through the nineteenth century, the breech-loading rifle, its charge detonated by means of a hammer falling on a percussion cap containing the newly discovered and very volatile fulminate of mercury, rather than by setting fire to loose gunpowder in a pan by means of a spark struck by flint off steel, reached a point in its development where it was able, finally, to supersede the muzzle-loader. There had been breech-loaders developed earlier, of course, but they were either of questionable efficiency, or were too expensive to be widely adopted. Gunmakers and inventors soon began to suggest ways in which a repeating gun,

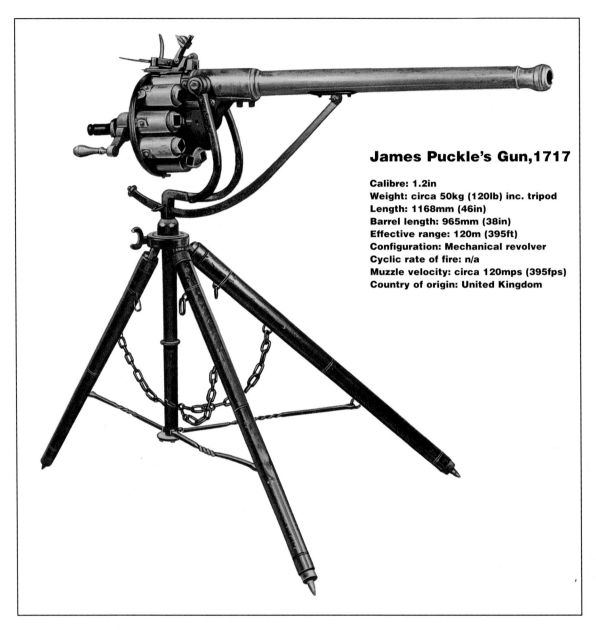

James Puckle's Gun, 1717

Calibre: 1.2in
Weight: circa 50kg (120lb) inc. tripod
Length: 1168mm (46in)
Barrel length: 965mm (38in)
Effective range: 120m (395ft)
Configuration: Mechanical revolver
Cyclic rate of fire: n/a
Muzzle velocity: circa 120mps (395fps)
Country of origin: United Kingdom

with one charge after another presented to the breech from some sort of hopper or magazine – either by turning a crank or rocking an actuating lever backwards and forwards – could be made to operate. By this time there was no lack of expertise in the design and manufacture of mechanisms adequately precise for this purpose – seed drills were a good example – but the innovators were to be let down by a factor outside their control: the basic deficiency of contemporary ammunition. Thus, the mechanical

machine gun was a notion somewhat ahead of its time, though only by (at most) a decade, as we shall see.

THE UNITARY CARTRIDGE

The first unitary cartridges designed for breech-loading had actually been produced a half-century earlier by the Swiss, Samuel Johannes Pauly (or Pauli), who worked in Paris. In fact, Pauly's chief interest was in improving the breech-loader itself, but in order to do that, he realised, he first had to devise a

means of containing projectile, charge and detonator in one package. In 1810 or 1811 he produced a cartridge with a rimmed base of soft metal with a body of paper, like shotgun shells were until the 1960s, when plastic replaced cardboard. Priming was primitive for, the percussion cap proper not yet having been invented, the only method available was to place a small amount of very sensitive fulminate in an open pan in the head of the cartridge. In order to make sure the priming stayed in place, Pauly was forced

Gatling Model 1868

Calibre: .5in
Weight: 64kg (140lb)
Length: 1220mm (48in)
Barrel length 626mm (26in)
Effective range: 400m (1320ft)

Configuration: Mechanical multi-barrel revolver
Cyclic rate of fire: Circa 300rpm
Muzzle velocity: 400mps (1320fps)
Country of Origin: United States

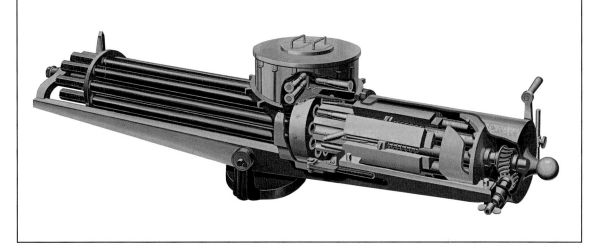

to utilise a flush-standing breech, pierced to take a spring-loaded firing pin, and the hammer-like extensions seen on his guns are in fact just cocks for concealed strikers. Pauly employed a young Prussian gun-lock maker, Johann Nikolaus von Dreyse, to make the guns he designed; employee was to go on to become rather better known than master, thanks to his bolt-action needle gun, which enabled the Prussians to beat the French very decisively in the war of 1870–1. Curiously, the fact that the brass heads of the cartridges expanded when the charge was detonated, to form a gas-tight seal at the breech – which was probably the most important aspect of his work – seems to have gone unremarked for many years, and the problems of achieving an efficient seal (or obturation, as it is properly known) were to hinder the development of the breech-loader as a result.

Later, Louis Flobert in France and then Daniel Wesson in the USA improved on Pauly's basic design – at least marginally – by enclosing the primer in the cartridge's rim. The rim-fire cartridge had a basic defect, however: its material strength. In order for the blow from the hammer to be able to detonate the primer, the case of the cartridge had to be

both thin and soft; in larger calibres the heavy charge necessary to propel the projectile often then proved sufficient to split the case. In addition, it was difficult to ensure the even distribution of primer around the cartridge's rim, and this often resulted in misfires, while the relatively high proportion of primer-to-propellant that was necessary frequently caused the rim to split and even to separate from the case proper, which normally rendered the weapon unusable without the attention of an armourer.

BOXER AND BERDAN

In the end, there were to be many false starts made and not a few false paths followed before the reloadable cartridge with a replaceable primer became a practical reality, even though all the components of a successful design, and all the workshop techniques to realise it, were available as early as 1840, or even before. Noting the contributions made by George Morse, who constructed tubular brass cartridges with wire 'anvils', against which percussion caps could be detonated, the annular gap left when the cap was fitted being filled with a rubber retaining ring, we can pass on to the work of the two men, both military officers, one British and the other

American: Colonel Edward Mounier Boxer of the Royal Laboratory at Woolwich, and Colonel Hiram Berdan, late of the elite Sharpshooters Regiment of the Union Army. It was these two – with considerable help from assistant technicians, who no doubt contributed much to the development process while actually doing the work involved in manufacturing prototypes, since neither Boxer nor Berdan was an engineer or gunsmith – who designed and produced the first truly effective reloadable centre-fire cartridges with set-in primers, Boxer in 1866 and Berdan two years later.

In practice, Boxer's cartridges (which were made up of coiled brass walls, a drawn brass head cup drilled to take the primer, and a separate anvil to strike it on, and a perforated iron disk – nothing more than a washer, really – which served as the extraction and seating rim) proved to be less than perfect under the rigours of active service. On firing, the cases often swelled and jammed in the chamber, and the iron rim was all too easily torn off by the extractor claw. They were assembled by hand, and inevitably, faults in the process meant misfires; annoying on the firing range, this was life-threatening in battle, as the British Tommy all too often found out to his cost.

Gatling Model 1878

Calibre: .45in Gatling-Gardner
Weight: 34kg (75lb)
Length: 965mm (38in)
Barrel length: 610mm (24in)
Effective range: 500m (1640ft)

Configuration: Mechanical multi-
barrel revolver
Cyclic rate of fire: Circa 300rpm
Muzzle velocity: 400mps (1310fps)
Country of Origin: United States

It is important to realise that in order for it to function properly, the cartridge had to be an accurately dimensioned component of the gun itself, albeit a disposable one. Thus, until such time as production engineering had reached a stage where accurate repetitive machining of components had become commonplace, there was really no way that satisfactory cartridges could ever have been produced.

Berdan's major contributions were to see that the anvil for the primer could be formed as part of the case itself, and that cases could be drawn from the solid and then machined to fit precisely, thus avoiding the major problems which beset Boxer's early ammunition. Surprisingly, Berdan didn't take the obvious next step and patent the design for a primer to fit his cartridge cases; that was left to A.C. Hobbs of the Union Metallic Cartridge Co. in 1869. In Europe, Werder in Bavaria (and somewhat later the Mauser brothers in Germany) also began to devise unitary cartridges on the

■**BELOW: Machine-gun teams of the British Army during the Second Afghan War, 1878-80. Their .45in-calibre Gatling guns are fitted with Broadwell drum magazines.**

Boxer/Berdan model, and within just a few years it became clear that a *de facto* standard had evolved.

At this stage, all cartridges were rimmed or flanged, the rim rather than the form of the cartridge and projectile locating the round in the breech. This continued to be convenient while single-shot weapons were the norm; later it became a liability. If rimmed rounds are wrongly packed into a box magazine, with the rim of the first round behind that of the second, they won't feed; rimmed rounds loaded into a belt (usually) have to be withdrawn to the rear before they can be chambered. The answer to both these problems was the rimless round, the neck of the cartridge case (which of course was of slightly greater diameter than the projectile it contained) and its overall length determining its accurate seating within the chamber, with all that entailed for headspacing and extraction. However, it was some years before this was suggested, by the Swiss, Rubin. The introduction of the rimless round would be very important to the future development of machine guns – more so, in fact, as we shall see in due course, than it was to that of rifles and pistols. However, for the moment, the rimmed, centre-fire Boxer/Berdan cartridge represented a very significant step forward indeed.

THE FIRST MECHANICAL GUNS
There were many varieties of mechanical machine gun developed during the early 1860s; the best – though the term is relative – was probably the Ager or Alger, which first saw action with the Union Army at the battle of Fair Oaks (Seven Pines, to the southerners) on the last day of May 1862, during the American Civil War. In all, the US Army bought something over sixty Ager 'coffee mill' guns (described by salesman J.D. Mills as 'an army in six square feet'). They were single-barrel 'revolvers', fed by gravity from a vertical hopper to a cylinder composed of chambers which were actually troughs arranged around a central spindle. The cartridge – charge and projectile, only – was loaded into a hollow steel tube, which was pierced at its head and fitted with a percussion cap. This disposable chamber – for that is what it was, in effect – was allowed to fall from the hopper into a trough at the nine o'clock position and carried round to twelve o'clock, where it was locked in

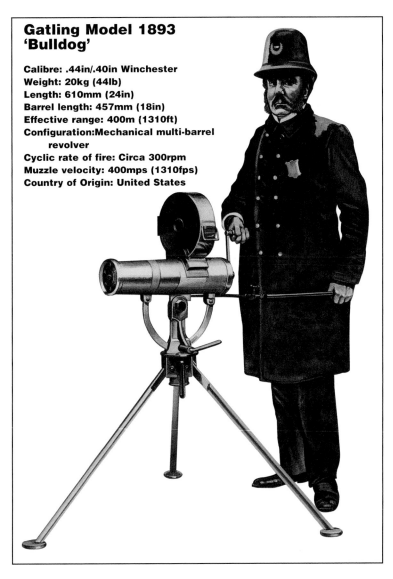

Gatling Model 1893 'Bulldog'

Calibre: .44in/.40in Winchester
Weight: 20kg (44lb)
Length: 610mm (24in)
Barrel length: 457mm (18in)
Effective range: 400m (1310ft)
Configuration:Mechanical multi-barrel revolver
Cyclic rate of fire: Circa 300rpm
Muzzle velocity: 400mps (1310fps)
Country of Origin: United States

alignment with the barrel and fired. Further rotation ejected (or more accurately, spilled out) the now-empty cartridge holder, which was later reloaded and reprimed.

The Ager had its weaknesses – precise enough alignment of the cartridge carrier with the bore of the barrel was chief among them – and the other first-generation mechanical machine guns were even less reliable. None managed more than a short burst, a few rounds at best, before deformation – which was almost their defining characteristic – led to a jam. It was not until the best-known of the mechanical machine gun pioneers, Richard Jordan Gatling, turned to the

metallic unitary cartridge that a significant improvement in performance came about, and then it was to be accompanied by a major variation in operational technique.

ENTER DR GATLING
Gatling was a professional inventor with a string of successes to his credit, chiefly in the field of agriculture, who later qualified as a doctor of medicine. He was originally from Carolina but long settled in Indiana. There is nothing to show that he ever practised medicine, and his main interest lay in mechanical devices; by 1861, when the outbreak of the war between the states prompted him to turn

his attention to the machine gun, he had already made a small fortune out of his successful horse-drawn seed drill. His first attempt at developing a gun was much like Ager's in concept – a single-barrelled revolver, employing cartridge carriers – and may well have been nothing more than a modified copy. Gatling experienced the same sort of frustrating difficulties as his contemporary, and for just the same reasons. Considering the matter further, he concluded that only unitary metallic cartridges were likely to prove satisfactory, like those then being produced by Wesson and others, loaded into the gun by means of a modification of the sort of bolt action used in rifles such as the Spencer and the Henry, in which it was actuated by an under-lever and locked in place by a toggling action, rather than being turned to engage a lug. However, he was unable to see how to make the process work at a rate of fire appreciably greater than that which a skilled rifleman could achieve.

The solution he adopted was to employ a multitude of barrels, each with its own chamber, arranged and rotating axially around a central rod, in a fashion similar to the 'pepperpot' pistols which were still in occasional use, a method which also removed the problem of aligning chamber with barrel. Another of Ager and Gatling's contemporaries, Ezra Ripley, had already produced a volley gun which used this principle. Gatling's contribution was to show how such an arrangement of barrels could be fed with fresh ammunition from a hopper or magazine. The chamber was reloaded while it was away from the firing mechanism and then rotated into alignment with it. The loading and firing process was controlled by the profile of a simple fixed cam, against which the assemblage of barrels, chambers and spring-loaded bolts was rotated; the fresh cartridge dropped into the open breech at the twelve o'clock position was progressively driven forward into the empty chamber during the rotation downwards towards the six o'clock position, where it was fired and was then extracted, and ejected on its way back up again. The 'operator' merely turned a handle to actuate the machinery while his helpers kept the hopper magazine topped up with ammunition. Gatling was awarded US Patent No. 36,836 in November 1862 for this device. As he said in 1865 (and he was actually understating the case by that time): 'The gun can be discharged at the rate of two hundred shots per minute and it bears the same relation to other firearms that McCormack's Reaper does to the sickle or the sewing machine does to the common needle. A few men with it can perform the work of a regiment.'

GATLING'S BREAKTHROUGH

There was considerable interest shown in his invention, but no sales resulted until early in 1864, when General Benjamin F. Butler of Baltimore, Maryland, ordered 12 guns in .58in calibre (with tapered bores) along with 1000 rounds of ammunition for each one, at a total cost of $12,000. Both guns and ammunition were to be manufactured by McWhinney, Rindge & Company of Cincinnati, Ohio, the firm Gatling had enlisted as his partner. Butler used the guns at the siege of Petersburg, Virginia, in June 1864, with considerable success. However, even that practical trial failed to generate steady sales, perhaps because of the hefty price tag but more probably due to the

■LEFT: By 1878, the Gatling Gun had started to gain acceptance, as this cover illustration from the prestigious *Scientific American* magazine shows.

Martigny *Mitrailleuse*

Calibre: 11mm Chassepot
Weight: 140kg (308lb)
Length: 1370mm (54in)
Barrel length: 1050mm (41.3in)
Effective range: 400m (1310ft)
Configuration: Volley gun
Cyclic rate of fire: n/a
Muzzle velocity: 410mps (1345fps)
Country of Origin: France

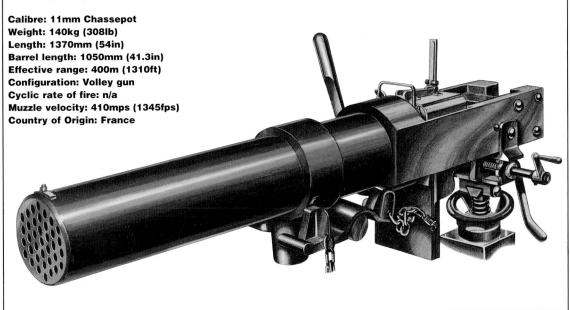

implacable resistance of the Chief of the Ordnance of the US Army, Colonel J.W. Ripley. It was to be two years more before the Gatling gun was officially accepted (though by then the US Navy had already acquired some), and by that time Gatling had refined the design considerably, and had succeeded in increasing the cyclic rate to a steady 300 rounds per minute (rpm) and regularly achieved twice that in his own trials.

The Model 1865, as the modified gun was known, was first made in 1in calibre, with six barrels, and fired either solid projectiles or shells containing 15 .25in balls. In 1866 the US Army ordered 50 such guns together with a further 50 chambered for the .5in round which Colonel S.V. Bénét, (a name which will crop up again later in our narrative; Bénét was to go on to become Chief of the Ordnance, his son a leading figure at Hotchkiss, qv), had developed at the Frankford Arsenal, this time with 10 barrels. By now, Gatling had severed his connection with McWhinney, Rindge & Company, which was an artisan workshop, unsuited to the sort of precision repetition machining necessary to produce the gun, and turned to James Cooper, who was also based in Frankford, a move which was to result in a considerable improvement in the product.

Cooper, however, didn't have the capacity to produce the guns for the army in the time available, and the order went instead to The Colt Patent Fire Arms Manufacturing Company, by then established for almost a quarter-century in a purpose-built factory in Hartford, Connecticut, where all the most modern industrial working practices were employed, and not a few of them developed. Colt's was to produce Gatling guns and spare parts for the US military until 1911, by which time they had been superseded by the true (that is, self-powered) machine gun as defined by Maxim and developed by him and others. Gatling continued to develop his own gun; he was to produce a variety of other models, including the shortened 'Bulldog' version, the Model 1893, with 18 inch long barrels, powered by an electric motor instead of being cranked by hand (a development to which we will return in time) and even one which can be considered a true machine gun since it was powered by propellant gas bled off from a vent in each barrel.

THE GATLING'S PERFORMANCE

Just how effective was the Gatling gun? There are two measures to be taken. Firstly, how accurate was it, and what sort of cyclic rate of fire could it achieve?

And secondly, how reliable was it? Let us examine that second factor first. At that time (that is, during the 1870s), when the world's major military powers were first becoming aware of the new weapon's possibilities, there was an unofficial and quite unorchestrated campaign in full swing against it, mounted by a disparate group of senior military men from many different countries who were united in one regard: their hatred for a machine which they believed threatened, in two senses, the very existence of the soldiery as they knew it. This campaign was still in full swing as late as the onset of World War I, by which time, as we shall see, there was no room whatsoever left to doubt the machine gun's capabilities; ironically, by wilfully failing to recognise the potential of the machine gun it was probably responsible, at least in part, for the deaths of millions of men. This group never failed to talk down the Gatling at every opportunity, stressing its vulnerability to jams and misfeeds, and describing the dreadful effects of such failures on soldiers who placed their faith in it rather than in their own skill at arms: 'The sand of the desert is sodden red, / Red with the blood of a square that broke, / The Gatling's jammed and the Colonel dead / And the regiment blind with the dust and smoke', as the poet Sir

Hotchkiss Gun

Calibre: 1.5in
Weight: 124kg (273lb) (gun only)
Length: 1370mm (54in)
Barrel length: 710mm (28in)
Effective range: 400m (1310ft)
Configuration: Mechanical multi-
 barrel revolver
Cyclic rate of fire: Circa 60rpm
Muzzle velocity: 400mps (1310fps)
Country of Origin: United States

Henry Newbolt wrote, after just such an incident occurred during the Hazara campaign of 1890. There were indeed considerable grounds for this fear, as the gun *was* susceptible to a serious jam if a spent (or misfired) cartridge case failed to eject – as a result of the case splitting and tearing, for example – and a fresh round was then forced into the (still occupied) chamber (a circumstance over which the 'operator' would have had no control at all, particularly in the heat of battle, since it was something of which he would have had no warning). Hiram

Maxim was later to use this failing to prove the superiority of his self-loading gun over the hand-cranked machine gun, pointing out that in his gun, a round not firing normally would immediately cause a stoppage, since it would not supply the energy necessary to cycle the action, and would thus not result in a jam requiring the attention of an armourer.

A CONCLUSIVE TRIAL

Reliability apart, the Gatling soon proved very effective indeed. The problem cited above was the only serious flaw the

Gatling had; and though it was an error of principle, it was actually directly related to the quality of the ammunition available, and became less of a problem as time went on and cartridges became more reliable. In a trial conducted by the US Army in October 1873, at Fort Monroe, Virginia a .42in calibre Gatling gun was compared with a 12-pounder breech-loading bronze field gun firing time-fused spherical case shot (shrapnel shell), each round containing 82 .69in lead musket balls, and an 8in siege howitzer firing similar shot, this time containing 486 musket balls. The three guns fired at a canvas target approximately 3m (9ft) high by 15m (48ft) wide, at ranges of 460m (500yds) and 730m (800yds) and each was in action for one and a half minutes at a time. At 460m (500yds), the Gatling gun got off 600 rounds, and hit the target 557 times. The 12-pounder 'Napoleon' fired seven times – and therefore launched a total of 574 musket balls – and scored 55 hits. The siege gun fired four rounds – a total of 1944 balls – and scored 112 hits. Then the guns moved out to 730m (800yds), and repeated their exercise. This time, the Gatling gun scored 534 hits, the Napoleon 35, and the siege howitzer none at all.

However, not all trials were as conclusive as this; an *ad hoc* affair staged in Gibraltar pitted a Gatling of the Royal Navy against a team of 18 riflemen from a British infantry regiment; it is reported that while the Gatling got off more rounds in a given time, the riflemen scored more hits – and they were armed with relatively slow-to-fire Martini-Henry rifles with falling block actions, which had to be reloaded manually with each shot. One hundred Prussian infantrymen couldn't outshoot a Gatling gun at 800m (875yds) at Karlsruhe in 1869; they fired 721 rounds in a minute, and hit a 1.8m (6ft) by 22m (72ft) target 196 times, while the Gatling gun fired 246 times and scored 216 hits.

GATLING TRIUMPHANT
At that same Fort Monroe trial, a gun – equipped with the gravity-feed drum magazine developed by another failed machine gun pioneer, James G. Accles – fired 100,000 rounds over a three-day period; it is clear that the Gatling's reliability had been much improved, largely, one suspects, as a result of the adoption of the Berdan solid-drawn centre-fire cartridges having been adopted. The Accles drum, which had its axis horizontal, parallel with that of the barrels, was later joined by a larger, 400-round capacity version produced by Broadwell, a series of vertical hoppers set around a central shaft, which turned sequentially as each one emptied. The latter became standard equipment in the British Army and Navy, while the double-track 'stick' hopper devised by L.F. Bruce early on in the gun's development remained popular in the USA.

Within five years, Gatling's gun had become widely accepted. He had sold

large quantities to the US Army and Navy, to those of Great Britain (made under licence by Armstrongs), to the armies of Imperial Russia (where it was also produced, in the Tula Arsenal), and to Japan, Turkey and Spain. Prussia considered the gun and rejected it; Austria showed little interest, producing a mechanical machine gun of its own, which was only marginally effective at best, though a private firm in Vienna purchased a manufacturing licence from Gatling, and did well with it. Even before

1864, Gatling himself had driven the French from his door by refusing to supply a single gun for evaluation, offering instead to fill a minimum order for 100, presumably at the same inflated price he had supplied Butler and the government – which had a well-defined and very urgent need for new, up-to-date weaponry, given that war with Prussia already looked inevitable – took this proposal as an insult. Instead they developed further a design for an updated version of the already archaic volley gun,

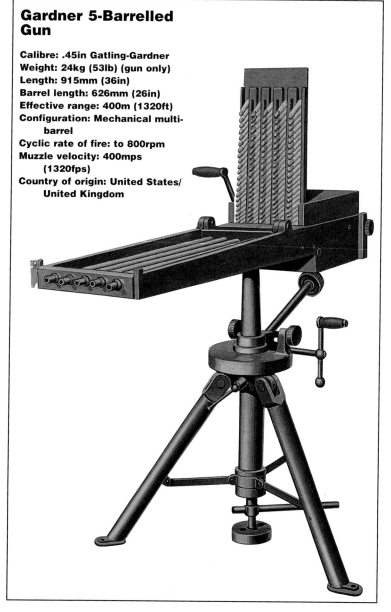

Gardner 5-Barrelled Gun

Calibre: .45in Gatling-Gardner
Weight: 24kg (53lb) (gun only)
Length: 915mm (36in)
Barrel length: 626mm (26in)
Effective range: 400m (1320ft)
Configuration: Mechanical multi-barrel
Cyclic rate of fire: to 800rpm
Muzzle velocity: 400mps (1320fps)
Country of origin: United States/ United Kingdom

submitted to them a decade earlier by a
Belgian infantry officer, Captain T.H.J.
Fafschamps, who called his gun the
mitrailleuse, a word derived from the
French for grape-shot (perhaps telling us
something about the way in which he
envisaged it being employed).
Modification was entrusted to
Fafschamps' collaborator, an engineer
named Joseph Montigny, and it is by his
name that the resultant gun was known.

THE MONTIGNY *MITRAILLEUSE*
Even from quite close up, the Montigny
Mitrailleuse looked like a field artillery
piece; its 37 rifle-calibre barrels were
enclosed in a tube, and it was mounted
on an artillery carriage and loaded in a
single action by means of a plate
cartridge holder which located a cartridge
in each barrel. The plate itself was
located vertically in a slide transported
backwards and forwards by the action of
a side lever, the return (ie, forward)
stroke cocking the action by holding off
an array of firing pins. All barrels were

fired simultaneously in the first version,
which went into service in 1867, and a
trained crew could get off perhaps 12
volleys in 60 seconds – a notional rate of
fire of something over 400rpm, rather
superior to that achieved by the Gatlings
of that time. Its unwieldiness (a gun on
its carriage weighed close to 3.048 tonnes
(three tons) and required a team of six
horses), combined with the French High
Command's insistence that it be
employed as an artillery piece, ensured
that it was never popular with troops. A
version modified by de Reffye came into
service in 1870, just in time for France's
disastrous war against Prussia; the most
significant improvement allowed the
gunner to fire the barrels sequentially,
the rate controlled by cranking a rear-
mounted handle; de Reffye also ordered
the guns reworked to accept the same
ammunition as the standard infantry
rifle, the Chassepot, and replaced the
loading lever with a more robust worm
screw. The guns in use in 1870 were
known as the de Reffye *Mitrailleuses* in
consequence. Where they were used
creatively – at the battle of Gravelotte, on
18 August 1870, for example – the
Mitrailleuses were effective, but in
general they were not. They proved
themselves in the popular rising which

followed the war, when they were turned
on insurgents in the streets of Paris, with
devastating effect, thanks to the most
important streets being wide, straight
thoroughfares and excellent fields of fire,
just as the far-sighted Baron Haussmann
had intended when he laid them out
during the rebuilding of the city after the
revolution of 1848. By the time of the
Franco-Prussian War, the unitary brass
cartridge had been perfected (though one
would not have known it in that conflict;
one side used Dreyse needle-guns, the
other the essentially similar Chassepot,
both of which used 'soft' cartridges), and
thus the problems of feeding ammunition
at speed into the breech had been
eliminated in the most satisfactory way.
Gatling had a large share (but not a
monopoly) of what was still a small
market, despite his pricing policy – guns
that Colt's made for him for around $700
he sold for over twice that. Others, such
as Claxton, were making essentially
similar weapons (and Claxton had even
sold some to the French) but more
importantly, other newcomers were
turning their attention to the field.

THREE NEW DESIGNS
In 1871, Benjamin Berkeley Hotchkiss of
Watertown, Connecticut, showed off a

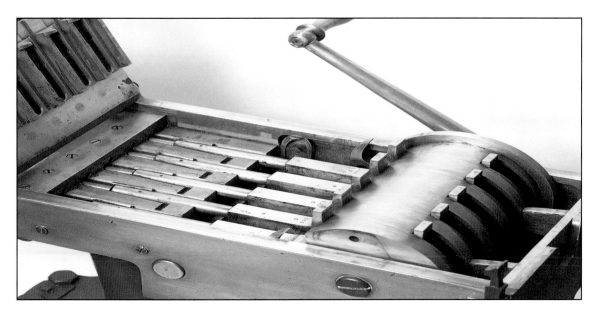

■ABOVE: A five-barrel Gardner gun of
circa 1880. More reliable than the
Gatling, and both simpler and lighter
than the Nordenfelt, it was more
popular with the British in particular.

five-barrelled revolver cannon in 1.5in
calibre, which was designed to fire
explosive shells at a relatively slow cyclic
rate – not much over one per second.
Described as a copy of the smaller
Gatling, in fact its operating principle
was subtly different; it fed rounds of
ammunition to a single breech and
thence into the chamber of the barrel
adjacent to it. Hotchkiss found that his
gun was considerably more popular in
Europe than in his native United States
(Armstrongs, for example, bought a
licence to produce it for the Royal Navy),
and soon emigrated to France. The
company he founded there, which later
employed Laurence Bénét as its chief
engineer/designer, was to become a major
force in machine gun manufacture, and
the only one successfully to make the
transition from producing mechanical,
hand-cranked guns to manufacturing
true machine guns.

Also in 1871, a Swedish engineer
named Helge Palmcrantz demonstrated a
manually operated machine gun which
was a cross between the Gatling and the
Montigny *Mitrailleuse*; it had a
horizontal array of barrels to which
rounds were fed from a vertical hopper,
the breeches being opened, the spent case
ejected and a fresh round chambered and
fired by the reciprocating action of a
lever. This may sound somewhat
laborious, but a system of gears ensured
a mechanical advantage which translated
into an acceptable cyclic rate of fire. The
invention was taken up by another

Swede, the financier, Thorsten
Nordenfelt, who coupled his name with
that of the designer, and then
eliminated the latter as soon as the
gun had been perfected. The Nordenfelt
gun, as it thus became known, was
taken up with enthusiasm by the
British Navy amongst others, and
employed, alongside the Hotchkiss, the
Gatling and the Gardner (see below) to
defend against the new-fangled high-
speed torpedo-boats which had
appeared to threaten the
invulnerability of the capital ship. It
was produced in many different
configurations and calibres and had
between two and 10 barrels but the
most common were in 1in calibre,
firing solid steel projectiles weighing
207g (7oz) and .45in calibre, employing
the cartridge developed for the British
Gatlings. The latter round was also
specified for the similar but rather
simpler multi-barrelled gun William
Gardner of Toledo, Ohio designed in
1874. The Gardner gun was lighter
than its rivals, particularly in the two-
barrelled version the British Army
preferred, and weighed just 45kg.
(100lb), including its tripod, and was
hence much easier to transport. It was
no less deadly, however – a twin-
barrelled gun tested at the Washington
Navy Yard in 1879 fired 10,000 rounds
in 27.5 minutes, and a 5-barrelled
version achieved a cyclic rate of 812
rounds per minute (rpm) when tested
by the Royal Navy.

A SHORT-LIVED SUCCESS

By the end of the 1870s, the manual
machine gun, as defined by Gatling,
Hotchkiss, Nordenfelt and Gardner, had
become a regular and important item in
the armoury of virtually every 'civilised'
nation on Earth. It had changed the
nature of land warfare – though by no
means as radically as is sometimes
suggested; the guns were not light,
mobile or handy enough for that; but they
had stimulated both thought and
discussion. Its day was not yet over, and
even at the end of the nineteenth century,
and the start of the twentieth, it was still
to be found on the battlefield, but by
1884, it had been rendered technically
obsolete by the invention of 'a quiet,
scientific gentleman, living in Kent' –
Hiram Stevens Maxim. The principle
Richard Gatling employed in his gun was
to be revived briefly during World War I,
when externally powered machine guns
were suggested as a means of overcoming
the problems associated with firing
through the arc of an aircraft's propeller
and again in the 1960s, as a means of
increasing the cyclic rate of fire of an
aircraft's guns. This time the suggestion
was taken much more seriously, and a
new genre of weapon was developed as a
result, as we shall see in Chapter Five.

CHAPTER 2
TRUE AUTOMATIC WEAPONS

The machine gun can perhaps be said to have been the first great American invention, though Whitney's cotton gin and McCormick's reaper-and-binder have their supporters; three out of the four effective manual repeater guns were conceived there, and most of the important first-generation automatic guns were also the work of Americans.

All the important pioneers found their real fame in Europe, however. Both William Gardner and Benjamin Hotchkiss left their native land to move there, and were followed later by Hiram Stevens Maxim, Laurence Bénét, John Moses Browning and Isaac Newton Lewis. Maxim was by far the most important of these, if only by virtue of primacy, though Browning was indisputably the more talented gunmaker; Bénét was to become a most important force in France as Hotchkiss's protégé and successor, while Lewis only ever had the one design to his credit (and that, in fact, was actually conceived by someone else, as we will see when we come to examine it).

Hiram Maxim was a man of many parts; born in Maine in 1840, he worked as a boy at his father's watermill which, as well as grinding corn, provided motive power for a machine shop where he learned how to work in both wood and metal, later perfecting his skills as an apprentice carriagemaker with a local firm. In his autobiography, *My Life*, he maintained that he first started thinking about machine guns at the age of 14,

■LEFT: Simple, but horribly effective. The air-cooled, belt-fed machine gun as perfected by John Browning just after World War I, and unchanged in over 80 years.

when his father Isaac described to him an idea he had had for a lever-operated, belt-fed single-barrelled repeating gun, and asked him to make both drawings and a model of the new weapon. He did so, and showed them to a gunmaker in nearby Bangor, who said he believed that the gun would work, but that he himself did not have the tools necessary to make it. An uncle who owned a small engineering works in Massachusetts, whose opinion was also sought, was rather more blunt; he said it would cost $100 to make and the result would not be worth 100 cents. Maxim's interest waned, and was then apparently rekindled briefly some 12 years later, in Savannah, Georgia, when he was introduced to a group of men at target practice with Springfield rifles, and was invited to try his hand. He was able to shoot quite as well as the best of them, he tells us modestly, though he was surprised to find that the rifle gave him a very powerful kick. From this he derived the inspiration for a repeating gun actuated by the energy of its own recoil.

It's tempting to suggest that Maxim made up the story – it seems extremely unlikely that a young man of 26 who had grown up in the USA of that period had never fired a shot before, or if he had not, that he could instinctively shoot as well as a group of Civil War veterans – but it is clear that he did, at some point or other, conceive the notion of harnessing

Maxim Gun

Calibre: .303in
Weight: 18.2kg (40lb) (gun only)
Length: 1180mm (46.5in)
Barrel length: 720mm (28.25in)
Effective range: 2000m (6600ft) +

**Configuration: belt-fed, recoil-
    operated, water-cooled**
Cyclic rate of fire: circa 600rpm
Muzzle velocity: 600mps (1970fps)
Country of Origin: United Kingdom

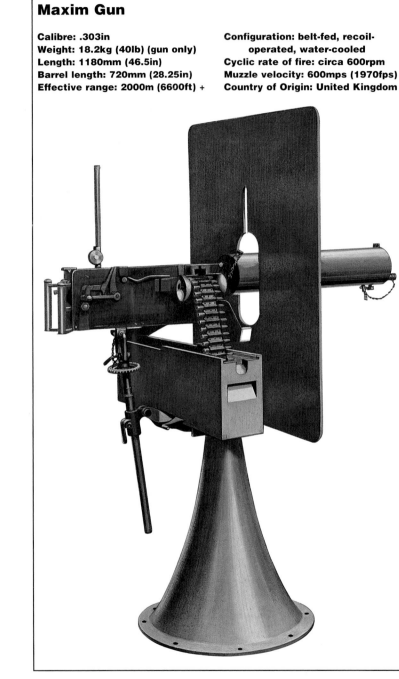

generation and the regulation of electric current to his credit. In fact, his success in rivalling the paragon Thomas Alva Edison so disturbed Edison's backers that they approached Maxim with an almost incredible offer: he was to go to Europe for a period of 10 years on behalf of the United States Electric Lighting Company, at a salary of $20,000 a year (a very substantial sum indeed), to 'report on new European developments in the field' but under no circumstances to make any new electrical inventions himself. Maxim accepted.

A CHANGE OF DIRECTION

The inspiration to switch to the design of firearms came, Maxim later said in an article in the London *Times*, from a conversation with an American acquaintance in Vienna in 1882: ' "Hang your chemistry and electricity", he was told. "If you want to make a pile of money invent something which will enable these Europeans to cut each others' throats with greater facility!" '

Presumably this prompted Maxim to resurrect the idea he had had in 1866 for a recoil-operated repeating gun, for by the time he settled in London in 1883 he had already produced a drawing for a magazine-fed automatic rifle reloaded by recoil action. Well aware of the necessity of a patent, Maxim soon submitted an application for an invention 'designed to utilise the kick or recoil of the rifle, or other arm, for operating the breech-loading mechanism, and constructed in such a manner that when the arm is discharged, the recoil stores up sufficient energy in a spring or springs to operate the mechanism for extracting the exploded cartridge shells, for cocking the arm, for transferring the cartridges from the magazine to the rear of the barrel, forcing them into the barrel and closing the breech'. He took care to cover a wide range of other possibilities, too, in the three-page document which formed the basis for British Patent No. 3178, dated 26 June 1883.

THE MACHINE GUN'S WORKINGS

Before examining the development of Maxim's gun, it would be as well to consider the various ways in which a gun can be made to cycle its own action using the 'waste' energy produced by firing a round. Two methods use the recoil directly; the others make a secondary use of the gases which propel the projectile to the target, either directly or indirectly.

the physical energy of a gun's recoil to eject the spent cartridge, feed a new one, close the breech, cock the action and release the firing pin, continuing through that cycle for as long as the trigger was depressed and the ammunition held out.

It was to be almost two decades before Maxim put the idea into practice, and in the meantime he had become very successful indeed, with an illustrious career as an inventor, with important patents in the field of electricity

■RIGHT: A Maxim gun, manufactured there as the Tikkakoski Model 09-32, in Finnish Army service during the Winter War of 1939–40, which was fought against the Soviet Union.

THE SHORT RECOIL SYSTEM

In the short recoil system (the one Maxim adopted), the gun's barrel and breech block move back together over a short distance (usually less – sometimes much less – than 2.5cm (1in)) before they are unlocked and separate. The momentary delay before the breech is opened allows the residual pressure in the chamber to drop to a point where it is safe to open the breech without danger of rupturing the cartridge case. At this point the barrel's rearward passage is arrested, but the breech-block is unlocked from it and continues on its way, the extractor ensuring that the spent cartridge case goes with it and is expelled. The breech-block's motion compresses a spring, which reverses its travel as soon as the point of equilibrium is reached, cocking the firing mechanism, collecting a fresh cartridge from the magazine or belt and ramming it into the chamber on the way back to the firing position, where it is

relocked to the barrel. We mentioned earlier a certain difficulty with rimmed cartridge cases loaded into belts; it is this: it is necessary to extract the entire round from the belt on the rearward

■BELOW: Two soldiers of the Cameron Highlanders with a British Maxim on a Mark 2 tripod, probably in 1914. The belt is actually loaded with blank ammunition.

Maxim 'Pom-pom'

Calibre: 37mm
Weight: 186kg (410lb) (gun only)
Length: 2130mm (84in) (gun only)
Barrel length: 876mm (34.5in)
Effective range: 1000m (3300ft) +
Configuration: belt-fed, recoil-
**   operated, water-cooled**
Cyclic rate of fire: Circa 200rpm
Muzzle velocity: 850mps (230fps)
Country of Origin: United Kingdom

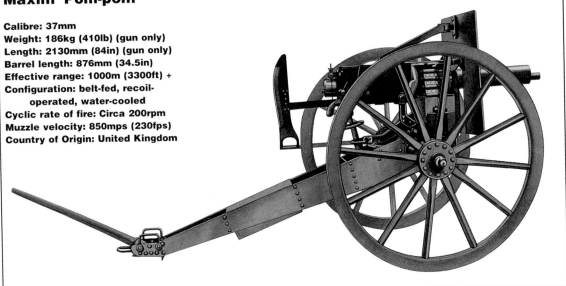

stroke because it cannot be pushed through the loop. Thus the travel of the breech-block must be marginally greater than twice the length of a round of ammunition. Rimless rounds are usually linked together by what are effectively spring clips, into what are known as disintegrating belts; they can be pushed forward directly, and that same action separates the belt into its component links, so that the entire operation is simpler.

THE LONG RECOIL SYSTEM

The long recoil system differs in that the barrel and breech-block assembly are driven back together rather further than the entire length of a round of ammunition. A return spring then drives the barrel back into the firing position, while an extractor on the face of the breech-block grips the empty case, which is ejected as soon as it is free. The subsequent forward action of the breech-block then strips off a fresh round and drives it into the chamber, cocking the action and then, if the trigger is still depressed, firing the next round, and so on while the ammunition supply lasts.

GAS ACTUATED SYSTEMS

The simplest of the mechanisms for gas actuation is known as the blowback system; the breech-block is held closed by the action of a spring alone, with no

locking lugs or toggles. On detonation of the cartridge, the breech stays closed until the pressure in the chamber overcomes the breech-block mass, at which point it flies backwards and cycles the action in exactly the same way as a recoil-powered gun. Clearly, this is a simpler solution, in mechanical terms, than the recoil-action gun, and is thus both cheaper and easier to manufacture and maintain. There have been more-or-less successful attempts to delay or retard the blowback system, the simplest of which relies on the breech-block having to overcome an artificially introduced mechanical disadvantage before it is free to start its cycle. Very few rifle-calibre machine guns have ever been constructed along these lines, and those that have, have been less than completely successful, for the energy their ammunition delivers is simply too great to be controllable in this way, but most sub-machine guns or machine pistols, which employ pistol ammunition, are so actuated. More commonly, rifle-calibre machine guns are actuated indirectly, by propellant gas tapped off the barrel at a point close to the muzzle, which then acts on the face of a piston in a cylinder which in turn acts on the breech-block or bolt (we use those terms interchangeably), driving the assembly towards the rear and unlocking and then cycling the action in the process. In this case, the quantity

of gas employed can be precisely regulated – by limiting the size of the hole which taps into the barrel, or controlling the length of time during which it can impinge upon the piston – and the force applied thus controlled.

MAXIM'S LOCK AND ACTION

Maxim's system relied on a toggle – a pair of pivoted levers with one arm longer than the other, hinged together so that they could work only in one sense, like the human knee joint – to lock the breech-block and barrel together. After the short backwards movement of barrel and breech-block together, this toggle was 'broken' downwards by its passage over a shallow camming surface in the upper plate of the receiver, and from that point on the block continued to the rear on its own against the tension of a side-mounted coiled spring called the fusee, which pulled the assembly back during the return stroke, resetting the toggle and relocating the barrel and breech-block in battery in the process.

The action actually fed the new round – a rimmed round, we will recall – in two stages: a round was pulled free from the belt, which passed through the receiver above the plane of the breech, by a cartridge holder, which also, simultaneously, pulled the spent casing out of the chamber. The cartridges – both live and spent – were held by their rims in a machined vertical slot. Before the breech-block started on its forward stroke the cartridge holder dropped, ejecting the spent casing and bringing the fresh round into line with the breech; when it was chambered, it returned to the upper position, continuing to grip the rim of the now chambered round at its lower end. The various ways of locking the two main components of the gun together are the chief defining characteristics of the different types of automatic weapon, and we shall examine the major variations in detail in due course.

MAXIM'S 'FORERUNNER'
By the time Maxim's first patent had been granted he was already hard at work on the design of his first machine

gun, the 'Forerunner'. He had already clearly made the intellectual leap which allowed him to understand why the manual machine guns were unsatisfactory, as we noted above. The point can be restated here more explicitly: in the automatic gun, whether the self-loading was accomplished by recoil action or by gas pressure, the operation is self-regulating; if a round fails to fire, it stops the action of the gun, just as automatically as a successfully fired round initiates the loading and firing of the next. The gunner can then manually eject a faulty round (chambering another round and cocking the action in the process) and continue firing as before; the misfire does not result in the gun becoming jammed solid

and thus useless. Maxim's insight – and his embodiment of it – negated that last remaining reason for not accepting the machine gun as a fully fledged weapon of war.

Maxim was granted Patent No. 3493, on 16 July 1883, for his 'Forerunner' machine gun, a belt-fed, recoil-action weapon with a somewhat different operating cycle than that described above, using rimless cartridges of Maxim's own design and manufacture, employing an adjustable hydraulic damper to vary the gun's rate of fire. Maxim was by no means satisfied with the design, and it served chiefly to allow him to claim patent protection on its main features. As he said: 'No one had ever made an automatic gun before; the

Skoda M1909

Calibre: 8mm Austrian
Weight: 44kg (20lb)
Length: 1070mm (42in)
Barrel length: 525mm (20.75in)
Effective range: 1000m (3300ft) +
Configuration: belt-fed, delayed
       blowback-operated, water-
       cooled
Cyclic rate of fire: 425rpm
Muzzle velocity: 618mps (2030fps)
Country of Origin: Austria

coast was clear. Consequently I was able to take out a number of master patents, to show every conceivable way of working an automatic gun, and to get very broad claims.'

Six months later he was to broaden further his original patent base (for a gun operated by recoil action) to include actuation by means of muzzle gases with Patent No. 606, of 3 January 1884. Though he never continued down that track himself, others did, and Maxim, believing their 'inventions' to be plagiarism of his own, became a keen litigant as a result, but see below.

THE 'PROTOTYPE' MAXIM

The 'Prototype' followed the 'Forerunner', and differed from it in one important particular: it used standard .45in Gatling-Gardner rimmed cartridges as employed by the British armed forces, thus introducing an essential element of standardisation into the weapon. The 'Prototype' was first fired on 24 January 1884 – Maxim recounts how he loaded a half-dozen cartridges into a belt and fired them off in less than half a second – at the workshop he had then recently set up at 57D Hatton Garden, in the heart of

London's jewellery district. Its high rate of fire was equal to that achieved by the Gatlings then in use, but produced problems of its own: the barrel rapidly became overheated (the .45in Gatling, of course, actually fired only one tenth as many rounds through any one barrel in any given time). In order to control the temperature of the barrel, Maxim surrounded it with a distinctive water jacket, which was to become a feature of almost all future Maxim guns, though the 'Lightweight' of 1887 and the 'Extra Light', unveiled in 1895, were exceptions, albeit not particularly successful ones. To all intents and purposes, Maxim's design was finished by the end of 1883. It was not yet perfect, certainly, but very little further actually needed to be done to it, and that chiefly by way of simplifying the mechanism in order to make it cheaper to manufacture and maintain. It suffered still from an inability to maintain sustained fire without stoppages, but the

■**BELOW: In the foreground, French Army troops armed with an M1914 Hotchkiss gun in 8mm calibre, mounted on a Model 16 tripod, near Roye in March 1918.**

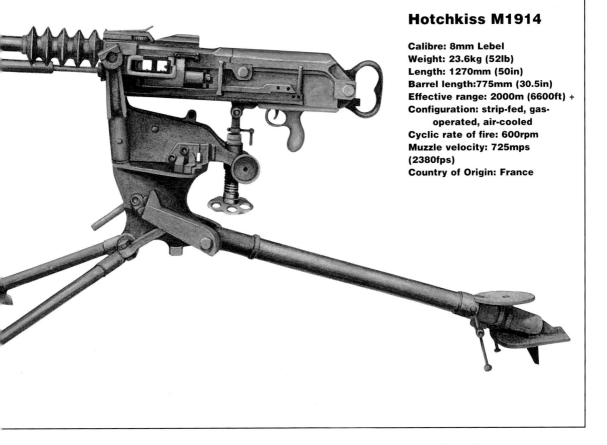

Hotchkiss M1914

Calibre: 8mm Lebel
Weight: 23.6kg (52lb)
Length: 1270mm (50in)
Barrel length:775mm (30.5in)
Effective range: 2000m (6600ft) +
Configuration: strip-fed, gas-
operated, air-cooled
Cyclic rate of fire: 600rpm
Muzzle velocity: 725mps
(2380fps)
Country of Origin: France

prime cause of that lay outside Maxim's control, in the quality of the ammunition available; he eventually overcame the problem by securing a supply of more reliable government-made cartridges.

A further problem involving ammunition was less easily solved. Up to that time, cartridges were still charged with so-called 'black powder', that is, gunpowder: a mixture of potassium nitrate, sulphur and carbon. It worked efficiently enough as a propellant, but had major drawbacks: it gave off copious quantities of smoke, thus obscuring the gunner's view of the target, and left behind a residue which quickly fouled the barrel. Maxim tried to circumvent the former by devising a means of collecting the smoke and 'purifying' it before releasing it into the atmosphere, but there was nothing he could do to counteract fouling. For a while it looked as if Maxim's gun might just turn out to be inherently flawed through no fault of its own, like the early mechanical machine guns before it, but then, in 1885,

with the sort of serendipity which seemed to characterise much of the Industrial Revolution, a French chemist, Paul Vielle, developed a new propellant, a combination of cellulose and gelatinised nitroglycerin, which produced no smoke to speak of, and solved the problem once and for all by a much more satisfactory means (see *The World's Great Rifles* for a full account of the development of smokeless powder – an essential component in the history of modern firearms).

Maxim also experienced problems caused by the sheer weight of a belt of .45in-calibre ammunition, which itself tended to cause feed problems, and these he tried to overcome by substituting a positively indexed drum magazine, not unlike the Broadwell drum used on the Gatling gun in appearance, but actually very different in nature. It proved to be a short-lived interest for Maxim, but a very similar system was later adopted by Isaac Lewis for the light machine gun which bears his name. Maxim eventually

solved this problem in a more straightforward way, by fitting a box-like ammunition tray to the underside of the gun, reducing the unsupported length of the belt from just over 1m to 30cm (roughly 3.5ft to 1ft).

THE 'FIRST PERFECT GUN'
More modifications to the basic gun design followed, leading to the 'Transitional' of 1885, and then to the Model 1887, sometimes called informally 'the first perfect gun' and described in the company's catalogue as the 'World Standard' gun. Important among those changes were those required to alter the characteristics of the gun's action to take account of the different pressure curve of the new slower-burning smokeless powder and to cope with the reduced recoil produced by smaller-calibre rounds. The first small-calibre guns made were the 130 supplied to Austria in 1889 (see below), which used the 8mm x 50 cartridge with a cordite charge (that same year the British Army adopted the

Lee-Metford magazine rifle in .303in calibre, but still, initially, with black powder as the propellant), and Maxim produced other 'RC' (rifle-calibre) guns, particularly in 7mm, 7.5mm and 8mm chamberings, for other European customers. He also produced what came to be known as the 'pom-pom', from the noise it made (its cyclic rate of fire was under 200 rounds per minute), in 37mm calibre, designed to fire the same sort of 450g (1lb) shells for which the Hotchkiss revolver-cannon was chambered. Maxim and later Vickers manufactured them in relatively small numbers (just over 760 in all, between 1895 and 1916 and 14 produced during the first year went to

■ RIGHT: Japanese sailors on the island of Guadalcanal in 1942, armed with a Type 92 machine gun in 7.7mm calibre – a modification of the French Hotchkiss which Japanese forces originally used.

Type 92 (1932)

Calibre: 7.7mm Shiki 92
Weight: 55kg (122lb)
Length: 1160mm (45in)
Barrel length: 700mm (27.5in)
Effective range: 2000m (6600ft) +
Configuration: strip-fed, gas-operated, air-cooled
Cyclic rate of fire: 450rpm
Muzzle velocity: 715mps (2350fps)
Country of Origin: Japan

Taisho 3 (1914)

Calibre: 6.5mm Arisaka
Weight: 28kg (62lb)
Length: 1155mm (45in)
Barrel length: 750mm (29.5in)
Effective range: 1500m (5000ft)
Configuration: strip-fed, gas-
operated, air-cooled
Cyclic rate of fire: 400rpm
Muzzle velocity: 760mps (2500fps)
Country of Origin: Japan

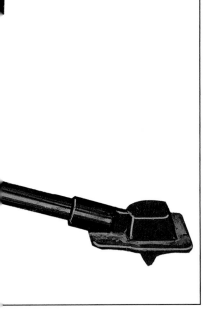

the Transvaal, and were used to very good effect against British troops during the Boer War; see below), but Krupp and later DWM also produced them. Most were used on board ship or as anti-aircraft guns.

The .45in Maxims were short-lived; they were produced chambered for both the Gatling/Gardner cartridge ('GG'), for the Royal Navy, which had large stocks of that type and for the round used in the British Army's standard rifle to 1889, the falling-block Martini-Henry ('MH') employed. Initially, Maxim had considerable difficulty in getting his gun to work with the smaller, lighter rifle-calibre ammunition, which produced less recoil. He experimented with a recoil enhancer at the muzzle, and that was employed on re-barrelled guns originally built to accept .45in ammunition, but the problem was definitively solved only by quite drastically reducing the weight of the reciprocating parts, including the barrel, though recoil enhancers were later used to increase the cyclic rate of fire of rifle-calibre guns. The guns would not work at all with the first type of .303in ammunition, which was filled with black powder; it was not until the filling was changed to cordite, in 1891, that Maxim began producing 'RC' guns for the

British Army. It was 1915 before the last British .45in-calibre guns were converted, however, and some were in use even later than that in India.

The first guns Maxim submitted to the British Army for official testing went to the Enfield proving grounds (a location we shall come to know well) in March 1887. The specifications called for a gun weighing less than 45kg (100lb) and able to fire 400 shots in one minute, 600 shots in two minutes and 1000 shots in four minutes. The three Maxims, in .45 MH calibre, all performed satisfactorily, and after also passing the standard sand and rust tests were purchased on the spot. Two were 27kg (60lb) standard models, but the third was a special lightweight version of just 18kg (40lb), and fitted with a separate reservoir to augment the water jacket around the barrel. Maxim put a specially constructed belt of 3000 rounds through this gun at a rate of 670 rounds per minute (RPM), non-stop, and this, he said, 'was the commencement of my success as a gunmaker'.

SELLING THE MAXIM GUN
Maxim also started looking for markets further afield. That same year he heard of trials having been conducted at Thun by the Swiss Army, to choose between the

Taisho 11 (1922)

Calibre: 6.5mm Arisaka
Weight: 10.2kg (22.5lb)
Length: 1105mm (43.5in)
Barrel length: 480mm (19in)
Effective range: 1500m (5000ft)

**Configuration: hopper-fed, gas-
    operated, air-cooled**
Cyclic rate of fire: 500rpm
Muzzle velocity: 760mps (2500fps)
Country of Origin: Japan

Gatling, the Gardner and the Nordenfelt, which the Gardner had won comfortably, and Maxim wrote asking to compete against the winner. That second Swiss trial was to have an interesting sequel in terms of the tactics of machine-gun employment.

The object of the trial was to test the guns' rate of fire and their accuracy over 200m, 500m and 1200m (220yds, 550yds, and 1312yds respectively). That longest range worried Maxim somewhat, for the gun he had brought from England was chambered for an 11mm German cartridge, whereas the Gardner was chambered for a 7.5mm cartridge, more predictable at longer ranges. His fears were groundless; on the day, the Gardner's demonstrator elected not to fire at the longest range. The Gardner, which required a crew of four, fired first, and got off 333 rounds in a little over a minute at the shortest range, Maxim replying with a similar number in less than half the time, and with considerably greater accuracy. At 500m the Gardner jammed and, in their haste to clear it, its crew spilled most of their ready ammunition onto the sand of the gun pit;

they took almost four minutes to fire off their allotment as a result. The Maxim performed as before.

DEVASTATING AT LONG RANGE
Now, 1200m (1312yds) is a considerable distance; the unaided eye cannot make out individual human figures, and even an object as large as a family car is hardly more than a speck. Maxim's account of the third firing test speaks for itself: 'The officer in command asked us to fire at a dummy battery of artillery at a distance of 1200m [1312yds]. At first I was quite unable to see the target, and the officer informed me that it was the blue streak that I could see in the distance. The sights on the gun had only been marked up to 1000yds [914m], and I therefore set them about where I thought it ought to be [for the distance] and marked it. I told Mr Vickers [Albert Vickers, his partner] that if we fired off the whole 333 rounds at once, we might not hit the target at all; they might fall short, or they might pass over the top. The officers wished to see how many hits we could make in one minute. The gun-mounting was provided with two stops to

limit the travel from left to right, so I adjusted these so that the gun just covered the length of the target, which might have been two or three hundred feet and having put a belt of 333 cartridges in position, I sighted the gun for what I thought would be a little high and fired about one hundred rounds, sweeping the gun slowly round from left to right. I then changed the sight to the point that I had marked and this time I fired rather more than one hundred shots, swinging the gun round as I fired; again I changed the sight to what I thought would be a little too low, and fired the remainder . . . All this was done in slightly less than a minute. After a wait of about twenty minutes, the telephone rang and we were told that we had technically killed three-quarters of the men and horses. I asked Mr Vickers if he supposed they expected us to kill the whole of them; he said he did not know, but shortly we were approached by the officer in charge, who said enthusiastically: "No gun has ever been made in the world that could kill so many men and horses in so short a time!" and they gave us an order.'

In fact, it was not the gun's accuracy which distinguished it, but rather its ability, as Maxim had just demonstrated, probably unwittingly, to establish a controlling field of fire. It was a short intellectual step to the realisation that a number of guns working together could create interlocking and overlapping fields of fire, and thus control quite large areas, and this soon became part – actually, a very major part indeed – of established infantry tactics.

When it became clear that the guns could operate equally effectively in the indirect fire role (that is, using the ordinary trajectory of the rifle-calibre bullet to hit targets the gunners could not see; a British .303in round of the World War I period fired at a target 2560m (2800yds) away, its maximum lethal range by calculation (the bullet had a velocity of 140mps (459fps) at that point), reached a maximum height of 183m (600ft) in the process, and was descending at an angle of 21 degrees when it struck), the real worth of the machine gun on the battlefield was immeasurably increased. We shall return to this point later.

SMALL BEGINNINGS
The initial Swiss order was for just one gun, in 7.5mm calibre; the most important thing about it was probably Maxim's realisation, while making it, that the 'World Standard' gun of 1887, designed for .45in and similar calibre cartridges, needed considerable modification to work with less-powerful ammunition. The Swiss Army later ordered more guns from Maxim, initially for defence of the St Gotthard Pass but later also to create machine-gun troops for each of its four cavalry brigades. Towards the turn of the twentieth century, the Swiss turned to Maxim's (then) German agent, DWM, for their supply of machine guns – numbered in the hundreds – and when World War I came, began themselves to produce the DWM Model 1909 at the Bern Arsenal, manufacturing eventually a total of over 10,000 between 1915 and 1946.

From Thun, Maxim and Vickers travelled to La Spezia, where the Italian Navy had also held a trial of machine guns, this time selecting the Nordenfelt. There was to be no comparison shoot-out, but Maxim was simply asked to beat the

■ ABOVE: The Japanese Model 93, a heavy machine gun in 13mm calibre, was similar not only in character but also in performance to the American Browning M2.

record the Nordenfelt had set which, he records, was 'a very simple matter'. He was then asked to throw the gun into the sea, leave it there for three days and then recover and fire it with no preliminary cleaning. The gun performed just as well as it had when factory-fresh. They left it there and returned to London, bearing an order for 26 'World Standard' guns in 10.4mm Vetterli calibre. Similar trials in Austria later that year produced a similar result – and eventually the order for 130 guns in 8mm calibre. Maxim returned to London and began to look around for much larger workshop premises.

'THE MYSTERY MAN OF EUROPE'
In confronting the Nordenfelt gun in Italy and later in Austria, Maxim had, wittingly or not, gone up against perhaps the most unscrupulous member of an unscrupulous trade: the 'Mystery Man of

■ABOVE: A painfully posed French infantry platoon, armed with M'07 'St Etiennes'. A poor gun by any standards, it was developed to save money on licence fees to the Hotchkiss company.

Europe' (as he was styled by wartime Prime Minister, David Lloyd George, in the House of Commons), Basil Zaharoff, Nordenfelt's chief salesman. Zaharoff may have been singularly lacking in morals, but he knew a good thing when he saw one; after a desultory attempts or two at sabotaging the Maxim gun and its growing reputation (one such apparently involved bribing a Maxim Gun Company machinist to ruin the casing of a gun destined for a trial and rivet on a repair patch in such a way that the gun was bound to jam as soon as it commenced firing; another, more subtle, approach was to mix with journalists watching the Maxim firing from a distance and inform them that it was the Nordenfelt gun on trial) he set about trying to engineer a merger between the Nordenfelt Guns and Ammunition Company, the

manufacturing and trading company Thorsten Nordenfelt had set up in England, and the Maxim Gun Company.

THE MNG&AC
The Maxim Nordenfelt Guns and Ammunition Company (MNG&AC) commenced trading on 18 July 1888, with Maxim and Nordenfelt as joint managing directors, and with members of the Vickers family and financier Lord Rothschild as directors, production being shared between the Nordenfelt plant in Erith, Kent, and a site Maxim had recently acquired in nearby Crayford. Maxim finally had an engineering base which matched the promise his revolutionary new weapon showed. Due to a variety of factors, however, it was 1896 before the new company turned a profit, and by then day-to-day management had been taken out of Maxim's hands and entrusted to a German-born businessman, Sigmund Loewe, brother of the man who had earlier been granted the licence to manufacture Maxim guns in Germany.

By that time also, Thorsten Nordenfelt had long been forced out, resigning his directorship in January 1890 and selling his £200,000 holding back to the company. He committed professional suicide soon after by purchasing the rights to a Swedish hybrid automatic/manual machine gun called the Bergman, thereby breaking the agreement he had signed in 1888 to desist from armaments manufacture except on behalf of MNG&AC for the subsequent 25 years. The Bergman gun never worked satisfactorily anyway, and Nordenfelt soon slipped into obscurity.

The company later changed its name to Vickers Son & Maxim (VSM), and later still, on Maxim's retirement in 1911, became simply Vickers Ltd, the most important arms manufacturer in Britain at the time, remaining so well into the future, producing naval vessels, aircraft and tanks, as well as small arms.

UNORTHODOX METHODS
Loewe proved to be an enthusiastic salesman, as well as a talented manager,

and his accidental death in 1901 cut short a very promising career. It was he, and not, as is usually reported, Hiram Maxim, who liked to demonstrate the automatic gun's power in a somewhat unorthodox fashion – by cutting down mature trees with it. He is recorded as having shown off the gun in this peculiar fashion on several occasions in the company of the Chinese Ambassador to Britain, at the house of the celebrated cookery-book writer Mrs Beeton, which Loewe had rented. His daughter later recalled that 'squads of Chinese dragging machine guns about and firing them with more relish than discrimination were to be found at all daylight hours' in the five-acre grounds of the house, an account

confirmed by the official Vickers company history, which says: 'Loewe shared the Chinese Ambassador's pleasure in the sport of cutting down trees by machine-gun fire, and all through the summer days the glades and lawns were decorated by groups of silk-robed figures engaged in this delightful pastime.' What the neighbours thought seems not to have been recorded.

Aristocratic fascination with the machine gun was no new thing; Maxim recorded a stream of titled visitors to the old Hatton Garden workshop, all of them eager as could be to fire the gun for themselves. The Prince of Wales, the Duke of Cambridge (then Commander-in-Chief of the British Army, so he at least

had a professional, and not just prurient, interest), the Dukes of Devonshire, Edinburgh, Kent and Sutherland all came, and later it was to be the personal intervention of the German Kaiser Wilhelm II himself (at the prompting of his cousin the Prince of Wales) which prodded the German Army into accepting the gun. 'That is the gun – there is no other,' he said, after firing it and coming close to wiping out his entire General Staff in the process. The gun was fitted with a device that automatically tracked it round through a pre-set arc as it was fired, and the Kaiser had inadvertently set it in motion. Maxim's quick thinking saved the day, and he thereafter deleted the device, except by special order.

M'07T16 St Etienne

Calibre: 8mm Lebel
Weight: 25.75kg (57lb)
Length: 1180mm (46.5in)
Barrel length: 710mm (28in)
Effective range: 2000m (6600ft)

Configuration: belt-fed, gas-operated, air-cooled
Cyclic rate of fire: 400rpm
Muzzle velocity: 725mps (2380fps)
Country of Origin: France

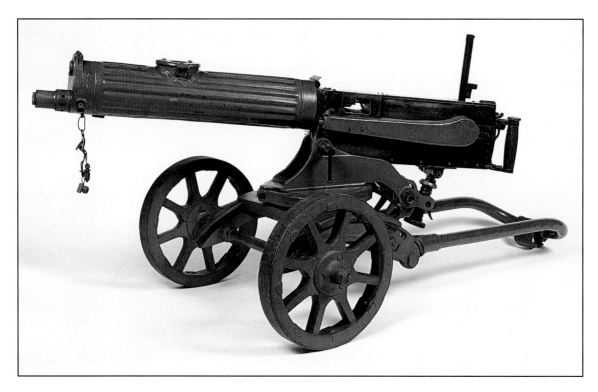

■ **ABOVE: A Russian Model 1910 Maxim gun, probably built at the Tula Arsenal in World War II, when production of this model was at its height. It is mounted on the Sokolov wheeled carriage.**

THE MAXIM IN AFRICA

The Maxim guns which the British Army bought – in surprisingly small numbers – from 1887 onwards (and adopted officially as the Gun, Machine, Maxim, Mark I) soon saw action in Africa, at the time of the 'Scramble for Africa', when the 'Dark Continent' was being carved up by Europeans, the British very much to the fore. The process had been going on for some time, of course; Gatling and Gardner guns, in particular, had done their share too, but they were cumbersome and difficult to transport over trackless terrain. The Maxims, at 27kg (60lb) – a tripod, tools and accessories weighed in at around the same – were much more portable, and they were used to subdue the indigenous tribes with terrible effect. Many of the soldiers and 'Colonial Policemen' who used them wrote to MNG&AC, praising the efficiency of its product in glowing terms. Said one grateful trooper:

'The Matabele never got nearer than 100yds [914m]. They were led by the

Nubuzu Regiment, the King's bodyguard, who came on, yelling like fiends and rushing on to certain death, for the Maxims far exceeded all expectations and mowed them down literally like grass. I never saw anything like these Maxim guns, nor dreamed that such things could be: for the belts of cartridges were run through them [150 in each belt] as fast as a man could load and fire.'

Elsewhere, far to the north in the Sudan, the British had somewhat belatedly, according to many, finally sent an army under Kitchener to avenge the murder of General Charles 'Chinese' Gordon at Khartoum in 1885. The Dervishes, as the local people were known, quite incorrectly, employed the charge *en masse* as their only tactical formation, and to the Maxim guns, this was meat and drink. The decisive battle of the campaign came at Omdurman, on 2 September 1898, when 23,000 British and Egyptian soldiers faced more than 50,000 Dervishes; the butcher's bill makes almost incredible reading – the natives lost at least 15,000 killed, and perhaps the same number wounded; the British lost five officers and 85 other ranks. The reason for the disparity was simple – the British 1st Brigade deployed six Maxim guns, the 2nd Brigade another

four. These 10 guns, which between them consumed some 34,000 rounds of ammunition, were officially credited with having caused fully three-quarters of all the casualties.

Hiram Maxim was later knighted, having renounced his American citizenship so that he could enjoy the honour, in recognition of the part his guns had played in the triumph in the Sudan.

WAR WITH THE BOERS

Almost a year to the day after the successful conclusion of the Sudan campaign, the British Army found itself at war again in Africa, right at the other end of the continent, and this time the enemy was not natives armed with spears and a grasp of tactics which was straight out of the Dark Ages, but Europeans with Mauser repeating rifles and Maxims of their own, who proved themselves to be masters of mobile warfare. This is considered the first time machine gun-armed armies had faced each other (though both sides in the short Spanish-American War of 1898 had possessed Gatling guns, and the American forces then fighting the Moro insurgents in the Philippines were using Gatlings against Maxims, often to very poor effect indeed) and it was, as Rudyard Kipling was to comment presciently in *The Captive*, published in 1903, 'A dress-parade for Armageddon'. The Boers' 37mm 'pom-pom' Maxims proved to be particularly effective against British field artillery detachments, often reducing them completely before they could get into action.

British infantrymen were sent into the set-piece battles such as Magersfontein, Colenso and Paderberg with no better tactics (though with considerably better discipline) than the Khalifa's Dervishes had employed against them in the Sudan; they advanced over open ground with fixed bayonets, and were cut down in swathes by the machine guns of defenders they couldn't even see. The tactics of close-quarter battle which General James Woolf had devised after Culloden in 1746 and used so successfully against the French in Canada, and which successive British generals had adopted throughout the nineteenth century, were finally beaten, though few in London – or, indeed, in any of the other capital cities of the world – would yet acknowledge the fact, and it was to take a further decade and the bloodiest, most costly war the world had ever seen to drive the message firmly home. With the benefit of hindsight, it is incredible that the British Army, which had been instrumental in obtaining proof that the machine gun was absolutely lethal when deployed in defensive positions, had not itself learned the lessons it had taught so widely and so effectively, but that was true not only in 1899, but also in 1914.

A HARD LESSON HALF LEARNED
Britain won the war against the Boers in South Africa thanks to its overwhelming military and economic might, but not by finer fighting skills, better leadership or superior weaponry. In many ways, that conflict was anomalous and anachronistic – the guerrilla tactics the Boers used, hitting the enemy and then withdrawing before he could strike back – were totally at odds with the training of contemporary armies, including the British, even though they had been used with good effect – and named – by their Spanish allies in the Peninsular War almost a century earlier. The war in South Africa wasn't a realistic precursor of the First World War at all except in certain particular (though that doesn't mean that the specific lesson that machine guns were overwhelmingly lethal at long- as

well as short-range should have been ignored), but the Russo-Japanese War of 1904–1905 was – and that was totally disregarded, too.

THE MAXIM COPIED
However, if the world's military leaders were content to ignore the power of the machine gun, armaments manufacturers were not. As we have seen, Maxim soon licensed his gun for manufacture in Germany (actually, to two firms; before reaching an agreement with Ludwig Loewe, Maxim had already negotiated one with Krupps. He was able to 'persuade' the latter to produce only 37mm 'pom-poms', and leave the manufacture of rifle-calibre guns to Loewe, which was already a force in the armaments market despite having started out producing sewing machines. The company took over some shares in Mauser in 1886, and had also manufactured Gardner guns under licence from Pratt & Whitney, to whom Gardner had sold out). The company later became DWM (Deutsche Waffen- und Munitionsfabrik), and the major force in small-arms production in Germany; as well as machine guns and rifles it produced both the Mauser C96 and the Luger pistols. Initially it produced exact copies of British Maxims, but later, particularly after 1898 when the licence agreement lapsed, and DWM began paying VSM a simple royalty, DWM began to introduce innovations of its own. Imperial Russia obtained a licence to produce Maxims, too, and its successor-state, the Soviet Union, ended by producing something in excess of 600,000 of them, right up the end of World War II in 1945; Nationalist China produced around 40,000 from 1935 on; Colt's made less than 200 in the USA and, somewhat ironically, the British Government, too, obtained a manufacturing licence and produced Maxim guns of its own at the Royal Small Arms Factory (RSAF) rather than buying them from the company, ostensibly, at least, because production at MNG&AC was erratic. Production of the 'Gun, Machine, Maxim, 0.45in (Mark I)' began in 1891, and continued in a variety of forms for 26 years until 1917. In that time, the RSAF turned out 2568 Maxim guns, for which it paid Maxim Nordenfelt and its successors a royalty of £25 per gun. As well as improving the flow of finished guns, production at Enfield had another huge advantage – it brought

down the price of the gun dramatically; the lowest unit cost achieved was during the year 1902–03, when .303in RC guns were produced for £47/10/4d (£47.52), compared with considerably over £250 from MNG&AC and its successors, a huge saving even when the licence fee was added in.

THE AUSTRIAN CHALLENGER
Producing Maxim guns under licence wasn't entirely satisfactory, largely because it was still unnecessarily expensive. The Loewe agreement was reckoned to be quite realistic; MNG&AC paid half the tooling costs, all the manufacturing costs, the wage bill and the expenses, and the two companies split the profit, two-thirds to Maxim, one-third to Loewe. Soon the search was on for a means of enabling a gun to operate automatically which wasn't covered by Maxim's various patents – no easy matter, for the American had been as comprehensive as he knew how in his claims. The first to offer an alternative was the giant Skoda company of Pilsen, in Bohemia, the 'engine room' of the Austro-Hungarian Empire, which was probably the biggest arms producer in the world at that time. In 1888, the Grand Duke Karl Salvator and an army Colonel named Georg von Dormus were granted a patent for a machine gun which operated on the delayed blowback system, the delay in this case being brought about by a pivoting block reminiscent of that used in the Martini rifle, together with a large coil spring acting in compression. Skoda obtained the rights to this design, and produced the *Maschinengewehr Modell 1890* in 8mm calibre. The company improved on it (but not significantly, for the basic design was flawed) in the *Modell 1893* and it was accepted by the Austro-Hungarian Army and Navy. The M1893 was an air-cooled gun, its ammunition fed from a vertical hopper, with an ingenious rate-of-fire regulator in the form of a pendulum arm with a sliding weight suspended below the receiver – a somewhat unnecessary feature, since the maximum rate of fire was something less than 250 rounds per minute (RPM) anyway. It was one of these guns and not, as is usually reported, 'an Austrian Maxim', together with a Nordenfelt gun in .303in calibre and a Colt M1895, which was the mainstay of the defence of the legation area of Pekin during the Boxer Rebellion of 1900.

to suggest, by the pressure of the propellant gas in the gun's barrel acting on the breech mechanism. Maxim always insisted that the Browning/Colt design infringed his 1884 patents, which he had renewed wherever possible, and there is little doubt that he was right, despite Browning trying to obscure the issue with a complicated arrangement of levers designed to make it appear, at least, as if the gun was based on a different operating principle. Maxim was capricious, however – he tried everything he knew to force Colts to acknowledge that the M1895 infringed his patents, but said not a word against the Hotchkiss guns which appeared in the same years (see below) which did so equally clearly!

The Skoda gun went through three more evolutions, acquiring a cooling water jacket and a 30-round gravity-fed box magazine in place of the earlier hopper, in an effort to overcome feed problems, in 1902. This was never much of a success either, and an unconventional belt-feed system was substituted in its reincarnation as the *Modell 1909*. This was in fact a comprehensive redesign. At last the rate-of-fire regulator was finally abandoned and largely by brute force the cyclic rate was increased to around 450 rounds per minute. The Salvator-Domus system last saw the light of day (but never front-line service) as the Skoda *Modell 1913*, by which time it had been superseded in Austro-Hungarian service by the gun Wilhelm Schwarzlose designed for Österreichische Waffenfabrik-Gesellschaft Steyr (see below), and it had also been challenged in the meantime by a belt-fed gun using the long recoil principle and firing a specially designed 5mm-calibre round, designed by Karl Krnka in 1899 for Waffenfabrik Roth of Vienna. Unlike most guns of its day, the Roth gun could be fired in either full-automatic or semi-automatic modes, but it never got beyond the experimental stage. Krnka was an early pioneer of what we

ABOVE: British machine gunners in action with a Vickers Class C gun on the Somme front in 1916. The gas hoods were ineffectual and served only to reduce the men's fighting capacity.

today call the sub-miniature calibre for military weapons, and also produced rifles chambered for the 5mm round.

BROWNING'S FIRST GUN

Meanwhile, in Hartford, Connecticut, the management of Colt's had realised that the Gatling guns it was still producing were basically things of the past, and that technology had moved on. The company eventually bought an air-cooled, gas-actuated gun designed by a talented young gunsmith, the Mormon John Moses Browning of Salt Lake City, Utah, on which he had obtained a patent in 1891, and put it on the market as the Model 1895 'Gas Hammer' machine gun. Browning is widely and justifiably held to have been one of the most competent gun designers of this or any other period, but it is fair to say that the Colt Potato Digger, as it was sometimes known, did nothing to enhance his embryonic reputation. Unlike the Maxim guns (if we exclude the designs Maxim patented in 1884), it was operated, as its name tries

Gun, Machine, Vickers, .303in Mark 1 (Class C)

Calibre: .303in
Weight: 18kg (40lb)
Length: 1155mm (40.5in)
Barrel length: 725mm (28.5in)
Effective range: 2000m (6600ft) plus; later 3000m (10,000ft)
Configuration: belt-fed, recoil-operated, water-cooled
Cyclic rate of fire: 600rpm
Muzzle velocity: 600mps (1970fps); later 730mps (2400fps)
Country of Origin: United Kingdom

Neither did he bother with the obvious infringement of his original patent in the locking toggle of the automatic pistol Hugo Borchardt designed in 1893, while working for Ludwig Loewe & Cie, and which Georg Luger later also adopted.

Browning's design appeared somewhat cumbersome; its operating mechanism was partly external – a swinging arm mounted beneath the barrel, the fore end of which was driven down and back through 90 degrees by gas pressure acting on a short piston, forcing a secondary linking arm to open the breech, extract the spent cartridge case and load a new one, cocking the gun at the same time. Its rather eccentric action looked clumsy, but was actually very

smooth and progressive. It was fed by a cloth belt similar to that used by the Maxim, each one with a capacity of 250 rounds.

The Colt Model 1895 was originally produced in 6mm calibre, chambered for the round rifle designer James Lee had chosen for the straight-pull bolt action rifle he sold to the US Navy that same year, and first saw action with the US Marines during the landings at Guantanamo Bay in Cuba in 1898. It was subsequently sold to the US Army and to a number of overseas customers – particularly Italy and Spain – in a variety of calibres. It was to become a favourite with Volunteer mounted infantry units fighting with the British

Army during the Boer War, who preferred it to the Maxim by reason of its much lighter weight.

While it was effectively obsolete long before World War I, a lighter variant manufactured by Marlin-Rockwell in .30in-06 calibre and designated the M1918 'Marlin' (in which the ponderous under-lever was finally replaced by a straight-acting piston, Maxim's patent having long-since expired) saw service with the US Air Corps and in armoured vehicles. The M1918 was itself a derivative of an interim development, the M1914, supplied by Marlin to the governments of Imperial Russia and Italy, amongst others (though never in large quantities) which was eventually

Type 97 (Japanese) Vickers Gun (Aircraft Mounting)

Calibre: .303in
Weight: 18kg (40lb)
Length: 1155mm (40.5in)
Barrel length: 725mm (28.5in)
Effective range:2000m (6600ft) +

Configuration: belt-fed, recoil-operated, air-cooled
Cyclic rate of fire: 600rpm
Muzzle velocity: 600mps (1970fps)
Country of Origin: Japan/United Kingdom

modified by a Swedish engineer, Carl Swebilius, to become the M1918. Several thousand even found their way to Britain during the 'Lend-Lease' days before the United States entered World War II, and were used for anti-aircraft defence on coastal merchant ships.

AMERICAN MAXIMS

The Colt gun and a Maxim in similar calibre, together with two Gatlings and a Hotchkiss, were compared by the US Navy Board in 1895, and to Maxim's horror, the Colt proved superior to his own tried-and-tested design, chiefly, it must be said, due to the eccentric characteristics of the 6mm cartridge. This had some of the attributes of the modern magnum load, being very heavily charged; consequently chamber pressure was very high, which made it impossible

to extract the spent case soon enough to maintain the normal rate of fire.

Perhaps the most important outcome of the 1895 trials was that the Gatling gun was finally shown to be decisively out-classed by the new generation of automatics (even if two years earlier Gatling had fitted an electric motor to one of his guns and persuaded it to fire at an almost incredible rate of 3000 rounds per minute), and when trials recommenced, only the Colt, the Hotchkiss and various different models of Maxim, all of them now in a more appropriate .30in calibre, were left. The trials were, in point of fact, quite useless, and were doomed to be so even before they began, because there was no one individual on the selection board powerful enough to bully his fellow members into risking their collective

careers by wholeheartedly recommending the purchase of any one (potentially fallible) gun over its rivals. As a result, five years later the still-undecided US Army found itself with antiquated Gatlings and a very few 6mm Colts facing Filipino rebels armed with Maxim guns. It was to be late in 1903 before the US Army finally accepted that neither the Colt nor the Hotchkiss – nor a late-comer, the Danish Schouboe/Madsen light automatic rifle – could really come up to the standard set by the Maxim, and ordered 50 Model 1901 'New Pattern' guns in .30in calibre from VSM for field testing, at a price, including tripod, tool box and belt-filling machine, of $1662.61 each – guns which were essentially similar in nature to those they had first tested some six years before. All the long-drawn-out selection process had achieved

Vickers Class D (Aircraft mounting)

Calibre: .303in
Weight: 18kg (40lb)
Length: 1155mm (40.5in)
Barrel length: 725mm (28.5in)
Effective range: 2000m (6600ft) +
Configuration: belt-fed, recoil-

operated, air-cooled
Cyclic rate of fire: 600rpm
Muzzle velocity: 600mps (1970fps)
Country of Origin: United Kingdom

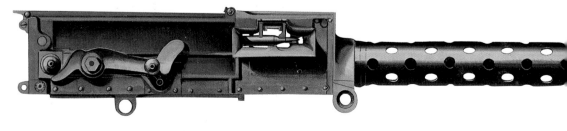

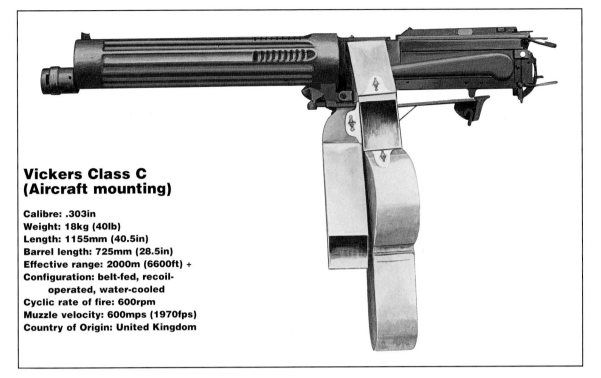

Vickers Class C (Aircraft mounting)

Calibre: .303in
Weight: 18kg (40lb)
Length: 1155mm (40.5in)
Barrel length: 725mm (28.5in)
Effective range: 2000m (6600ft) +
Configuration: belt-fed, recoil-
    operated, water-cooled
Cyclic rate of fire: 600rpm
Muzzle velocity: 600mps (1970fps)
Country of Origin: United Kingdom

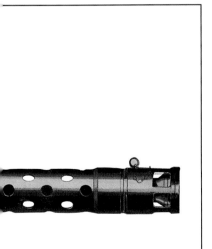

was to deny the American armed services the use of the most effective infantry weapon in the world for half a decade.

Vickers, Son & Maxim built a total of 90 Model 1904 guns, as the slightly modified American version was to be known, and then had to rework them all when a new version of the .30in cartridge (the slightly shorter but much longer-lived M1906, usually called the .30in-06)

was introduced to replace the .30-.03in. By that time, Colt's had signed a contract to make Maxims under licence, the first order from the US Army being placed with them on 25 October 1905. In all, Colt's were to make 197 Maxim Model 1904 guns for the US military (and a 198th, from unused parts, un-numbered and unproofed, which was eventually presented to the Museum of Connecticut History). Production ceased in 1909, when the much lighter but fragile and complex Bénét-Mercié Machine Rifle, Model 1909 replaced the M1904.

The Maxims were said to be unpopular in the US Army because of their weight. A gun and tripod weighed 65kg (142lb), an increase of over 10 per cent on similar British and German guns thanks to the American insistence on over-engineering everything. They were quickly relegated to storage, and many never saw the light of day again until 1914, when they were used for training purposes.

IN SHORT SUPPLY

By the time the United States belatedly entered World War I in 1917, her Army's machine-gun inventory comprised just 1305 'modern' machine guns – 665 Hotchkiss/Bénét-Mercié Model 1909s (see below); 287 Maxim Model 1904s, and 353

Lewis light machine guns, the latter mostly issued to troops guarding the frontier with Mexico – plus a handful of Gatlings and Colt Model 1895s. That, quite frankly, was both scandalous and unbelievable, a sad state of affairs which was compounded when the only gun available to issue in significant numbers to the American divisions arriving in France proved to be the *Fusil Mitrailleur Modèle 1915*, called the Chauchat after the chairman of the committee which oversaw its design, and certainly the worst machine gun of that or any age ever to gain official approval. There was a gleam of light on the horizon, though: orders had been placed with Colt's for the manufacture of 4125 Vickers Class C guns, the Maxim's eventual successor, though none had yet been delivered, and the similar Browning water-cooled recoil-operated gun (see below) was soon to be adopted as the M1917.

AMERICANS IN PARIS

In France, the company established by Benjamin Hotchkiss, with a factory at St Denis in the northern suburbs of Paris, had prospered. Before his death in 1885, he had begun to explore ways of circumventing Maxim's patents, to no good effect, and when he brought the

■LEFT: An Austrian Brandenburg two-seater scout, fitted with fixed- and flexibly mounted Schwarzlose machine guns, which have been converted to air cooling.

young Laurence Bénét from the USA to become his Chief Engineer, he, too, concentrated on the problem without any greater success. It was to be solved from an external source, eventually, when in 1893 an Austrian cavalry officer, Baron Odkolek von Augezd, brought to St Denis a prototype of a gas-operated machine gun. Hotchkiss & Cie promptly bought the design outright and put it on to the market, considerably modified by Bénét (he adopted a locking method based on that which the Scots-Canadian rifle designer James Lee had devised for his straight-pull bolt-action rifle, with a lug forced out of the bolt to engage in a recess in the receiver) as the *Mitrailleuse Hotchkiss Modèle 1895*, in 8mm Lebel

calibre, its ammunition presented, rather unsatisfactorily, in 24- or 30-round metal strips. Two years later the French Army adopted it as the M'le'97, by which time it had gained brass fins on the barrel, to help dissipate the heat generated in firing it. It was succeeded by the M'le 1900, with modified barrel fins and a new type of tripod, with traverse and elevation, and just before the outbreak of World War I by the M'le 1914, which dispensed with a somewhat complex safety system and had a better tripod still. This was the machine gun with which the French Army went to war in 1914. The M'le 1900 was also adopted by the Japanese, who used it to very good effect in the war against Russia in

1904–1905 and later modified it themselves to become the *3 Nen Shiki Kikanju*, chambered for the 6.5mm round developed for the Arisaka rifle. The main failing of the gun was its non-adjustable headspacing, which meant that ejection was somewhat unpredictable. Colonel Nambu Kijiro, the doyen of gun designers in the country at the time, changed the design of the ejector system, substituting a mechanism which was basically that of the Lewis gun, but without complete success. Nonetheless, the Type 3 machine gun was subsequently modified only very marginally to accept much more powerful semi-rimless 7.7mm ammunition and was reissued as the Type 92 in 1932 and was subsequently reissued again, this time chambered for the rimless 7.7mm round, as the Type 99 in 1939. This was the most widely used machine gun within the Japanese Army during World War II, and was still to be found in active use in the Far East as late as the 1980s, despite

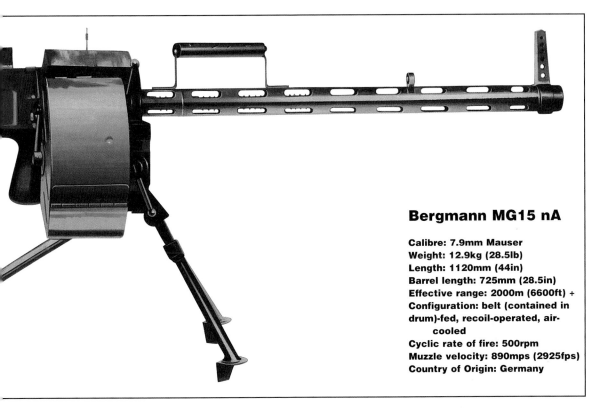

Bergmann MG15 nA

Calibre: 7.9mm Mauser
Weight: 12.9kg (28.5lb)
Length: 1120mm (44in)
Barrel length: 725mm (28.5in)
Effective range: 2000m (6600ft) +
Configuration: belt (contained in drum)-fed, recoil-operated, air-cooled
Cyclic rate of fire: 500rpm
Muzzle velocity: 890mps (2925fps)
Country of Origin: Germany

being massively over-engineered, and as a consequence, very heavy.

The basic principle of the Hotchkiss was quite simple; a pivoting locking flap secured the bolt to the barrel until gas bled off from the latter, less than half way down its length, and acted on it, unlocking the action and permitting residual gas pressure in the barrel and chamber to push the bolt backwards to begin cycling the action. As we have noted elsewhere, there is no doubt that it actually infringed the strict letter of Maxim's 1884 patent, but due to the vagaries of patent law, and the differences in the way it was applied between one country and the next, Maxim's protection may not have been complete. In its final form, as the M'le'14, a not altogether successful attempt was made to improve on its weakest feature: the 30-round cartridge strips. They were reduced in length to hold just three cartridges, which could be linked together into a flexible belt. That at least made the gun better suited to use in aircraft and armoured vehicles. This unsatisfactory feature apart, the Hotchkiss was a reliable sustained-fire weapon, particularly in its final form,

and hence was popular with the men who had to depend on it. It was still in service at the outbreak of World War II. Its cyclic rate of 600 rounds per minute (rpm) was comparable with that the rifle-calibre Maxim guns achieved.

'IMPROVED' HOTCHKISSES

There were two totally unnecessary and entirely unsuccessful attempts made to 'improve' on the Hotchkiss design in France, neither of which actually addressed the gun's only real deficiency, its ammunition feed system – the M'le'05, known, from its place of origin, as the Puteaux, which stayed in service for just two years before being relegated to reserve, and the M'le'07 'St Etienne', developed at the government arsenal in that city, which was based on the M'le05, but was even more hopelessly flawed – the design group which developed it seems to have taken a perverse delight in extensively modifying existing features to the point where their reliability was impaired to breaking point. It, too, was soon consigned to obscurity, this time in the Colonies, from which it never re-emerged. These two failures were, however, by no means the worst the

French could do during this period, however, as we shall see when we come to discuss briefly, in a subsequent chapter, the *Fusil Mitrailleur Modèle 1915* light machine gun, the execrable 'Chauchat', in a subsequent chapter.

A heavy machine gun in 11mm calibre, which Hotchkiss developed as an infantry weapon, but which was actually employed almost exclusively against German observation balloons, firing incendiary ammunition (and which became known as the '*Modèle de Ballon*' as a result) was adequate enough in that role, but otherwise not a spectacular success. Its main achievement was to inspire the US Army to look at the entire concept of heavy machine guns – an initiative which was to lead to the development of the Browning .5in-calibre weapons which we shall examine in more detail later.

IMPROVED MAXIMS

It was 1911 before Sir Hiram Maxim retired, but from around the turn of the century he had played only a very small part in the affairs of VSM, and from 1901 new machine gun patents were not registered in his name. Detail improvements were made in new models produced in 1901 and 1906. The most significant were the introduction of a device allowing adjustment of the headspace – the distance between breech-block and cartridge head at the moment the gun was fired – the redesign of the feed block and the substitution of much lighter components in high-tensile steel and aluminium, which allowed the weight to be reduced to just over 18kg (40lb). When the gun was substantially redesigned, two years later, to become the .303in calibre Vickers Class C, the weight was further reduced, to 14.5kg (32lb), but the most important change made by Chief Designer George Buckham was to turn the lock upside down, so that the toggle broke upwards, into what had been wasted space behind the feed mechanism. He also introduced an angled tail to the rear toggle arm, which acted against a roller in the receiver side wall, which broke the toggle joint rather more effectively than the original camming surface. The easiest way to tell a Maxim from a Vickers gun is by the depth of the receiver – in the former it was almost 150mm (6in) deep, and in the latter, just

two-thirds of that, little more than the diameter of the water jacket around the barrel. The new gun, which was adopted as the Gun, Machine, Vickers, .303, Mark I in 1912, was to stay in service with the British Army until the early 1960s, when it was replaced by the L7A1 General-Purpose Machine Gun (see Chapter 5), chambered for the 7.62mm x 51 NATO standard round and was not declared officially obsolete until 1968. There was very little modification to the basic gun in all that time, though a new bullet form with a recessed 'boat-tail' rear was developed for it, which increased its range by 914m (1000yds) to 4115m (4500yds) with a marked improvement in effectiveness in the indirect-fire role as a result. Versions for use in aircraft were produced – from 1916 – in air-cooled form; the modification was simply a matter of replacing the water jacket with a perforated protective shroud. The aircraft-mounted Vickers were never entirely satisfactory, and soon lost out to Brownings, except in Japan, where they were extensively employed into World War II. Vickers also produced versions of the basic gun, still employing what was

essentially Hiram Maxim's original action, in larger calibres – .5in and, experimentally, 1in – and as a 40mm anti-aircraft gun, though that latter falls somewhat outside the scope of this work. The company also produced two quite different machine guns – the Vickers-Berthier light machine gun, to be dealt with in the next chapter, and the Vickers 'K', also known as the Vickers Gas-Operated, or VGO, which will be described here later. The few Maxims which remained, together with the Vickers guns, were the only sustained-fire machine guns employed by the British Army and its Empire allies during World War I. By the end of hostilities in 1918, the British had deployed a total of perhaps 3000 Maxims and just under 71,500 Vickers Class Cs.

FOREIGN MAXIMS
Imperial Russia bought Maxim guns in considerable numbers from both MNG&AC and its successors and from DWM in Berlin – Maxim himself showed off his World Standard gun in St Petersburg in 1888, and that demonstration immediately produced an

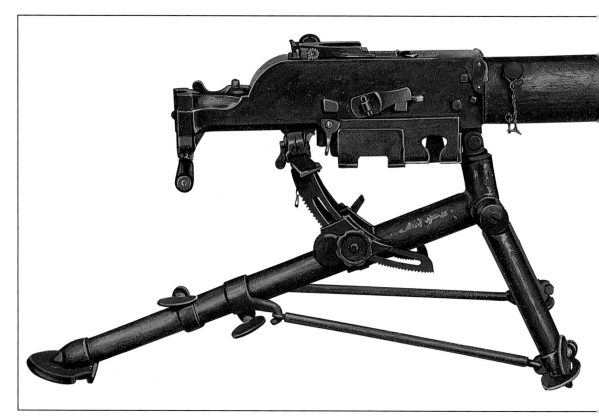

order from the Director-General of Artillery for a dozen guns in 10.6mm calibre. The Imperial Russian Navy – threatened, just as were all its counterparts, by fast launches armed with the newly perfected locomotive torpedo – followed suit, and began ordering guns in larger quantities. It was 1899 before the Russian infantry saw the value of the innovation, and they turned to DWM for their guns, buying the commercial Model 1894 in '3 line' .30in calibre (a line was approximately .25mm [.104in]), introduced in 1891, which was to become known as 7.62mm x 54R after the Soviet Union adopted the metric system following the revolution of 1917. That round, like the essentially similar British .303in, was to continue in use through both the world wars of the twentieth century (and was in fact still being employed, in the Dragunov sniper's rifle, over a century after its

■RIGHT: 'The Devil's Paintbrush' and 'The Grim Reaper' were just two of the more fanciful names for the German Maxim, the MG08, seen here on its characteristic, versatile sledge mount.

Schwarzlose M07/12

Calibre: 8mm Austrian
Weight: 20kg (44lb)
Length: 1070mm (42in)
Barrel length: 525mm (20.75in)
Effective range: 1000m (3300ft) +
Configuration: belt-fed, delayed blowback-operated, water-cooled
Cyclic rate of fire: 425rpm
Muzzle velocity: 618mps (2030fps)
Country of Origin: Austria

introduction), despite the inherent disadvantages of the rimmed form already mentioned.

RUSSIAN GUNS
Domestic production of Maxim guns began at the Tula Arsenal in 1905; the guns were direct copies of the German Model 1894, with the heavy brass water jacket and feed block which were that model's defining features, with one important exception: they employed the Vickers 1901-pattern lock. Production soon switched over to a copy of the Vickers New Light gun of 1906, which we may recall still employed the original downwards-breaking toggle lock and the deep receiver. This was to become the definitive Russian Maxim, as the *Pulemyot Maxima obr 1910* (Maxim machine gun, model of 1910 – PM 1910); it was produced in vast numbers until the last year of World War II, and was still to be found in second-line service well into the 1980s in the less advantaged Soviet client states. Most were mounted on the 'Sokolov carriage' – a pair of small-diameter wheels supporting a turntable to which the gun was secured. The wheels could be swapped for sled runners for winter operations; the only important

modification introduced to the gun itself was to the same end – the water jacket was equipped with a very large diameter filler, which allowed snow to be crammed into it. Maxims in service with the Finnish Army were similarly equipped.

During the 1920s, the Red Army attempted to transform the Maxim gun into a light machine gun, just as the Germans had tried to do in 1915. Two designs were executed, one by Tokarev and the other by Kolesnikov, both of which were air-cooled with lightened receivers and were tested, but neither was found to be acceptable.

SWISS MAXIMS
Switzerland, too, after initially buying guns from Maxim, turned to DWM, and then began to manufacture them themselves. In this case, they settled on a copy of the German commercial Model 1909 in 7.5mm x 54 calibre, despite the fact that Vickers were by that time selling the much-improved version. Production started at Waffenfabrik Bern in 1915, and continued until 1946, during which period a total of over 10,000 MG11s, as the guns were known, had been produced, both for home use and for export, particularly to Persia (present-day Iran), which bought 2000. The

Swiss-made Maxims, perhaps unsurprisingly, given that country's reputation for precision, are generally regarded as the best ever produced, in terms of finish and parts-fit.

CHINESE COPIES

In the latter years of the nineteenth century, before the Boxer rebellion of 1900, MNG&AC supplied a considerable number of guns, most of them in .303in calibre, to Pekin (Beijing) and to various Chinese provincial governments. After the rebellion, the trade stopped. When Nationalist China came into being in 1912, DWM was able to sell a small number of Model 1909 guns there, but before the end of World War I, that trade, too, had dried up. It was not until 1935 that the Nationalist Chinese, under the supervision of German engineers, put the gun, in its 1909 German form, into production for themselves as the Model 24, still in 7.92mm x 57 calibre. Some 40,000 were manufactured before the factory producing them was overrun by the Japanese after the invasion of 1937. The standard of fit and finish was high – not as good as the Swiss Maxims, nor, perhaps, as those manufactured pre-war by DWM, but certainly superior to those produced in Russia. Virtually all the guns were later converted to 7.62mm x 54R Russian-calibre after the Communist take-over – a relatively simple operation

which required a small amount of machining to the receiver and feed mechanism to accept the larger-diameter rimmed M1891 cartridge case and for the barrels to be changed. There was ample metal in the components to allow the machining operations to be carried out without weakening them. Many Model 24 guns were to be employed in Korea and in Vietnam in later years

GERMAN MAXIMS

By the turn of the twentieth century, DWM, the other main producer of Maxim guns at the time, had largely gone its own way, the agreement made between MNG&AC and Loewe & Cie having expired in 1898. It had begun to introduce minor modifications of its own into the gun produced as the Modell 1901, which the German Army adopted as the MG01. The German Navy had adopted the gun, in its earlier incarnation as the Model 1894, in the year it was introduced, but the home army delayed until 1899, and even then only bought very small quantities of what it called the MG99; it was not until two years later that it started to develop a coherent policy *vis-à-vis* the machine gun, and didn't become entirely convinced of the 'new' weapon's merits until after the Russo-Japanese War. There was no such reticence in the German colonies, however – like most 'white' armies the

Germans had soon realised the value of machine guns against 'native hordes', as one commentator put it. The Army purchased larger quantities of the somewhat lighter MG08 up to World War I (it had a total of just over 4900 on hand on 3 August; the British Army, which was smaller, had far less) and then started buying them in huge numbers.

The MG08 was to stay current until the end of World War I, when the production of automatic weapons in Germany was forbidden under the terms of the Versailles Treaty, by which time DWM and the State Arsenal at Spandau had produced about 72,000 of them. DWM made no attempt to replicate the new adjustable lock Vickers installed in 1901 until it introduced the commercial Model 1909 (which the German Army ignored), and at no time did it adopt the new inverted lock with which the Vickers guns produced after 1908 were fitted; thus, it is easy to tell a German Maxim of World War I vintage from a British gun of the same period, simply by the depth of the receiver, though there are other distinguishing marks, of course, particularly the maker's name on the 'fusee' spring cover, and the method of mounting the guns was quite different. The British used a tripod, the Germans a sled mount or *schlittenlafette*. Naturally enough, it is not so easy to distinguish a German Maxim from a Russian, Swiss or

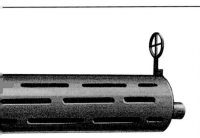

bellum-
chinengewehr Modell 14

e: 7.92mm Mauser
t: 9.8kg (21.5lb)
1: 1225mm (48.25in)
length: 705mm (27.75in)
ve range: 2000m (6600ft) +
uration: belt-fed, recoil-operated, air-
ooled
rate of fire: 650-750rpm
velocity: 890mps (2925fps)
ry of Origin: Germany

■RIGHT: Despite their idiosyncratic
design, the Austrian Schwarzlose
machine guns were in service for a
long time; this one is in the hands of
Bulgarian troops during World War II.

Chinese gun. All the German Maxims
were chambered for the 7.92mm nominal-
calibre round adopted for the German
Army's rifles in the 1880s, but there is
some scope for confusion, since the naval
Maxims were referred to (and labelled) as
8mm guns. This came about due to the
German Navy's insistence on quoting the
nominal diameter of the projectile, which
was 8mm (0.32in), not that of the barrel,
which was 7.92mm (0.31in). The original
round was subsequently modified and
became the 7.92mm x 57 *Patrone 98*, the
standard German rifle- and machine-gun
cartridge of the two world wars.

THE MG08/15

A lightened version, the MG08/15, was
developed in 1915 at the Spandau
Arsenal, under the direction of Colonel
Friedrich von Merkatz, a member of the
German Army's Rifle Testing Commission
(*Gewehr-Prüfungskommission*), a body
with much greater responsibility than its
name would suggest. It was to become
the most widely distributed automatic
weapon in the German Army from early
in 1917, and something of the order of
130,000 were produced in all, at seven

different factories. By far the largest
number – over 50,000 – were produced at
Spandau itself, and the British came to
call it by that name. The MG08/15 was
intended to be used in the light machine
gun role – that is, carried into action by
one man, and used by him alone or
perhaps with one helper, or even to be
fired from the hip, while on the move. To
facilitate this, a shortened, 100 round-
capacity belt could be loaded into a
simple drum, which was clipped to the
receiver; this was not a drum magazine,
as such, but simply a container for the
belt. In fact, the 'light' gun wasn't *that*
much lighter than the original – 21kg

(46lb) with a full water jacket and bipod,
unloaded, as opposed to 26kg (57lb) for
the MG08 – but the provision of a rifle-
type buttstock, a pistol grip and
conventional trigger in place of the twin
spade grips and thumb-operated trigger,
and an integral folding bipod and a
carrying sling made it possible for a
strong, determined man to use it in the
newly defined role.

It was never as effective a weapon as
the much lighter air-cooled, drum-fed
Lewis guns, which were very highly
regarded by German troops, who were
very eager to get their hands on them
(and many were captured and turned on

FIAT-Revelli Modello 1914

Calibre: 6.5mm M95
Weight: 17kg (37.75lb)
Length: 1180mm (46.5in)
Barrel length: 655mm (25.75in)
Effective range: 1500m (5000ft)
Configuration: magazine-fed, delayed
      blowback-operated, water-cooled
Cyclic rate of fire: 400rpm
Muzzle velocity: 640mps (210fps)
Country of Origin: Italy

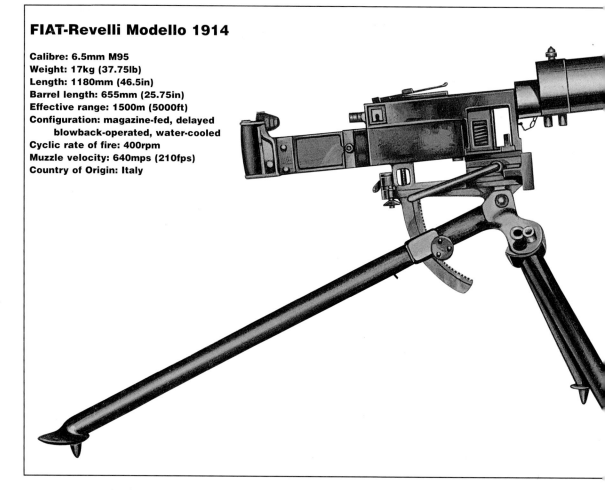

their erstwhile owners; there was even a German operating manual published for the weapon), but nonetheless they were to be the mainstay of a new sort of infantry fighting unit, the *Stosstruppen* (shock troops) who provided mobile fire support for squads of heavily armed infantrymen as they assaulted enemy positions using fire-and-movement and fieldcraft, in place of the steady, open advance culminating in a charge, which had cost so many lives during the earlier phase of World War I.

GERMAN AIR-COOLED MAXIMS
Just before the end of the war, an air-cooled version, with its water jacket replaced by a perforated shroud on which a carrying handle was mounted, was also developed, this time at the Erfurt Arsenal. The MG08/18, as it was known, was around 4kg (9lb) lighter than the ready-to-fire MG08/15, though there is

speculation that the real reason it was developed was not simply to save weight but also to counter the problem of the cooling water freezing and locking the gun's action or the converse – a lack of water or some other suitable liquid (urine, for example, was routinely employed as an expedient substitute). The barrel had to be free to reciprocate inside the water jacket, of course, in order for the action to cycle: the jacket was sealed at the muzzle by a simple gland. The British solved this problem, which they first encountered during the Boer War, by adding glycerine to the cooling water, increasing the strength of the recoil spring and fitting a recoil enhancer, but it still required at least half a dozen rounds to be hand-loaded and fired before the gun became hot enough to start cycling itself; when water alone was employed as a coolant in an unmodified gun, tests showed that it took

as many as 240 rounds before the gun would begin to cycle. The MG08/18 was issued only in small numbers, to mountain troops, cavalry and bicycle-mounted infantry, but records indicate that the production programme was to have been stepped up considerably during the winter of 1918, indicating that it was intended to issue the MG08/18 to line infantry troops too had the end of the war not intervened. The gun's main deficiency lay with the difficulty in changing its barrel – a necessity if an air-cooled machine gun is to be used in the sustained-fire role, as we shall see.

An air-cooled (*luftgekühlt*) version of the MG08 was produced for use in aircraft. This was an attempt, once again, to counteract the problem of the cooling water freezing and causing the gun to seize up, which naturally was even more pronounced in aircraft than it was on the ground thanks to the chilling factor

Fokker's mechanical interrupter gear, which – nominally, at least – allowed it to fire through the arc of a propeller, a subject to which we will return later.

THE 'UNIVERSAL' MAXIM
A further development of the Maxim principle, as we may call it, took place at the Erfurt Arsenal in 1916; this was an

mechanism – it was the forerunner of the MG34 and MG42, and thus one of the modern general-purpose machine guns. It used a copy of the much more efficient Vickers 1901-model lock and was therefore a rather better gun, technically speaking, than the MG08, but still failed to replace it (understandably; to have introduced it mid-war would have been

Perino M1913

Calibre: 6.5mm M95
Weight: 13.65kg (30lb)
Length: 1180mm (46.5in)
Barrel length: 655mm (25.75in)
Effective range: 1500m (5000ft)
Configuration: magazine-fed, combined recoil/ gas-operated, water cooled
Cyclic rate of fire: 500rpm
Muzzle velocity: 640mps (210fps)
Country of Origin: Italy

produced by airflow. But it was soon superseded by a similar version of the MG08/15, some 23,000 of which were produced, this time exclusively at Spandau. Neither was a pronounced success, either as a flexibly mounted gun for the observer, or when fitted with an early version of aircraft designer Anton

attempt to develop a 'universal' machine gun, capable of sustained fire but light enough to be employed as an LMG. The *Einheitsmaschinengewehr* was known as the MG16, but was made in trial quantities only and as far as can be ascertained, was never used in combat. In its broad principle – but not in its

impossible, in view of the amount of production that would inevitably have been lost during the changeover).

OTHER GERMAN GUNS
As well as Maxim guns it produced, DWM also set about producing machine guns of its own design, using the name

'Parabellum' (Latin for 'For War', which was its Berlin telegraphic address), which it also used for the 9mm automatic pistol designed by Georg Luger, and is also current now in the name given to the 9mm round developed for that pistol, probably the most widely used ammunition type ever (see *The World's Great Handguns* for a fuller description of both pistol and cartridge). Naturally, these guns, too, were chambered for the *Patrone 98* round. The first of them was the MG14, designed by Karl Heinemann

for use in airships and aircraft, which at last used a copy of the much-improved Vickers 1908-model lock, allowing the receiver to be much shallower. It was produced in both water- and air-cooled versions, the former for mounting aboard Zeppelins as defensive armament, the latter for use in heavier-than-air craft, where the airflow assisted the cooling process. Careful attention to the size and weight of its reciprocating components gave it a high cyclic rate – around 700 rounds per minute (rpm) – without

recourse to a recoil enhancer. A few MG14s found their way to ground forces. A version with a much narrower perforated barrel shroud was also produced, as the MG14/17, and it is widely held that Germany would have been well advised to have concentrated on developing the gun in this form – which weighed under 10kg (22lb) unloaded – as an LMG for the infantry, rather than concentrating on the heavy, cumbersome MG08/15, though perhaps the same caveat applied to the MG16 should also be applied here.

Two other types of machine gun were adopted to some degree or another by the *Reichswehr* during World War I – one developed by Bergmann, a name which we shall again encounter later when we come to examine the development of the machine pistol/sub-machine gun – and another by Rheinmetall as the Dreyse, while Gast and Becker produced designs for the German Air Force. A heavy machine gun, the TuF (*Tank- und Flieger*) in 13mm x 92 calibre, could be considered a joint venture of a sort, since it was intended for use against both armoured fighting vehicles and aircraft. The first two named are the most important, and we will deal with them in due course. Even the Bergmann and the Dreyse were overshadowed completely, but that came about as a result of the DWM-produced Maxim guns having become widely accepted before they were offered as alternatives, and not necessarily due to any incurable defects; their faults would have been rectified in short order had the MG08 not been available.

BERGMANN AND SCHMEISSER
Theodor Bergmann Waffenbau AG was an established name in weapons production in Germany before the War. The company had one outstanding asset: its design department, which included not only Bergmann himself, but also Louis Schmeisser, who had earlier designed a first-generation automatic pistol which the company had produced and sold in significant numbers around the turn of the twentieth century. Bergmann produced its first machine gun in 1902, though the patent which covered

■LEFT: A second-generation Browning, the M1917A1. Outwardly similar to the Maxim and its derivatives, it is fed from the left. The machine gunner is Francis Pershing, son of General 'Black Jack'.

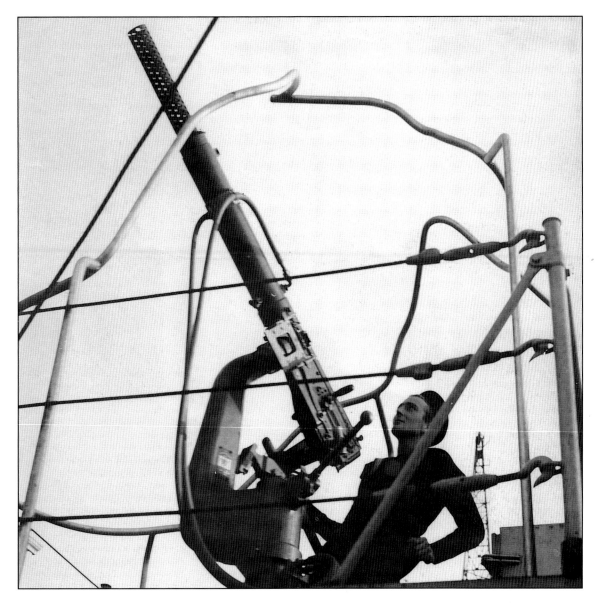

its action was taken out two years earlier. Like the established Maxim guns, it worked on the short recoil principle, but in this case locking was carried out by a swinging block below the breech-block. As the recoil propelled the barrel/block assembly rearwards by just 13mm (.5in), this locking block or wedge was forced down by a cam and released the breech-block to continue through its travel against the pressure of a spring, which then took over and returned it to battery, re-establishing the lock in the process by turning the locking block back up into position. The earliest models seem to

have used gravity to feed vertically cartridges contained in a metallic strip and later in a belt, but a later modification saw that system replaced by a 'conventional' (in the sense that it was the same as that used by the Maxim guns) withdrawal belt which fed from the right hand side.

The gun was eventually produced as the water-cooled MG10, and was tested extensively against the MG08; though it was both somewhat simpler and lighter – and German through and through – it got a lukewarm reception, largely, one suspects, due to deficiencies in the feed

■ABOVE: The .5in-calibre Browning was developed from the rifle-calibre gun to give infantry a weapon for downing observation balloons, and was also used to good effect against aircraft.

mechanism. It was adopted only after the outbreak of World War I, when machine guns of any type were in demand, but was still produced only in small numbers, and was known as the MG15. Later an LMG version was produced as the air-cooled MG15 nA (*neuer Art* – 'new pattern'), with a barrel identical to that fitted to the MG08/18, and a buttstock

(actually, little more than a recoil pad fitted at the rear of the receiver), pistol-grip and conventional trigger. It had provision to carry its ammunition belt in a drum like that employed with the MG08/15, and was commonly mounted flexibly on a lightweight tripod at around about its centre of gravity. It would seem that only around 5000 MG15 nA guns were ever produced.

SCHMEISSER MOVES ON

Soon after he had participated in the design of the Bergmann gun, Louis Schmeisser left the company and moved to Rheinische Metallwaaren- und Maschinenfabrik (which was to become Rheinmetall AG and later Rheinmetall-Borsig; we will employ the simpler name from the outset, though the change didn't actually come about until much later), where he was responsible for the design of the Dreyse MG10/MG15. Significantly, at least for Bergmann, his son Hugo did not follow him. He had as his assistant there a man who was to become equally important in the field of automatic weapons in Germany, Louis Stange. Dreyse, who we may recall had worked

with Pauly and produced the needle gun with which the Prussian Army annihilated the French during the short war of 1870–71, was long dead by the time Schmeisser produced the design for the new machine gun in 1907; Rheinmetall had acquired the rump which was all that was left of the company he started, and used his name for some of its products, including the machine guns it produced during World War I and for a short time afterwards. Many components of the new gun were, not surprisingly, perhaps, similar to that of the Bergmann, but instead of the locking block, the breech-block itself was cammed upwards at the rear during its initial travel by the action of a pivoted lever attached to the barrel extension, allowing its forward portion to drop, and unlock from the barrel in the process. Schmeisser employed both a recoil enhancer and a buffer, and achieved a high cyclic rate as a result.

The 'Dreyse' guns were water-cooled and tripod-mounted, though right at the war's end an air-cooled version sometimes known as the Dreyse *Muskete* (a term used in Germany at that time to

Browning M1917A1

Calibre: .3in
Weight: 15kg (32.75lb)
Length: 980mm (38.5in)
Barrel length: 610mm (24in)
Effective range: 2000m (6600ft) +
**Configuration: belt-fed, recoil-
    operated, water cooled**
Cyclic rate of fire: 450-600rpm
Muzzle velocity: 850mps (2800fps)
Country of Origin: United States

■LEFT: The Browning in its air-cooled form was to become the main rifle-calibre sustained-fire weapon of the US Army and Marine Corps throughout World War II and the Korean War.

mean a lightweight automatic weapon) was also in the course of development. It is suggested that some MG15s, as the final version of the water-cooled gun was known, were later converted to an air-cooled configuration, to become the Rheinmetall MG13, of which more below. In fact, the two guns were different enough in detail to have made this unlikely, though the Dreyse guns were certainly the basis for the MG13. Their best feature was probably the manner in which the receiver was constructed. It had a top cover hinged at the front which housed the mainspring, and which exposed the feed mechanism for cleaning when opened; the backplate and the rear section of the floor, which housed the entire firing mechanism, was also hinged at the front, and could be dropped down for disassembly. Their main deficiency lay in the rather complex and imprecise mechanism which advanced the belt and fed the cartridges into the breech. A spring-loaded claw withdrew the fresh round from the belt during the rearwards stroke, and then forced the cartridge downwards into a pair of feed lips in the barrel extension, helped by two spring-loaded guide fingers. The returning bolt then chambered the round. The reciprocating action of the bolt also served to advance the belt by means of a lever in the top cover. The barrel could be replaced in the field, but this operation was not by any means easy; it was removed and inserted through the receiver, after the backplate had been dropped out of the way and the bolt removed. It was not practicable to perform this operation if the gun had just been fired and the barrel was still hot.

Browning M2HB

Calibre: .5in
Weight: 38.5kg (84lb) (gun only)
Length: 1655mm (65in)
Barrel length: 1145mm (45in)
Effective range: 3000m (10,00ft)+
Configuration: belt-fed, recoil-
operated
Cyclic rate of fire: 450-550rpm
Muzzle velocity: 895mps (2930fps)
Country of Origin: United States

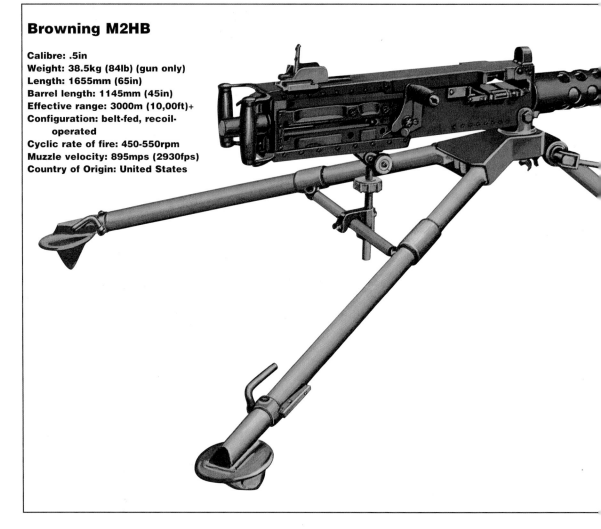

THE TWIN-BARRELLED GAST

The twin-barrelled Gast machine gun,
developed from 1916 but produced only in
the last year of the War by Vorwerk &
Cie, can best be described as an oddity. A
recoil-operated gun in rifle-calibre (that
is, chambered for the *Patrone 98* round),
the Gast fired each barrel alternately, a
pivoting connecting lever transforming
the rearwards motion of the recoil of one
mechanism into a charging motion in the
other; thus it needed no recoil springs,
save to act as buffers. It was fed by
paired spring-driven, vertically-mounted
drum magazines, each holding 180
rounds, and achieved a very high cyclic
rate of fire indeed – some 1200 rounds
per minute (rpm). The original intention
had always been to produce a gun for
flexible mounting in aircraft, but during

the last months of the war, when
weapons were at a premium, it was also
offered to the army, which turned it down
as unsuitable – reasonably enough, for its
rate of fire was far too high for land
warfare. At almost 20kg (44lb) without
ammunition, it was also judged to be too
heavy for infantry use (though at that
weight, it was considerably lighter than
an MG08), but its weight didn't present a
problem when it was mounted in an
aircraft. Perhaps 1500 Gast guns were
manufactured in all (of which 1340 were
certified as having been destroyed by the
Allied Control Commission) and it went
on test in early 1918, but was never
adopted officially. Curiously, the Allies
(that is, France, Great Britain and the
USA) knew nothing of the gun's existence
until the spring of 1919, and it was some

months more before they managed to
round up all the surviving examples.
Most were destroyed, but some were
retained for testing; all the test reports
subsequently produced spoke very highly
indeed of the design, but no further
development took place. It is thought
that work had begun on a version of the
Gast gun in 13mm TuF calibre just before
the war's end, though there is no
evidence that such a gun was ever
completed.

THE BECKER MACHINE CANNON

The gun Stahlwerke Becker produced,
which is probably better described as a
machine cannon than as a machine gun,
was in 2cm calibre, and intended for use
both in aircraft and to defend against
them. It was in service with anti-aircraft

■ABOVE: The Browning 'Fifty', originally developed for aircraft, but soon finding a home with the infantry, too; the heavy barrel came later, and allowed longer periods of sustained fire.

units and in Gotha heavy bomber aircraft and some large airships from 1917 onwards. Blowback operated and fed from a ten- or fifteen-round magazine, the Becker cannon achieved a cyclic rate of fire of about 300 rounds per minute (rpm). Each of the paired spade grips had its own trigger – that on the right was for single shots, while that on the left produced automatic fire. After the war, the design was sold to a Swiss firm, Seebach Maschinenbau, which subsequently sold it to the Oerlikon company; there it achieved its full potential, and went on to be one of the most important weapons in its class during World War II; both Germany and Japan used it as an aircraft-mounted weapon, while the British and US navies employed it as a light anti-aircraft gun aboard ship (the former alongside the 40mm Vickers pom-pom, which was the original 1-pdr gun rechambered).

AN AUSTRIAN NEWCOMER

We have noted how Germany's main ally in World War I, the Austro-Hungarian Empire, first adopted Skoda machine

■LEFT: The Browning M2HB is often found to be situated in or on vehicles, in pairs, with the feed mechanism of the right-hand gun switched to the other side.

guns, and then switched to a competing design put forward by Österreichesche Waffenfabrik-Gesellschaft, Steyr, in 1905. The gun in question, designed by Andreas Wilhelm Schwarzlose, who had already enjoyed a degree of success with semi-automatic pistols, was certainly more successful than the Skoda, but it, too, was somewhat eccentric in that it employed a simple retarded blowback action with an unlocked breech mechanism, the only one of its kind ever seen in a weapon designed to operate in the sustained fire role. Its mechanism relied on the mass of the breech-block, aided by a heavy spring and a jointed toggle arm which worked initially at a considerable mechanical disadvantage, to keep the reciprocating parts in contact with the barrel until such time as it was safe to open the breech. That meant that the barrel had to be short, to ensure that the bullet had left the muzzle by the time the components separated, and that in turn resulted in low muzzle velocity and relatively short range. In fact, the load of the cartridges, the length of the barrel and the mass of the moving parts were all very finely calculated – change any one of them and the gun either failed to cycle, or the action was extremely harsh and prone to failure; this was to prove a telling flaw, particularly in wartime, when cartridge loads were frequently approximate. Nonetheless, the *Modell 07/12*, the best of the Schwarzlose guns, was popular with the troops who used it (it was sold widely through eastern Europe, in a variety of rifle-calibre chamberings, the most common of which were 7.92mm German and 6.5mm Dutch, and first saw service in the Balkan wars of 1912–13), who liked its rugged simplicity. Its chief failing was a susceptibility to stoppages caused by poor quality ammunition, but that did not prevent it from staying in second-line service until World War II. It is said that M07/12 guns were in use well into the 1970s, in the hands of guerrilla bands, particularly in Africa; since their construction quality was high, and they were chambered for ammunition which was popular and relatively easy to obtain, that is certainly not impossible.

FIRST ITALIAN MACHINE GUNS

Though Italy had been the first country in the world to adopt the Maxim gun officially, after the La Spezia trials of 1887 – and subsequently bought hundreds, chiefly the 1901 'New Pattern'

gun to American specification, as well as almost a thousand Vickers Class C guns, when they became available in 1911 – there was also a small domestic machine gun development programme which led to an Italian-designed and -made gun eventually being adopted for the nation's armed services.

The first and most ingenious production was the design Giuseppe Perino patented in 1900. It was a hybrid recoil- and gas-operated gun chambered for the rather under-powered 6.5mm rifle cartridge (adopted by Italy along with the Carcano carbine in 1895), as were all the Italian machine guns after the turn of the century. Originally it was fed with ammunition by a metal chain contained in a drum magazine, but this system was later superseded by an even more unorthodox arrangement: a stack of five trays holding 12 rounds each. One of the most interesting features of the Perino was its system of assisted cooling: the barrel was enclosed in a fixed cylinder, and fitted with sealing rings reminiscent of those found on the piston of an internal combustion engine. The movement of the barrel in the cylinder forced cooler air across the breech and into the chamber via angled vents. A later arrangement enclosed both barrel and cylinder in a water jacket, and pumped water around the barrel. Perino tried in vain to interest not only his own War Ministry, and the British too, but met with limited success; the main drawback to the gun, which was judged to be robust and well engineered, was its weight: almost 23kg (50lb) without water or tripod. By 1913, Perino had reduced the weight by 9kg (20lb), but by that time it was too late.

THE FIAT-REVELLI

That same year Ansaldo, Armstrong & Co – a conglomerate arms manufacturer and shipbuilder with strong ties to the Armstrong company in England – acquired patents obtained by Giovanni Agnelli for a form of delayed blowback action and tried to interest the Italian Army in a light machine gun, with no success. FIAT, on the other hand, finally succeeded in breaking the effective monopoly which Maxim and later Vickers had established with another retarded blowback design from Bethel Revelli. This one was even more complicated than Agnelli's. As with all retarded blowback designs, extraction of the spent casing was an uncertain business, since there

was no possibility of primary extraction to unseat the spent casing, and to assist it each incoming round was oiled from a reservoir on top of the receiver. This had the secondary effect not only of attracting whatever dirt, dust and grit was available locally to ensure frequent stoppages but to achieve the same end in cold conditions (and we may recall that Italy's only land border is marked by the highest mountains in Europe) when the oil thickened to the consistency of grease.

Other, later, blowback rifle-calibre machine gun designs also employed oiled cartridges because they all suffered from the same problems (the same was not true of sub-machine guns, which, of course, use much less powerful propellant loads and straight cases) but this was an unsound and unsatisfactory solution to a basic weakness; there was a better one, and it was available, so to speak, right on FIAT's doorstep – machining flutes into the chamber wall to equalise the pressure inside and outside the spent case. The Agnelli gun had pioneered this method and employed it successfully, and it is more than somewhat surprising that FIAT did not licence this aspect of Agnelli's design for use in its own gun. In the case of the FIAT-Revelli, the stoppages due to swollen and split cases were perhaps welcome, for behind the oil reservoir an exposed buffer rod attached to the bolt (reciprocating with each round fired, thus up to 400 times per minute) acted against a stop only a few centimetres in front of the firing handles, which must have been a trifle disconcerting for the gunner, to say the least! Like the Perino, the Revelli used an unnecessarily complicated system to pass ammunition into the breech: a magazine (known in some circles as the 'Squirrel Cage') divided vertically into 10 compartments, each of which held five rounds. As each stack emptied, a pawl engaged an arm which pushed the magazine one step to the right, bringing the next stack into line.

Amazingly (or perhaps not; the Revelli gun had one insuperable advantage over its competitors: it was designed and made in Italy) the FIAT-Revelli Modello 14 was adopted by the Italian Army at the outbreak of World War I, and was still to

■**RIGHT: 12.7mm machine guns are the smallest calibre to be of any effect as anti-aircraft guns. These particular guns are Czech-made M53s in a towed quadruple mounting.**

be found in first-line service until the Italian capitulation in 1943, in World War II, its original water-cooling jacket having been discarded in favour of air cooling in a major modernisation programme instituted in 1935, which also saw the system of oiling each cartridge replaced by chamber-fluting, though imperfectly, and thus without any marked degree of success.

OTHER EUROPEAN GUNS

Elsewhere in Europe, a small number of other men, army officers, gunsmiths and speculative inventors, were also at work, trying to improve on existing designs – or at least, to change them enough to be able to secure patent protection for themselves. Few achieved much of note (and as we have already discovered, even some of the more famous amongst them only actually took retrogressive steps), though an essential element of one design, from Sweden, was to be incorporated much later into a number of very successful guns developed in other countries.

A SWEDISH INNOVATION

The *Kulspruta Kjellman* first appeared in 1907, manufactured in small numbers to a design executed by Rudolf Kjellman. Its novel feature was its locking system – two pivoting lugs or flaps on the bolt body which were forced into recesses in the receiver wall as the firing pin was pushed forward, thereby ensuring that a round could not be detonated prematurely before the assembly was locked. The main advantage to this simple system was the reduction in the mass of the moving parts, which meant that they could be made to reciprocate quickly, leading to a very high rate of fire. It was, in fact, the work of a Swedish Army officer named Friberg, who had conceived of it back in the 1880s and then taken the project no further; Kjellman didn't get far with it either – no order from the Swedish armed services was forthcoming – and the idea simply gathered dust, along with the few guns which embodied it (two models were in fact produced: an air-cooled LMG with a box magazine; and a water-cooled, belt-fed, tripod-mounted sustained-fire version) until the late 1920s, when an identical system was adopted in the Soviet Union by designer V.A. Degtyarev, who, with M. Kalashnikov (qv) was for decades the main driving force in Soviet automatic weapons design, for his

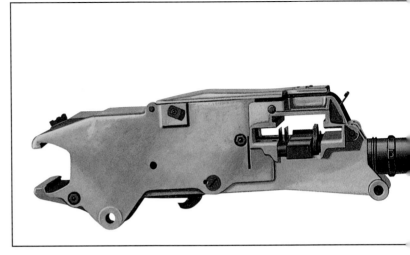

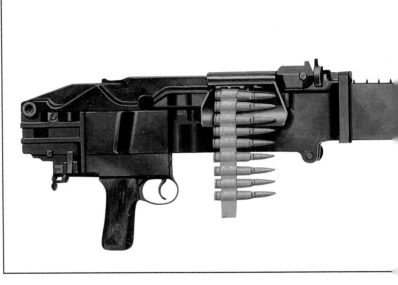

Ruchnoy Pulemyot Degtyareva pakhotnyi LMG (known in the west as the DP) and in the heavy DShK (*Degtyareva, Shpagina Krupnokalibernyi*) he conceived with G.S. Shpagin, and later still, in a considerably modified and refined form utilising rollers in place of flaps, for the superlative second-generation German general-purpose machine gun, the MG42, of which much more in Chapter Five. The gun Degtyarev designed in 1943 to chamber the new 7.62mm x 39 cartridge,

the RPD, used a variant of the same system, too – see below. It is not entirely clear whether Degtyarev or the designers of the MG42 breech-locking system (there is still controversy over their actual identity, see below) knew of Friberg and Kjellman's work; the German engineers certainly knew of Degtyarev's guns, and had had plenty of opportunity to study examples captured from Soviet-supplied government forces in Spain during the civil war there.

Rolls Royce Prototype Heavy Machine Gun

Calibre: .5in M2
Weight: 22.25kg (49lb)
Length: 1270mm (50in)
Barrel length: 1020mm (40in)
Effective range: 3000m (10,000ft)

Configuration: belt-fed, recoil-operated, air-cooled
Cyclic rate of fire: 1000rpm
Muzzle velocity: 715mps (2350fps)
Country of Origin: United Kingdom

BESA

Calibre: 7.92mm Mauser
Weight: 21.5kg (47lb)
Length: 1105mm (43.5in)
Barrel length: 735mm (29in)
Effective range: 2000m (6600ft)+

Configuration: belt-fed, gas-operated, air-cooled
Cyclic rate of fire: 750-850rpm
Muzzle velocity: 825mps (2700fps)
Country of Origin: Czechoslovakia/United Kingdom

BROWNING'S BEST

The majority of machine guns employed during World War I were, as we have seen, basically Maxims of one sort or another, the only notable exceptions being the idiosyncratic Austrian Schwarzlose, the Hotchkisses employed by the French Army and the Italians' Revellis. Only one other sustained-fire weapon used during that conflict deserves to be known as a great machine gun, and it was to go on to become

probably the most important of all during the extended period of global conflict which characterised more than half of the twentieth century. Fittingly, perhaps, given the real roots of the entire genre, it was American through and through.

We have already encountered John Browning as the author (some, notably Hiram Maxim, said plagiarist) of the odd and not particularly popular Colt M1895 'Gas Hammer'. In the intervening period, Browning had produced one of the best

automatic pistol designs yet, for the Colt which was to become widely known as the M1911; that design was produced in 1900 and perfected by 1905, and immediately afterwards – though by no means exclusively – Browning turned his attention back to machine guns. Though he had chosen gas actuation for the first of his designs, he abandoned that now, and opted for the short recoil system instead, though the method he chose to lock barrel and bolt together were rather simpler than Maxim's toggle – a vertical slide, which was taken out of engagement by camming surfaces within the receiver. He also incorporated an accelerator – a curved lever pivoted off-centre – which hastened the rearward motion of the bolt, once it was disengaged from the barrel. The rearwards motion also advanced the belt – which fed from the left hand side. This was most obvious point of difference from the Maxims and their derivatives, which all fed from the right (though left hand feed was always an option, and was incorporated in paired or ganged guns, as used aboard ship and in some aircraft). The provision of a pistol grip and finger trigger on the rear plate is another important recognition feature, though later guns, including those made by Browning's European partners, Fabrique Nationale in Belgium, were fitted with paired spade grips and a thumb trigger.

THE M1917

The basic design first appeared in the gun the US Army adopted as the Machine Gun, Caliber .30in, M1917. It was water-cooled and tripod mounted, and identical in character and performance to the British, German and Russian Maxims; some 56,500 were manufactured before the end of World War I (though few actually saw service; the first US Army units to arrive in Europe were equipped with French Chauchats – see Chapter Three – and the next wave had Vickers Class Cs in .30in-06 calibre) and it became the US Army's most important static automatic weapon. It was revamped in 1936 and issued as the M1917A1, though the modifications were of a minor nature. It succeeded where the Maxims and the derivative Vickers gun failed, however, for it successfully made the transition from water- to air-cooling. The M1919, as the air-cooled gun was designated, appeared just too late to see action in World War I, but was to have a very long combat career indeed, right through World War

II and beyond, as an infantry weapon, as a fixed and flexible tank machine gun, and, in somewhat modified form now known as the M2, mounted in aircraft of all types. The definitive version of the gun was the M1919A4, which was adaptable to both fixed and flexible mounts and was issued to both armour and infantry units (though the latter also received M1919A6s, from April 1943, fitted with a shoulder stock and a lightened barrel, and mounted on a bipod).

THE 'FIFTY CAL' BROWNING
The use of the designation M2 for the airborne version of the basic machine gun in .30in-06 calibre was to give rise to a certain degree of confusion, for the same designation was later applied to a heavier gun in .5in calibre, developed as a rival to the Hotchkiss 11mm 'balloon gun' at the request of the US Army (the changeover from model numbers which reflected the date of the weapon's adoption to one which reflected its place in the development programme came in the mid-1930s; all US weapons were then designated 'M1', 'M2' and so on, instead of by their date of adoption). The original Browning HMG was little more than a blown-up version of the M1917; it was introduced in 1921, and designated as the Machine gun, Caliber .5in, M1921. It too underwent some modification and was subsequently reissued as the M1921A1, and then as the M2. Just as the M1917 had been converted to air cooling, so was the M2, but this time there was no change of designation until it was given a heavier barrel, capable of longer periods of sustained fire (the original version could fire only 75 rounds before it needed a cooling-off period) when it became known as the M2HB. It was to be employed, like its smaller brother, by American forces and those of their allies on land, at sea and in the air, and enjoyed a very long life indeed – as the twentieth century drew to a close, and the gun entered its seventh decade of active service, it was still in production; for over 50 years, people had been trying to improve upon it, but few made any worthwhile headway, and from World War II onwards, it enjoyed pride of place as the western world's most effective heavy machine gun, either tripod-mounted for use by infantrymen, flexibly mounted in vehicles or aboard ships and aircraft, or in fixed mounts in aircraft and armoured vehicles. With a rate of fire

equal to that of the rifle-calibre guns but firing a much heavier projectile at greater muzzle velocity, its destructive power was considerable; it was – and is – widely held that any 'soft' target a Browning HMG could reach (and 'soft' here includes most buildings), it could destroy. The Browning M2HB was destined to become a benchmark by which other heavy machine guns would be measured, and we shall return to that topic in a later chapter.

OTHER HMGS
While the Browning 'fifty' as it was to become widely known, was the most significant of the heavy machine guns of World War II, it was not the only one in use by ground forces. In 1938, the Red Army introduced a heavy machine gun in similar calibre (12.7mm x 108 in this case; the Browning round was actually 12.7mm x 99). As noted above, the DShK (*Degtyareva, Shpagina Krupnokalibernyi*) as the new gun was known, employed the Friberg/Kjellman locking system; Shpagin's contribution was a somewhat over-complicated rotary feed mechanism, while Degtyarev had perfected the other elements of the design in a heavy gun known as the DK, which was produced in very limited numbers in 1934. The DShK made its appearance in 1938, and was used by the Red Army throughout the Great Patriotic War, as World War II was known in the USSR; in 1946 the rotary feed mechanism was swopped for the simpler and more conventional shuttle feed Degtyarev produced for the version of the RP which appeared that same year. He also took the opportunity to replace the fixed barrel with one which could be easily swopped. The DShK Model 38-46 went on to become the heavy machine gun of choice throughout the Warsaw Pact armies, and was also widely distributed to Soviet client states. The People's Republic of China produced a version known as the Type 54. The gun's main distinguishing feature was its heavily ribbed barrel and large muzzle brake. Not surprisingly, its performance was very similar to that of the Browning 50 – an effective direct-fire range of 2000m (2150yds) and a muzzle velocity of 860mps (2800fps). The round it fired was slightly lighter than that of the American gun at marginally over 44g (1.5ozs), but that did little to lessen its destructive power. Cyclic rate of fire was 575 rounds per minute (rpm), but for all practical purposes, something of the order of

■RIGHT: The Vickers Gas Operated or Class K gun was designed for use aboard aircraft, but during World War II was also mounted on vehicles of forces like the Special Air Service.

100rpm was closer to the mark. The same stricture applied to the Browning, of course.

The DShK was supplanted – though joined, is probably more accurate – in service in 1955 by an even heavier-calibre weapon, the Vladimirov (*Krupnokalibernyi Pulemyot Vladimirova* or KPV). This recoil-operated weapon was designed as a light anti-aircraft weapon, and appeared in single-, twin-, and four-gun mountings on a variety of different vehicles. It was chambered for a round first produced for an anti-tank rifle in 1941, in 14.5mm x 114 calibre, which fired a 64g (2.25ozs) projectile at a muzzle velocity of almost 1000mps (3280fps).

THE BRITISH HEAVIES
During the early 1930s, Vickers began producing a .5in-calibre machine gun, too, chiefly for use at sea and in armoured vehicles; it was basically a beefed-up Class C gun with various unimportant modifications – its recoil spring worked in compression, rather than in expansion, for example. A heavy-calibre version of the BESA tank machine gun (see below) was also produced, in 15mm x 104 calibre, for use as primary armament in the British Humber armoured car, but only slightly over 3000 were ever made. Rolls-Royce developed a prototype .5in HMG during World War II, too, with a breech-locking system based on that of the Friberg/Kjellman guns, but never took it to production, considering other activities to be more important.

NEW RIFLE-CALIBRE GUNS
With the benefit of hindsight, the 'pacification programme' which succeeded from the end of World War I in 1918 and was particularly manifest in Britain, France, and to a lesser degree in the United States of America, was hopelessly naive. It meant that in those countries, weapons development effectively ground to a halt, and even when it became obvious that Germany had recovered sufficiently to play a major part on the world stage again, in the early 1930s – and that her new rulers clearly had the will to do just that – still nothing was done to develop new, state-of-the-art

weaponry. Elsewhere, and particular in the Soviet Union where the Communist revolution had now firmly established control, the same conditions didn't apply, and weapons development continued apace. When the Allied powers, victorious after World War I, were called upon to defend themselves against resurgent Germany during the second round of the global conflict after 1939, they went out to fight with the same small arms they had used previously. It says a great deal for the design of those weapons that, by and large, they were up to the task at hand.

TWO FROM CZECHOSLOVAKIA

As a result of the virtual moratorium on weapons development in the UK, the most significant additions to the armoury

of machine guns there prior to World War II were in fact both imports, and seemingly from a somewhat unlikely source: Czechoslovakia, which only came into existence as a modern state with the break-up of the Austro-Hungarian Empire. The most important of them was the Bren light machine gun, which we will consider in the next chapter, but there was also the Besa, which was adopted as the secondary armament for Britain's tanks, though it had originally been intended to replace the Vickers Class C, in service with the infantry, too (in the end, the Besa was not thus deployed, due to lack of time – war was upon the British long before they expected it – and the troops had to soldier on with the by-then already venerable Vickers).

The Besa, known originally in its country of origin as the vz 37 and commercially as the ZB 53, was essentially similar to the Bren LMG (qv) save that its block locked into the barrel extension as well as into the receiver roof, but both were operated by means of the same sliding/tilting action – unsurprisingly, since the same designer, Vaclav Holek, was responsible for both (and also for the similar, later vz 52 LMG; see below). The heavier gun differed from the LMG in its method of actuation, however, employing a composite of short recoil and gas operation, known as the differential recoil system and sometimes called 'floating firing' or 'soft recoil' (and when we come to examine the development of machine

pistols, we will encounter a similar system known as 'advanced primer set-back'). In the differential system, the barrel/breech-block assembly was pushed back out of battery by the recoil a scant fraction of a second before the 'waste' propellant gas entered the cylinder from the barrel tapping and began to impinge on the face of the piston, pushing it back in its turn. This short recoil action was not, however, the means by which the Besa's block and barrel were unlocked from each other – the action of the gas-driven piston did that, in the normal way – rather, it was designed to reduce the battering the gun's mounting received ('reducing the trunnion load', in technical terms), since roughly half the recoil generated was thus absorbed, the rounds actually being fired while the barrel and block assembly was still moving forwards, fractionally before the end of the ejection/recocking/reloading cycle. Browning used a similar system in his

recoil-operated machine guns, and reputedly coined the phrase 'floating firing' to describe it.

Whatever the system is called, it certainly made for a smooth action, and in the Besa, a further innovation: reducing the length of the gas cylinder to the point where, at the limit of its rearwards stroke, the piston was withdrawn from it entirely, allowing the waste gases and any fouling elements they carried with them to exhaust to the atmosphere, reducing the build-up of deposits in the cylinder very considerably. The result was an excellent weapon, reliable and long lasting and renowned for its accuracy. Unlike the Bren, which was modified to accept standard British

service ammunition – that is, rimmed .303in rounds – the Besa was adopted in the original chambering, 7.92mm x 57. There are suggestions that the original ammunition was retained due to the shortage of time, but it seems at least equally likely that the difficulties in accommodating rimmed ammunition in a push-through belt were simply insoluble, and there was certainly no way the action of the Besa could be modified to withdraw the cartridges backwards before feeding them to the breech. In the end, it was easier to manufacture 7.92mm x 57 rounds in the UK, and since the gun was only ever used in armoured vehicles, logistical problems in ammunition supply were minimised. Holek went to considerable lengths to improve the gun's ergonomic efficiency; instead of taking his hand away from the trigger to operate the side-mounted

cocking lever, the Besa gunner merely had to release a catch and push the entire trigger/pistol grip assembly forwards so that the trigger sear engaged with a bent in the lower face of the piston, and then pull back, bringing the action to the rear where it was held until the trigger was depressed.

THE GAS-OPERATED VICKERS
The first use of air- instead of liquid-cooling, we may recall, was in guns designed for use in aircraft, where fire was likely to be sporadic, rather than truly sustained, and the air flow assisted in cooling the gun anyway. The Browning M2 was to be the best known of all the rifle-calibre aircraft guns, but a would-be competitor was produced by Vickers in the early 1930s as the Class K or VGO (Vickers Gas-Operated). This was essentially a development of the design

FIAT Modello 35

Calibre: 8mm
Weight: 19.5kg (43lb)
Length: 1270mm (50in)
Barrel length: 680mm (26.75in)
Effective range: 2000m (6600ft)
Configuration: belt-fed,
        gas-operated, air-cooled
Cyclic rate of fire: 450rpm
Muzzle velocity: 790mps (2600fps)
Country of Origin: Italy

the Frenchman Adolphe Berthier had produced and patented a decade earlier, which the British company put into production as the Vickers-Berthier LMG, and which came close to being accepted by the British Army as its squad automatic weapon. The VGO, like its forerunner, was a simple design incorporating a bolt which was locked, like that of the Bren, by being tilted or cammed up into a recess in the receiver top. The main difference between the VGO and the VB lay in the magazine – the latter had a 'banana' box, like the Bren (the excessive curvature was due to the profile of the .303in rimmed round), while the VGO had a 96-round fixed pan magazine – a drum laid on its side, similar in form, though not in principle, to that of the Lewis gun (qv The Lewis gun's drum rotated; the Vickers' did not). In the event, it was used only in limited numbers by the RAF, but proved highly popular with mobile infantry units such as the Long-Range Desert Group and the Special Air Service Regiment, which employed them as singletons and twins mounted on pintles in jeeps and light trucks against targets on the ground; their very high cyclical rate of fire (up to 1000 rounds per minute, achieved by reducing the weight of the reciprocating parts to a minimum, and paying close attention to their finish) ensured that the maximum amount of damage could be caused in the minimum amount of time.

■LEFT: The Breda Modello 37 was an idiosyncratic design, but proved reliable during World War II. Captured examples were used by Allied troops in large numbers.

THE BREDA MODELLO 37

With the benefit of hindsight, we can often look back over the history of an invention and note how, all too often, an undesirable feature passed from one generation to the next apparently without any thought being given to eradicating or correcting its faults, and the machine gun is certainly no exception. The gas-operated medium machine gun produced by Ernesto Breda, which was already a major industrial conglomerate. manufacturing a huge variety of products from aircraft to railway locomotives and rolling stock. The company adopted the gun as the *Mitragliatrice Breda Modello 1937* in 8mm, chambered for a newly developed round introduced two years earlier, was one such; it was not provided with a mechanism for effecting primary extraction of spent cases, and instead applied a light coating of oil, just like the FIAT-Revelli guns it replaced. Quite why its designers stuck steadfastly to this flawed principle is unclear, but the effect was exactly the same – the oil thickened in cold conditions, and picked up dust and dirt whenever possible. This was not the only idiosyncrasy the gun possessed; like earlier Italian machine guns, it also featured a rather extraordinary means of handling its ammunition. In this case, it was in the form of a strip-like tray, which was fed into the gun from the left; the peculiarity was that instead of ejecting empty, spent cases and disgorging an empty tray, the mechanism of the gun carefully reinserted them into the tray again, as it emerged from the other side of the receiver. Much has been made of the soldiers who used the M1937 having to then unload the empties from the tray before they could reload with fresh rounds, but it seems that this was not actually the way the system was planned to work – the 8mm rounds were not used by any other weapon in the inventory (except the upgraded M1914, in which they were loaded into belts), and it was planned that trays full of empties should be returned to the factories from which they came for reloading, having been preserved in good condition in the meantime. There was certainly one valid feature to this procedure: it ensured that hot spent brass didn't fly around and get under foot – an important consideration in armoured vehicles, where the gun was originally designed for, and for which it may even have been actually designed, but less important to infantryman. Despite these oddities, the Breda M1937 stayed in service with Italian Forces throughout World War II, and even gained a reputation for reliability; it was routinely employed by Allied troops who captured large numbers in North Africa and liked the extra punch given by its somewhat heavier than normal round.

THE SOVIET UNION

As we have noted, the main force in Soviet automatic weapons design during the inter-war period was Vasily Alexeyevitch Degtyarev. His first significant achievement was the *Ruchnoy Pulemyot Degtyareva pakhotnyi* LMG (known in the west as the DP), a simple design which used a modified form of the locking lugs of the Swedish Kjellmann, which we shall examine in more detail alongside other light machine guns in the next chapter. During World War II, it was suggested that there was a need for a company-level support weapon capable of delivering a greater volume of fire than the drum-fed DP or the 'modernised' version, the DPM, and in 1944, the year the latter appeared, the three designers who had been responsible for that modernisation, Dibinin, Poliakov and Shilin, were given the task of producing such a weapon with the minimum possible delay. With this criterion uppermost, they chose to produce a gun based on the DPM, but with a simple belt feed mechanism – really no more than a diagonal slot, which translated back-and-fore motion into side-to-side when used to guide a lug on the reciprocating portion – in place of the mechanism for holding the drum in place, though wisely the entire top plate together with the feed mechanism could be removed, and one equipped to hold a drum substituted; thus, the RP-46 (*Rotnyi Pulemyot obr 1946*), as the new weapon was to be designated, could also be used in the assault role without the necessity of a 'number two' to carry the box containing the belt. The chief difficulty they had in executing the design was, once again, the necessity of withdrawing rimmed rounds to the rear from a closed-loop belt before they could be rammed forward into the breech, but the problem was solved relatively simply, by using a pair of jaws on the feed slide to grip the rim of the fresh round and extract it against the pressure of a spring-loaded depressor arm mounted under the top cover, which then pushed the cartridge down and forwards into the feedway, where the bolt drove it into the waiting chamber. The new gun was actually completed too late to see service in World War II, and was eventually adopted, as its designation suggests, in 1946. It was later also adopted by the Peoples' Republic of China as the Type 58, and by North Korea as the Type 64.

The RP-46 was never entirely popular with the Red Army despite being – on paper, at least – a better weapon than the DP/DPM it replaced. Even while it was still in the development phase, Degtyarev himself was working on an alternative design, utilising the rimless 7.62mm x 39 'intermediate' cartridge which was designated the M1943 (for no really good reason, as far as can be ascertained; it wasn't actually adopted – and perhaps not even fully developed – until considerably later; see *The World's Great Rifles* for a comprehensive description of how this round, destined to become one of the most widely employed ever, was developed). The M1943 round had one distinct advantage over the M1891, of course: it was rimless, and so could be chambered directly from a disintegrating belt. But there was a drawback. It was distinctly underpowered for the combined tasks of driving the action and lifting the belt to feed a fresh cartridge. This was to cause Degtyarev more than a few headaches, and resulted in a number of modifications before the design was wholly satisfactory.

While it was classified as a light machine gun (RPD stood for *Ruchnoy Pulemyot Degtyarova* – 'Degtyarev Light Machine Gun'), the RPD actually fell between two stools – it was belt-fed, but the quick-change barrel of the later DP/DPM and the RP-46 (in which the mechanism was made both simpler and more efficient) was deleted, and instead, gunners were 'trained' to restrict their rate of fire to under 100 rounds per minute (rpm). It takes very little imagination to foretell how that training would have stood up under combat conditions. The RPD was itself soon supplanted by the RPK, a true light machine gun which employed the turning bolt action Mikhail Kalashnikov designed for the AK-series assault rifles, (and we shall consider that, too, in greater detail in the next chapter), and it was joined by a true general-purpose machine gun using a modified form of the same action, the PK, which was to prove itself a very well-thought-out automatic weapon indeed, and which we shall examine alongside its rivals, the GPMG/FN MAG and the M60 in Chapter Five.

Notwithstanding the relative merits of all these newcomers – which were all light guns, in fact, no matter to what the use to which they were put – the Red

Army still relied for sustained automatic fire on its PM1910 Maxims. By the middle years of World War II, it had become clear, however, that they were deficient, and should be replaced by a modern design. The one chosen was the work of Peyotr Maximovitch Goryunov, and was very much less the 'son of Maxim' than was its creator! To begin with, it was air cooled and gas actuated, with an easily changeable barrel, a simple and sturdy design making use of tried and tested components, like many of those the Red Army, knowing the intellectual standard of the majority of its soldiers to be low, was to adopt.

A NEW SOVIET MMG

The *Pulemyot Stankovyi Goryunova obr 1943* (Goryunov Heavy Machine Gun, Model 1943, usually known as the SG or SG43) was chambered for the old M1891 rimmed 7.62mm x 54 round, and its 'heavy' designation is thus misleading. It employed the standard Maxim-type withdrawal belt, and Goryunov got around the perennial 'back and forth' cartridge feed problem by the same means as was employed in the RP-46 (it is unclear for which gun that mechanism was actually designed) and the means of advancing the belt was the same also employed in the RP-46. Locking was achieved by a tilting block similar to that used in the Czech-designed Bren and Besa, but in this instance, the block tilted sideways, and locked into a recess in the right hand sidewall of the receiver. The delay necessary to ensure that pressure in the chamber had dropped to a safe level was also brought about by a similar method to that employed in the Czech guns – by working the breech-block by means of a post at the rear of the piston, which acted in a slot in the bolt body; the time it took the piston post to traverse the length of the slot caused the delay, and the first contact caused the block to be cammed out of its recess, whereupon it was free to travel to the rear and then forwards again, to complete the cycle. To compensate for fouling of the piston, a simple three-position track-type gas regulator was fitted, the tracks being of uniform depth by varying in width.

The gun fired from the open breech position, the breech-block being held to the rear with the fresh round in the feedway, and the whole assembly released by the trigger, first to chamber the round and then fire it, instead of the round being loaded and the block locked

together with the barrel and only the firing pin held off against its spring by the trigger sear. This system has the major advantage of allowing cooling air to circulate within the chamber while the gun is not actually in operation, and to ensure that there was no round actually in the breech for any extended period while the gun is hot. Sustained-fire weapons which fire from the closed breech position and which carry the fresh round loaded into the chamber always run the risk of heat build-up there leading to premature ignition or 'cook-off', a most undesirable effect, and few second-generation guns were so designed.

In the event, World War II was almost over before the SG43 was actually ready for service, and for the most part the Soviet troops had to make do with the PM1910 after all. The changeover was made fairly rapidly thereafter, however, and the SG43 and later the SGM, (denoting 'modernised', though the modifications were actually minor) became the regulation sustained-fire weapon for the Red army and its Warsaw Pact satellites, as well as for the Soviet client-states in the Middle East and elsewhere. The cocking handle was moved from between the rear spade grips to a position on the right hand side of the receiver, dust covers were fitted to the feed and ejector apertures, and the barrel gained longitudinal cooling fins; an interim modification had seen the simple wedge-type barrel lock replaced by a micrometer screw, which allowed fine adjustment of the headspace. A version for mounting in and on vehicles was developed as the SGMT, with a firing solenoid on the backplate in place of the conventional mechanical trigger. The People's Republic of China manufactured it as the Type 53/Type 57, and versions also came from Czechoslovakia, Hungary and Poland. A variety of ammunition types were produced, including armour-piercing (AP), semi-armour-piercing (SAP), and incendiary, as well as tracer and common ball in two weights, 9.6g (148 grain), and 11.8g (182 grain). Muzzle velocity was 800mps (2600fps), and the effective range was comparable with other similar guns – around 1000m (1094yds) directly, and up to four times that in indirect fire. The SG43's rate of fire was fairly standard, too – 650 rounds per minute (RPM) cyclical, and effectively perhaps half that. The gun had a fairly long sight radius – 850mm (33.52in) – and was accurate as a result.

TOWARDS THE GPMG

One thing will have become clear by now: the day of the water-cooled medium machine gun and heavy machine gun was over. Water jackets were simply too cumbersome, and water-cooled guns too heavy, to be truly effective except in static defensive positions, while water was actually only a poor coolant at best, prone to freezing in cold conditions, and beginning to boil after just a few hundred rounds had been fired. The last new successful water-cooled gun to be introduced was the Browning M1917, and as we have seen, that gun lost its water jacket early on, and became a real success only after it had been converted to air cooling. All the successful new designs introduced after the end of World War I were, without exception, air-cooled, and most, as a result, had easily changeable barrels; it became an accepted part of machine gun drill to swap barrels after some few hundred rounds had been fired, and most designers took that into account (though some, inexplicably, did not make the process easy or straightforward – the abysmal original procedure for changing the barrel of the M60 GPMG is a case in point, as we shall discover in due course in Chapter Five). Gas actuation took over from recoil actuation during the same period – light machine guns were almost exclusively gas-operated, and the virtues of that system, chiefly its greater degree of controllability, soon became apparent. Thus, by the time the machine gun had been in common use for 40 years or less, the original form – water-cooled and recoil-operated – had already given way to the forerunner of the modern GPMG. It was to be some time yet before the concept came of age, but the winds of change had already begun to blow.

■ BELOW: The Soviet Union developed a replacement for the PM1910 Maxim at the end of World War II; The People's Republic of China put it into production as the Type 57, shown here.

CHAPTER 3
THE LIGHT MACHINE GUN – A TACTICAL IMPERATIVE

The introduction of the machine gun changed the nature of warfare virtually instantaneously; its ability to control wide areas at long range from protected defensive positions reduced the old attack formations to a bloody shambles time and again. To combat it, a new scheme of infantry attack was required, combining a revised assault plan with the firepower of automatic weaponry.

The plan was simple enough to devise and put into practice; instead of advancing in strictly policed lines and at a regulated pace across a battlefield already pounded into featureless uniformity by artillery barrage, infantrymen would now be split into squads of up to a dozen under the control of a junior NCO, each one supporting its neighbours with covering fire. Having foregone the preparatory barrage in favour of surprise, the assault was thus able to use the natural features of the terrain – hedgerows, walls, ditches, dead ground, etcetera – as well as darkness to keep out of the enemy's line of sight and line of fire until his positions could be assaulted or cut off and neutralised. The fieldcraft was simple, but the key to the exercise was firepower.

Some of the machine guns which would eventually come to be used in this role had actually been around for some time before World War I broke out. We

■LEFT: The modernised, miniature-calibre 5.45mm Kalashnikov in its light machine gun form, the RPK, is shown here equipped with an image-enhancing sight system.

have already mentioned, at least in passing, the American Lewis gun, the Danish Schouboe/Madsen and the Franco-American Bénét-Mercie *Modèle '09*. There were others, too – but they had never been taken up wholeheartedly. Even as late as 1916, far too many highly placed individuals still considered the machine gun to be an artillery piece, albeit in miniature, and were convinced that it should obey the same sort of rules of engagement and deployment that applied to field guns.

As far as can be ascertained, the tactical breakthrough actually came at Riga on the Eastern Front, where a German officer named von Hutier put into practice a scheme devised at German General Headquarters, using Madsen LMGs as the basis of mobile firepower. Success at Riga led to the formation of specialist *Stosstruppen* units on the Somme front and at Verdun. These, too, were armed with Madsen guns initially, many of them captured from Russian cavalry units and re-chambered for the standard German rifle round, but they were soon equipped with the new lightened MG08/15 described in the previous chapter. The success of these

Madsen Let Maschingevaer

Calibre: 8mm M89
Weight: 9kg (20lb)
Length: 1145mm (45in)
Barrel length: 585mm (23in)
Effective range: 1000m (3300ft)
Configuration: magazine-fed, recoil-operated, air-cooled
Cyclic rate of fire: 450rpm
Muzzle velocity: 715mps (2350fps)
Country of Origin: Denmark

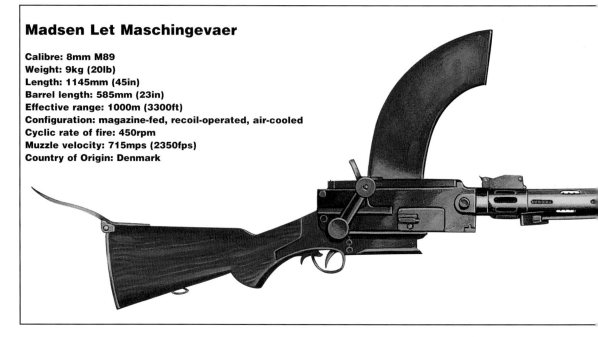

new assault units caused a general – and very drastic – rethink in armies the world over.

THE DANISH MADSEN

Dansk Industri Syndikat started making the light machine gun which became known as the Madsen, named after the Danish Minister for War of the day. The gun was actually invented by Schouboe, and was manufactured initially by the Rexer Arms Co. just on the turn of the twentieth century – by 1903, the model was being tested by the US Army against the Colt Model 1895 and the 'New Pattern' Maxim Model 1901 – and they were to go on doing so for over 50 years, despite it never having been selected as a primary weapon by any major military power (though it was sold in over 30 countries, sometimes in quite large numbers; for example, before World War I, both the Russian and the German armies had procured the gun in quantities sufficient for extensive testing). It had a most remarkable action based on that of a rifle which was not even easily adapted to repetition fire, but which had to be loaded manually with each fresh round – the Martini – and on paper, at least, lost out badly to designs which employed far simpler reciprocating bolts and in the absence of a bolt, the Schouboe design incorporated a separate rammer mounted on a pivoted arm to

strip the fresh round out of the vertically mounted spring-loaded magazine (which was to become the standard for units of that type), and chamber it, as well as a separate extractor/ejector to extricate the spent case. The whole assembly was driven by recoil (but neither to the short-nor to the long-recoil pattern). The barrel and block assembly moved back together a scant 12.7mm (.5in), and then rode up onto a horizontally set, non-recoiling switch plate; the extractor/ejector then levered the spent case out of the chamber, below the breech-block, and ejected it through the bottom of the receiver; a stud on the block, which was still travelling rearwards, then cocked the hammer against the pressure of a coiled spring, whereupon the block was forced down and the pivoted rammer arm fed a round into the now-exposed chamber. The breech-block was now free to move forwards again, and following the track in the switch plate, returned to the closed position, leaving the hammer cocked and ready to impact upon the firing pin. It perhaps sounds unnecessarily complex (and one authoritative analyst wonders that it functioned at all), but when compared to some locking actions it was actually quite simple and straightforward. The gun which embodied it was notably reliable as a result, at least, with rimless ammunition. The British tested it in a

version adapted to take rimmed .303in rounds and were disappointed at its performance. It achieved a cyclic rate of around 450 rounds per minute (rpm), though its real rate of fire was very much less than that of course – perhaps 120 rounds per minute (rpm) – and its ballistic performance depended on the type of round for which it was chambered; unloaded weight was just 9kg (19.8lb) or some 3kg (6.6lb) lighter than the Lewis gun, 1kg (2.2lb) lighter than the later Bren. The basic gun was produced in a variety of forms, with a bipod and buttstock, for infantry use, and with a pintle mounting and spade- and pistol-grips for use in aircraft. Some *Let Maskingevaer Madsens* (Madsen LMGs) captured by German forces when they overran Denmark in 1940 were even converted to accept belted ammunition under a modification programme instigated by the German Air Force.

MCCLEAN AND LEWIS

At around the same time that Schouboe was developing his gun, a physician in the US mid-western state of Iowa was neglecting his medical practice in favour of a career in the more lucrative field of arms manufacture. Samuel McClean moved to Cleveland, Ohio in the mid-1890s, took out his first patent for an 'improvement' to an existing machine gun in 1898 and by the turn of the century

had set up the McClean Arms and Ordnance Company. In or around 1903 he produced the prototype of a lightweight, air-cooled gun weighing under 9kg (19.8lb) which he claimed was simpler, and with fewer parts, than the Hotchkiss M'le'00, and over the next three to five years is reputed to have fruitlessly spent over $500,000 of his own and investors' money in trying to perfect the design and sell it to the US military establishment. In this author's opinion, that sum has probably been considerably overstated, but the basis for the assertion is probably accurate, for by 1906 McClean was broke, and had lost control of his company.

At this point, a US Army officer named Isaac Newton Lewis entered the picture. Lewis had two tenuous claims to fame: he had designed a successful rangefinder for the artillery, and had become embroiled in a very public dispute over the quality of US ordnance with a senior officer, General William Crozier, which had resulted in his being posted to 'limbo' – initially San Francisco, later Puget Sound. Crozier was to have a further profound effect on Lewis's life, but that was still in the future; in 1904 the young Captain was rehabilitated and returned closer to the centre of things, at Fort Monroe, Virginia, where he ultimately

held the post of Commander. During this time, Lewis apparently 'began to realise his true value to the world of science', as one somewhat uncritical biographer put it. In 1908 we find him obtaining approval from the Secretary of the Army to act as a paid consultant to the McClean Arms and Ordnance Company. He was to become a prime mover in the dealings which followed, and in the scheme which saw McClean ousted and divested of the rights to his own inventions. Within three years, Lewis had produced a design of his own for a lightweight, air-cooled gun, using the mechanism McClean had devised, and with not a little aid from O.A. Huberty, McClean's own assistant and machinist. McClean was later to claim – in a lawsuit begun 1920 and not completed until 1924 – that Lewis simply appropriated his basic design, made changes to the cooling system (see below) and devised a new pan-type indexing drum magazine. He lost his suit when Lewis demonstrated that essential parts of the design were based on common concepts, and not protected by patent (though if that were actually the case, it is difficult to see how Lewis himself can have felt that he had any valid protection for *his* design), and thereupon disappeared from view.

■BELOW: German troops sent to the Austro-Italian front to stiffen their allies are shown here armed with Mauser bolt-action rifles and Madsen light machine guns.

Lewis Gun Mark 1

Calibre: .303in
Weight: 11.8kg (26lb)
Length: 965mm (38in)
Barrel length: 665mm (26.25in)
Effective range: 1000m (3300ft)+

Configuration: magazine-fed, gas-operated, air-cooled
Cyclic rate of fire: 550rpm
Muzzle velocity: 600mps (1970fps)
Country of Origin: United States

■LEFT: Lewis guns were just as popular with German troops as they were with their British counterparts. Captured examples were highly prized trophies on both sides.

gun he eventually produced, which despite its considerable shortcomings was to become one of the most important small arms of World War I and beyond.

THE LEWIS GUN
The action of the Lewis gun was certainly different from anything previously seen, being based on a turnbolt design (something which, as we shall see, was to become very popular indeed later in the century). Gas passed from the barrel into a cylinder below it via a tapping and a simple two-position regulator; there it impinged on the face of a piston which was driven back. Meanwhile, a rack on its underside engaged a pinion and so wound up a spiral recoil spring. A post on the piston's upper surface was permanently engaged in a slot in the hollow bolt; a helical cam path cut in the bolt, within which a fixed lug was located, rotated it as it was pushed back by the piston post, unlocking it before causing it to reciprocate, extracting a spent case, indexing the drum magazine and returning to chamber a fresh round in the process. The firing pin was fixed,

■RIGHT: Royal Marines man twin Lewis guns in an anti-aircraft mount aboard the 15in-gunned HMS *Valiant* in 1931, showing the lightest and heaviest calibres together in Royal Navy service.

LEWIS REBUFFED
By 1911, Lewis had produced a working gun (actually, he had produced five examples, made by hand at considerable cost), and proceeded to demonstrate them to the US Board of Ordnance, the head of which was William Crozier. Certainly, the guns were not perfect, but equally certainly the faults in them, which were all to be corrected during series manufacture, did not warrant the Board's decision to reject them out of hand. Lewis, piqued beyond endurance by his old enemy's final fling ('slapped with rejections by ignorant hacks' was how he put it), promptly moved, lock, stock and barrel, to Europe, where he set up in business firstly in Belgium, and later in

the UK, where he became rich thanks to the massive royalty payments he extracted from the British government for the gun which they took up in 1915. As a result of the Board of Ordnance's decision to reject the Lewis gun, the US Army was to go to war against Germany with the impossible and entirely unsuitable French Chauchat, (much to the delight of the French government, which sold the US guns which it could not otherwise give away).

So much for the achievements of Isaac Newton Lewis. Were he indeed little more than a plagiarist, after all, he would not have been the first such in the field of machine gun design; more interesting – and more relevant – is the worth of the

Twin Lewis Guns (Aircraft mounting)

Calibre: .303in
Weight: 11.8kg (26lb)
Length: 965mm (38in)
Barrel length: 665mm (26.25in)
Effective range: 1000m (330ft)+
Configuration: magazine-fed, gas-operated, air-cooled
Cyclic rate of fire: 550rpm
Muzzle velocity: 600mps (1970fps)
Country of Origin: United States

■ABOVE: US Infantrymen armed with the M1 Garand rifle (left), and the BAR – the Browning Automatic Rifle – which was the US Army's LMG of choice from 1917 until its withdrawal in 1953.

and formed part of the piston post; it was held off by the trigger sear against the pressure from the volute spring. The gun fired from an open bolt. Lewis' self-proclaimed genius (he called his invention 'the best thing he had ever heard of in connection with a machine gun') lay in the cooling process he had developed – a steel tube surrounded the barrel from receiver to muzzle, and was spaced from it by an array of longitudinal aluminium fins. Lewis claimed that this arrangement forced cold air to pass the length of the barrel, sucked in at the receiver and expelled around the muzzle, in this way cooling the barrel. Guns produced by Savage in the USA and designed for use in aircraft lacked this arrangement, and were some 1.6kg (4lb) lighter, as a result; when, during World

War II, these guns were employed in the ground role (notably by the British Home Guard), they were found to be no less efficiently cooled than guns with the enclosed barrel, forcing the inevitable conclusion that World War I infantrymen were condemned to carry the extra weight about needlessly, because Lewis had wanted to make some show of 'his' design being radically different from McClean's. Poor Bloody Infantry indeed!

In its most common form, as the Gun, Machine, Lewis, .303in Mk 1, it actually weighed rather more than McClean's original version, almost 12kg (26lb). It could be fitted with drum magazines holding either 47 or 97 rounds of Mk 7 .303in ammunition, and fired at a cyclic rate of 550 rounds per minute (rpm), which translated to a real rate of around one fifth of that. There was no provision for firing single shots. It was produced in huge numbers – BSA in Birmingham, England manufactured over 145,000, and both Savage and Rockwell-Marlin in the USA also placed it in volume production,

if somewhat belatedly, to fill orders from the British Government, rather than their own. The US Army never did officially adopt the gun, except for use in aircraft; some were manufactured under licence by Darne in France for the French Army. It was widely held to be at its best when employed in aircraft and aboard ships and boats, where it didn't have to suffer the incursion of mud and dust that produced constant problems for the infantrymen who carried it into battle; its main drawback was its complexity, which produced what one commentator has described as an astounding variety of malfunctions and stoppages, and its ammunition supply mechanism was flawed and prone to misfeeding.

In the true LMG role, it was too heavy; but when all that was said and done, it was much quicker to produce than the Vickers Class C (though, thanks to Lewis's royalty, it was significantly more expensive – in 1915, a Lewis gun made by BSA cost the British government about £150, of which more than half went to Lewis himself; a Vickers Class C gun cost the government £100. By 1917, the cost had been reduced to a much more realistic level). By the time World War I ended, the Lewis outnumbered its rival in British service by something in the order of three to one. There were – nominally, at least – eight marks of Lewis gun adopted by the British between 15 October 1915, when they were first accepted, and 26 August 1946, when they were finally declared obsolete, but in fact only one version of the infantry/naval LMG (that is, with the barrel shroud and cooling fins) was ever produced, and the versions for use in the air, with the barrel shroud but no cooling fins, were all essentially similar. All versions could accept either a rifle-type buttstock or a spade grip, according to the use to which they were to be put. There were plans to produce an unshrouded version, similar in appearance to the Savage-Lewis but with a wooden foregrip, as an infantry LMG, but they were shelved. As we have noted elsewhere, Lewis guns were much sought-after by German troops, too.

BROWNING'S AUTOMATIC RIFLE

When Lewis first quit the USA he went to Belgium, where another expatriate American gunsmith, John Browning, had also set up shop, after a disagreement with his original partners, Winchester, about a self-loading shotgun. Browning soon established a close relationship with Fabrique National in Herstal-lez-Liège, originally set up by the Loewe company of Berlin to manufacture Mauser rifles, though he was also still connected with Colt in the USA. By this time – 1913 – Browning's work on the sustained-fire, recoil-operated MMG which was to

become the M1917 was well advanced, and he had begun work on a selective-fire weapon, capable of fully automatic fire or single shots, but this time magazine-fed and light enough – just – to be used as what we now call an assault rifle. For this, his third design for a machine gun, Browning reverted to gas actuation, and the result was to become both popular and successful. He adopted a simple locking system – a lug which protruded upwards from the body of the bolt, and which locked into a recess in the receiver top and was released by the toggle action of a link pin which also acted on the extractor to perform primary extraction before the bolt itself was propelled backwards to cycle the action. If anything, the original trigger mechanism, which could be set for single shots or repetitive fire or to safe, was rather more complex. It is a tribute to the simple effectiveness of the locking system that it was copied (albeit inverted) for use in one of the best of the general-purpose machine guns, the FN MAG, which was to be the sustained-fire weapon of choice for many of the world's armies for the last half of the twentieth century (see Chapter Five).

Universally known by its initials as the BAR, the Browning Automatic Rifle did not, however, satisfy its designer. He thought it fell between two stools, as it were, and strictly speaking, he was right. At over 8kg (18lb), including a full magazine, it was too heavy to be used as a rifle, certainly when fired standing, from the shoulder, and was not capable of any great accuracy even in single-shot mode, due to its open-bolt action, in which the reciprocating parts were held to the rear when the action was cocked, and slammed forward when the trigger

was pulled, inevitably moving the gun off the point of aim. In automatic mode it was too light, and hence again inaccurate, and its 20-round magazine meant it had to be frequently reloaded (but even so, a variant known as the M1918A2, which could not be set to fire single rounds, but which instead had two pre-set cyclic rates of automatic fire – 300 and 600 rounds per minute – was also produced). For all that it didn't satisfy Browning, it actually lived up to its design requirements very well indeed, because the concept of self-support it fulfilled called for a weapon capable of delivering significant firepower from the hip while the infantryman assaulted an enemy position at walking pace (or so went the theory, anyway). Some versions, the M1918A1 and -A2, which entered service in 1941, were fitted with bipods, which made them altogether better weapons; all were originally chambered for the .30in M1906 round.

The BAR was taken up by many countries throughout the world, and stayed in continuous front line service with the US Army and Marine Corps from its adoption in 1917 (it was first employed in combat on 13 September 1918) until the end of the Korean War in 1953, when, together with the then-standard M1 Garand rifle, it was replaced by the M14 rifle, which itself had a limited capacity for fully automatic fire. The last BARs in service with the US Army were withdrawn with the coming of the M60 general-purpose

■BELOW: The Browning Automatic Rifle became a much more satisfactory weapon in 1941, following the introduction of a bipod, fitted as standard.

Hotchkiss M1922
(Greek M/1926)

Calibre: 6.5mm Mannlicher
Weight: 9.5kg (21lb)
Length: 1215mm (47.75in)
Barrel length: 575mm (22.75in)
Effective range: 1000m (3300ft)

Configuration: strip-fed, gas-operated, air-cooled
Cyclic rate of fire: 450rpm
Muzzle velocity: 680mps (2225fps)
Country of Origin: France

machine gun in 1957. It was produced by Colt, Marlin-Rockwell and Winchester in the United States (and in small numbers by a variety of other companies, including IBM), and also by FN in Belgium, the State-owned Carl Gustav factory in Sweden and in Poland, in a variety of calibres and with quick-change barrels. And while the Thompson (qv) may have been 'the gun that made the twenties roar', not a few gangsters and law-enforcement agencies preferred the more predictable BAR – marketed commercially by Colt as the R75 and later as the Monitor – to the short-barrelled sub-machine gun. Among its more infamous victims were Bonnie Parker and Clyde Barrow.

HOTCHKISS LMGS
So urgent was the need for machine guns in the British Army during World War I that as well as purchasing huge numbers of expensive Lewis guns, the British turned to their closest allies (at least in

■LEFT: The Chauchat is widely held to have been one of the least satisfactory automatic weapons ever produced. Nevertheless, the US Army went to war with it in 1917.

geographical terms), the French, and obtained the right to manufacture the Hotchkiss *Fusil Mitrailleur Modèle '09*, taking it into service from 1916 as the Gun, Machine, Hotchkiss, .303in Mark I. The US Army adopted the same gun as the Machine Rifle, Bénét-Mercié, Caliber .30 M1909. To produce this lightweight gun (the term is relative; it weighed 12.3kg (27lb) unloaded, but that was little more than half the weight of the tripod-mounted M'le'00 or M'le'14 from which it stemmed) Bénét redesigned the locking mechanism, exchanging the flaps for a fermature nut into which both the barrel and the breech-block were screwed (by less than half a turn), which was rotated out of closure by gas pressure acting on a short under-barrel piston which had a helical slot cut into it, to translate reciprocating motion into rotation. Both British and American troops found the gun a useful addition to their armouries, and the former soon modified the strip feed system to accept the same pseudo-belt – actually short three-round strips joined by a flexible link – which Bénét had devised in an effort to improve the sustained-fire performance of the heavier Hotchkiss guns. Guns so modified became the Mark

I* Nos. 1 and 2 , and were still to be found in service with reserve units and the Home Guard in 1939; they were not finally declared obsolete until 1946. Hotchkiss Mark I* light machine guns also formed the secondary armament of Britain's first-generation tanks.

THE EXECRABLE CHAUCHAT
With a perfectly adequate LMG in the shape of the Hotchkiss M'le'09 at its disposal, it is something of a mystery why the French Army turned instead to what is, virtually universally, held to have been the worst automatic weapon of its – or any other – day. The *Fusil Mitrailleur Modèle 1915*, widely known as the Chauchat, after the man who headed the four-strong commission which accepted it for service sometime just prior to the outbreak of war – was a long-recoil-operated weapon. (The others were Suterre, Ribeyrolle and Gladiator and the gun was sometimes known by all their initials, as the CSRG, and also,when it was adopted briefly by Greece in the years after World War I, as the Gladiator). The barrel and breech-block remained locked together for the full extent of the rearward stroke, whereupon separation occurred and the barrel

Fusil Mitrailleur M'15 ('Chauchat')

Calibre: 8mm Lebel
Weight: 9kg (20lb)
Length: 1145mm (45in)
Barrel length: 470mm (18.5in)
Effective range: 1000m (3300ft)

Configuration: magazine-fed,
    recoil-operated, air-cooled
Cyclic rate of fire: 250rpm
Muzzle velocity: 700mps (2300fps)
Country of Origin: France

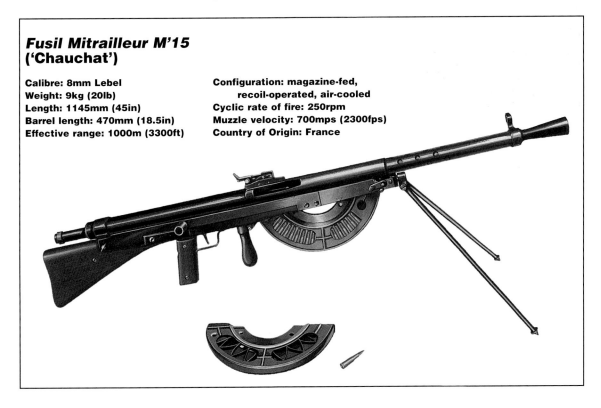

returned to battery, clearing the chamber by ejecting the spent round in the process. The breech-block was then released, stripping a fresh round out of the magazine and chambering it. It was not an action well-suited to a light gun such as the Chauchat – its weight, just 9kg (19.8lb) was perhaps its only virtue – and the problem was compounded by the poorly executed mass-production techniques used in its manufacture, which required that working tolerances be kept very large, and by the fact that the standard of raw materials available was generally low. The high rate of stoppages and jams caused by the poor fit of the components was exacerbated by the use of the totally unsuitable 8mm Lebel cartridge, the standard French Army issue of the day, which had a very pronounced taper and required the 20-round box magazine to be semi-circular in form.

Thanks to William Crozier's steadfast refusal to countenance the US Army procuring guns from Lewis – whom he always believed had attempted to make a fool of him in order to advance his own career – when the first 12 US Army divisions arrived in France in 1917, they were, almost incredibly, without machine guns of any sort. The French Government supplied 16,000 Chauchats in the original

8mm Lebel chambering to make good the deficiency, but this made for logistical difficulties of ammunition supply, and soon after, the French actually managed to sell their new allies 19,000 more, this time chambered for the American rimless .30in M1906 round, the guns thus modified being known as the US Machine Rifle, Chauchat, Caliber .30in M1918. This modification, while theoretically an improvement, in that it allowed the poorly feeding semi-circular magazine to be replaced by a parallelepiped box, actually made matters worse still, for the more modern round was considerably more powerful than the French M1886 cartridge it replaced (which, we may recall, was the first smokeless cartridge ever produced; pyrotechnology had moved on a long way in the meantime), and placed a further, often intolerable, strain on the already overloaded components.

THE *MITRAILLEUSE DARNE*

Ironically, the revenue the French government received from the US Army for the 19,000 Chauchats it foisted off onto was largely spent on Lewis guns! These were produced locally, in St Etienne, by the long-established firm of R&P Darne, which had gained a high reputation during the nineteenth century as makers of quality sporting guns and

rifles. Someone high in Darne et Cie clearly understood the proverb about horses for courses, however, and in 1917, the company produced a design for a lightweight, gas-operated, belt-fed gun manufactured by the simplest possible process and only crudely finished – a very radical departure from its previous practice, where no arm would have been permitted to leave the workshop until it was perfect, and an approach which was later to be adopted almost universally, much to the soldiery's disgust. The *Mitrailleuse Darne, Modèle 1918* was quickly accepted for service, and was put into production just across the Spanish border in the ill-fated Basque capital, Guernica, by Unceta Y Cia, where it could be manufactured at even less cost than in France. The Darne may have been manufactured at rock-bottom price to a very limited specification, but it was undeniably effective, particularly in the air, since it had a high cyclic rate of fire; it stayed in service with the French Air Force until the 1930s. An improved version, manufactured and finished to a rather higher standard, was even considered, just prior to World War II, by the RAF in the competition which saw the air-cooled Browning M2 accepted as the British Air Force's standard rifle-calibre machine gun.

Fusil Mitrailleur M'24/29 (Châtelerault)

Calibre: 7.5mm M29
Weight: 9.25kg (20.25lb)
Length: 1080mm (42.5in)
Barrel length: 500mm (19.75in)
Effective range: 1000m (3300ft)
Configuration: magazine-fed, gas-operated, air-cooled
Cyclic rate of fire: 500rpm
Muzzle velocity: 825mps (2700fps)
Country of Origin: France

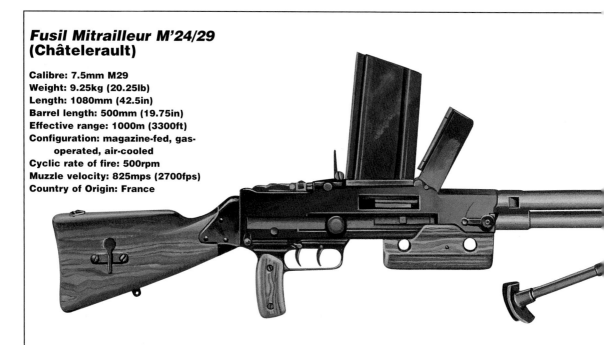

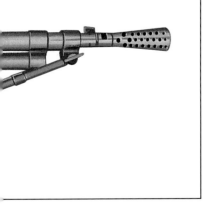

■ABOVE: French troops in Indo-China in the early 1950s with the Châtelerault LMG. The MAS36 rifle was an effective expedient support, its foresight set back with just that objective in mind.

The Darne was never a particularly sound infantry weapon for the same reason that it was successful in the air, but just like everyone else, the French knew that an effective light machine gun was essential to a modern army, and it desperately needed a replacement for the execrable Chauchat. The first alternative it was offered came from Hotchkiss, and was functionally a much slimmed-down version of the M'le'14, using the original flap locking mechanism, not the fermature nut of the M'le'09. Its main shortcoming was probably the 8mm Lebel cartridge for which it was chambered. It was offered either with the by-now standard Hotchkiss strip feed, or with a top-mounted 'banana' box magazine, reminiscent of the Madsen. It came with a bipod (with rather curious skid-like feet) and a sharply cut-off flash suppresser-cum-muzzle compensator, which was supposed to provide downthrust to stabilise the gun, but which seems to have been completely ineffective. It was never widely successful, though the Greek Army did take it up (as the M/1926 in 6.5mm x 54

Type 96

Calibre: 6.5mm Arisaka
Weight: 9kg (20lb)
Length: 1055mm (41.5in)
Barrel length: 555mm (21.75in)
Effective range: 1000m (3300ft)
Configuration: magazine-fed, gas-operated, air-cooled
Cyclic rate of fire: 550rpm
Muzzle velocity: 730mps (2300fps)
Country of Origin: Japan

Mannlicher calibre, a much more successful chambering) to replace its Gladiators.

THE 7.5MM CHÂTELLERAULT

The French Army did not adopt the new Hotchkiss (which was actually the last rifle-calibre automatic weapon that company developed). From this time on, the French Army's small arms were to be developed in national armouries, not by private business concerns; that arrangement continued until the French arms industry was reprivatised in the 1990s. Instead the French opted to switch from the by-now rather antiquated 8mm rimmed Lebel cartridge to a round with a better performance and a handier profile. The result was based broadly on the rimless 7.92mm round which had been the standard for the German Army since 1888, in 7.5mm nominal calibre, and was adopted in 1924. In fact, the new round proved somewhat deficient, and was replaced five years later by a modified version with a somewhat shorter case and a projectile weighing 9g (139 grains), delivering a muzzle velocity of around 825mps (2700fps).

It was probably something of an arbitrary decision as to whether a new

ABOVE: The Taisho 11th Year (11 Nen Shiki Kikanju), the first Japanese-made LMG and introduced in 1922, was essentially a Hotchkiss converted from strip- to hopper-feed.

light machine gun or a new rifle should be developed first in that calibre, but the existing service rifle, designed by Berthier as long ago as 1892, and much modified later, was at least functional, whereas the Chauchat was not, and the decision was made to concentrate on the LMG. In rather atypical fashion – for the French have been seldom known to adopt an existing solution when it was possible to devise a new one, particularly when the idea is foreign – the decision was made, therefore, to utilise the action of the BAR, small numbers of which had been procured during the war just ended. The most significant difference between the new design and the BAR was the position of its box magazine – on top of, rather than underneath, the receiver, which meant that a larger-capacity unit than the rather scant 20-round BAR magazine could be incorporated. Additionally, the gas tapping was located closer to the muzzle, and there was a recoil shock absorber located in the

buttstock, both of which contributed to the gun having a rather less violent action than its progenitor.

The new gun first appeared in 1924, and it was during prolonged testing of it that the decision to modify the M1924 round was taken. The gun was adapted too, and reissued as the *Fusil Mitrailleur Modèle 1924/29*, commonly called the Châtellerault, after the armoury where it was developed. Like the BAR which it so resembled, the Châtellerault was to remain in service until the 1950s. In 1931, a version of the basic gun without its rifle-type buttstock and with a 150-round capacity drum magazine mounted on the left hand side of the receiver was produced expressly for deployment in the static defences of the Maginot Line of forts, which stretched from the Swiss to the Belgian borders, and which the Germans who invaded the country in 1940 simply bypassed. The M'le'31, as it was known, also found employment in French tanks; it must be said that it was

a rather strange choice of weapon for static defensive purposes, for there was a limit to the amount of sustained fire a gun like the Châtellerault could be expected to produce.

THE LMG IN JAPAN

Having adopted the Hotchkiss as their first-generation medium machine gun, and subsequently opting to modify it and keep it in production long after it was technically obsolete, it comes as no surprise to discover that the Japanese also followed the Hotchkiss model – this time that of the M'le'09 – for the gun they adopted as the *11 Nen Shiki Kikanju* in 1922. The main modification was to the feed mechanism, but far from improving on the strip system, the result was a most peculiar and rather retrograde step. A hopper was situated on the left hand side of the receiver, into which up to six charger clips loaded with five rounds of 6.5mm ammunition, as used by the Arisaka rifle, were placed, and held down

by a heavy spring-loaded arm. A simple ratchet arrangement, actuated by the rearwards motion of the breech-block, pulled the bottom clip in towards the feed mechanism, which stripped out one cartridge after another, oiling them in the process – the gun had no primary extraction, and that process was highly problematical as a result – and ejecting the empty charger in due course. The attraction of this system was clear; it allowed any rifleman to supply the LMG with ammunition without having to load magazines or belts, but any advantage it might have conveyed was far outweighed by the problems inherent in the system itself. Despite its shortcomings, the gun was still in service up to 1945. A similar gun, but with a hopper enlarged to take 10 clips, was adopted as the Type 91, and was fitted to the first-generation Japanese tanks.

In 1936, Nambu – now in business for himself as the Nambu Rifle Manufacturing Company – modified the

design by replacing the hopper system with a 'banana' type magazine. It was still chambered for the 6.5mm Meiji 30 rifle cartridge, despite the introduction, some four years previously, of a more powerful 7.7mm semi-rimless round, and Nambu did nothing to improve the extraction system save that the oiling of the cartridges now took place as they were loaded into the magazine, and the gun was lighter and somewhat simpler as a result. He did, however, provide a quick-change mechanism for the barrel, and the gun looked, at any rate, very much like the Czech ZB vz26 and its successors (down to the finned barrel) or the Vickers-Berthier (see below). When a version chambered for the 7.7mm round (in fact, the improved rimless version introduced in 1939) finally appeared, in something of a hurry that same year, these deficiencies, however, had been addressed; there was now satisfactory primary extraction, and the cases no longer required oiling. The barrel

Lehky Kulomet ZB vz30

Calibre: 7.92mm
Weight: 9.6kg (21.25lb)
Length: 1160mm (45.75in)
Barrel length: 670mm (26.5in)
Effective range: 1000m (3300ft)+
Configuration: magazine-fed, gas-
**   operated, air-cooled**
Cyclic rate of fire: 500rpm
Muzzle velocity: 800mps (2650fps)
Country of Origin: Czechoslovakia

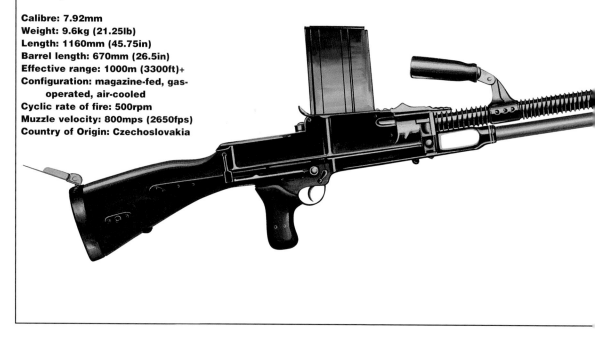

retention system received attention, too, and became something much closer to that of the Czech LMGs, with an interrupted-thread barrel nut rotated by a simple catch. It was an altogether better gun in consequence, but came rather too late, and substantially fewer Type 99 LMGs were produced than Type 96s.

In 1937, the 6.5mm Type 91 tank machine gun, with its unwieldy hopper feed, was replaced by a straightforward copy of the Czech ZB vz 26, chambered for the semi-rimless 7.7mm round. This decision was somewhat misguided, to say the least, for the way in which the gun was mounted prevented the barrel from being changed easily; over-exuberant gunners soon learned how easy it was to shoot out a barrel, as a result, despite the frequent halts necessary to change the 30-round capacity magazine.

GERMANY, POST-1918
As we have noted, the Versailles Treaty which officially ended World War I forbade Germany to develop new automatic weapons (and indeed, prohibited the cut-down German Army from holding more than 792 medium and 1134 light machine guns; those limits were subsequently increased to 861 and

1475 respectively, but by that time Germany had begun her descent into post-War chaos, and the numbers probably don't mean much. It's worth bearing in mind, perhaps, that the total number of machine guns handed over to the Allies after the Armistice of 1918 was of the order of just 30,000; even when the number of guns previously captured was taken into account, there was still a substantial discrepancy somewhere, and that meant that a lot of 'unofficial' German machine guns were still in existence; this was confirmed in 1945, when tens of thousands of World War I-vintage machine guns were discovered in German armouries). It was to be almost a decade and a half before Germany began openly to rearm, but in the interim, a considerable amount of development work went on, either in secret, or in countries prepared to turn a blind eye to the legality of the situation in return for a share of the product. Holland, the Soviet Union, Sweden and Switzerland were the most important of these, and as we shall see, Spain was to become an invaluable proving ground. In Germany itself, just one company – Simson & Cie of Suhl, just south of Erfurt – was permitted to manufacture machine gun parts and complete guns, though as we

■RIGHT: The ZB vz26, seen here in Czech service in the early 1930s, was the first in a very successful series of light machine guns to go into production.

shall see, a considerable amount of work done elsewhere was to be passed off as having come from the Simson factory.

Since the main thrust of the German effort in the field went into developing a true *Einheitsmaschinengewehr,* (a successor – though actually, only in spirit – to the aborted Erfurt-developed MG16, which we shall consider within the context of the general-purpose machine gun, in Chapter Five), there is ostensibly very little to say on the subject of light machine gun development in Germany during this period. In fact, there were a number of more or less successful LMGs developed, the best of them by German engineers working abroad, particularly in neighbouring Switzerland, and especially in Solothurn, where Rheinmetall made an important acquisition: Waffenfabrik Solothurn AG. Originally concerned with watch-making, the company converted to arms manufacture at some point soon after World War I. Rheinmetall gained control in 1929, and immediately began to put its own designs – machine guns

prominent amongst them – into limited production there. Rheinmetall had earlier made another important connection, with Steyr in Austria (and may eventually have acquired the company outright), and had also established a design bureau in Moscow, though that was concerned with artillery pieces and ammunition. By the time the National Socialists rose to power in 1933, and Germany began to take an active – and threatening – part in European affairs once more, Rheinmetall, which soon merged with Borsig, a manufacturer of heavy plant and locomotives, was very well placed indeed

to act as a major developer and supplier of armaments of all sorts.

THE RHEINMETALL MG13

In the previous chapter we touched briefly on the history of the almost-stillborn Dreyse MG10/MG15 and the even more elusive *Muskete*, and it is to that point which we must return now if we are to make sense of the development process which followed. The MG13 has been described as simply a rebuild of the old Dreyse guns left over from World War I, but there is no justification for that assertion. To begin with, Rheinmetall actually continued the development of those guns in a model the German Army designated the MG14 – a water-cooled MMG using the Schmeisser-designed dropping block action, firing from a closed bolt. This was on sale commercially as late as 1929. Thus, there would have been no real reason to have adapted earlier, less efficient guns. The confusion perhaps comes about as a result of the 'new' gun having a designation – MG13 – which seems to indicate an earlier origin, but there is well-reasoned speculation that the designation was an act of subterfuge, designed to convince the (by that time) fairly lax Allied Control Commission that the gun was an old design and thus exempt from the ban on new developments contained in the Versailles Treaty. It was a much lighter gun all round than the others, air-cooled from the start, with a perforated barrel shroud and a skeleton butt which could be folded to lie alongside the receiver. It was magazine- rather than belt-fed – originally it was fitted with a horizontally mounted 25-round box, but later a '*doppeltrommel*', a double drum or saddle drum, was also used. This magazine was originally developed for the MG15 (see below) and was also employed with the MG34 (qv). The MG13 was intended for bipod mounting and the support could be fixed either at the muzzle or near the receiver; when the lightweight *dreifuss 34* tripod with extendible legs became available, that, too, could be employed, though the ensemble's performance was poor – when fully extended for use against aircraft, for example, it required

■LEFT: The Wehrmacht took readily to the ZB vz26 (as it did to many Czech weapons and vehicles during the late 1930s), and put it into German service as the MG26(t).

ABOVE: The MG08/15, as its name suggests, was an attempt to adapt the MG08 Maxim to the LMG role, by the simple expedient of fitting it with a bipod, pistol-grip and shoulder stock.

the presence of a second man to kneel inside the tripod and hold it down. The much heavier, rigid *Lafette 34* tripod, developed for the MG34, was never modified for employment with the MG13. Like those of the Dreyse guns described in Chapter Two, the barrel of the MG13 could be replaced, but only via the receiver. The MG13 was equipped with a rocking trigger; pressure on the top portion gave single shots, while pressure on the bottom engaged a bar which disconnected the sear and gave fully automatic fire.

Taken together, these factors undoubtedly place the gun firmly in the LMG category; it was intended as a portable automatic weapon, to supply fire support during assault operations, but not for use in the conventional fixed-position, sustained-fire MMG role, even though it had the same theoretical ballistic performance, since it used the same ammunition as the heavier guns and had a barrel almost identically dimensioned. The MG13 saw limited service with the resurgent *Wehrmacht*

from about 1930 onwards; thus, it was almost immediately rendered obsolescent by the first-generation *Einheitsmaschinengewehr*, the MG34. It was produced only at the Rheinmetall plant at Sömmerda, and offered for sale (to the US government, amongst others) through Simson & Cie of Suhl as if it were their own product. It was never produced by Solothurn, though some aspects of its design were incorporated into weapons developed there.

THE SOLOTHURN GUNS

The first weapon to be produced at Solothurn was a blowback-action machine pistol developed jointly with Steyr from the wartime designs of Hugo Schmeisser, the MP18/1 and MP28/II (qv), known as the S1-100 and later as the MP34(ö), which we will examine in more detail in the next chapter. It is of passing interest here, though, for it was also offered with a longer, heavier barrel and a bipod mount for use as a light machine gun, despite being chambered for pistol rounds such as the 7.63mm Mauser and various 9mm loads. Next, however, came an LMG proper, developed at Sömmerda by Louis Stange and known originally as the Söda or Rh29. When the project was transferred to Solothurn, it became known as the S2-200; it was

never manufactured in quantity there – the Solothurn factory was small, and essentially reserved for development work – but rather at the Steyr works in Austria. The S2-200 operated on the short recoil principle. The barrel and breech-block were locked together by a collar (similar in nature to the fermature nut Bénét used in the French M'le'09, but with an interrupted thread, a much more effective form) and travelled together over a short distance of 19mm (.75in) during which time unlocking took place, releasing the bolt to continue its travel and cycle the action and the barrel to return to battery. The reciprocating mass was kept low, and with a strong recoil spring, a cyclic rate of around 800 rounds per minute (rpm) was attainable, though there is little, actually, to recommend such a high rate of fire in a weapon of this nature. Stange took account of this, and provided a selective fire capability by means of a rocking trigger, the mechanism of which was lifted straight from the MG13. The gun was magazine fed, the 25-round detachable box being located horizontally on the left side of the receiver. The barrel could be changed by a method not entirely unlike – though simpler than – that adopted for the earlier Dreyse guns; the buttstock, with the mainspring and guide attached, came free from the receiver with a simple half-twist; the barrel, locked together with the bolt, was a push-fit into the receiver from the rear, and could now be withdrawn backwards and replaced. It has been estimated that around 5000 S2-200 guns were manufactured between 1930 and 1935, when production appears to have ceased, and it was adopted by both the Austrian and the Hungarian armies, chambered for the already obsolete 8mm x 56 rimmed round. The majority of these guns were later reworked to take the standard German rifle cartridge – a simple enough operation, given that the two were very similar in dimension – at which point the curved magazines with which they were originally equipped were discarded in favour of the magazine designed for the MG13.

THE MG15 AND MG17

The S2-200 was hardly a significant gun in its own right; its importance lies, rather, in the contributions it made to weapons which came after it, notably the MG15 and the MG34. The former was

also developed at Solothurn for use in aircraft, and its locking method was identical to that of the S2-200. It was somewhat simpler than the earlier gun, however – there was no provision for single shots, for example – and thanks to a recoil booster at the muzzle, operated at an even faster cyclic rate. It fired from an open bolt, to improve cooling in the chamber (though it was difficult to ensure synchronisation with a weapon firing from the open bolt position due to the lag between pressing the trigger and the firing cycle commencing, and the MG15 was invariably installed as a flexibly mounted observer's weapon as a result). It was to become the German Air Force's standard flexibly mounted machine gun during its formative years, and was later pressed into service as a light machine gun on the ground, particularly after it had been superseded in the air by the MG17 and the heavier 13mm MG131. In order to provide greater ammunition capacity than was possible from a simple box magazine, the 75-round capacity *doppeltrommel* – a saddle drum magazine, essentially twin

spring-driven drums which incorporated a stepping mechanism which ensured that they fed alternately, to maintain the weight distribution between them as their load was expended – was developed for the MG15 and was later also used to increase the capacity of the MG13. The *doppeltrommel* was less than completely successful, for it was heavy and somewhat cumbersome to change in the confines of an aircraft's turret or cockpit. It required a special filling device which took up the tension on both drums' springs simultaneously. During World War II, most MG15s were replaced in aircraft, and were reissued to ground troops and fitted with a rudimentary tubular buttstock and either with a bipod, or adapted for mounting on the *dreifuss 34* traversing tripod, for use as light anti-aircraft guns. MG15s were also produced under licence by the Japanese,

■**BELOW: The MG08/15 may have been a hasty expedient, but it was effective for all that; this example was still in use in 1939 during German the invasion and occupation of Poland.**

for the army as the Type 98, in 1938, and for the Imperial Navy as the Type 1, in 1941, both apparently in 7.92mm x 57 calibre, rather than for the Japanese 7.7mm round, though that would seem rather anomalous.

An essentially similar gun, but of somewhat heavier construction, the MG17 differed chiefly in its ammunition handling – it was designed to be belt-fed. Otherwise, the chief difference between the two was the provision, in the latter, for synchronised operation. The bolt was released by the trigger in the normal way, but the firing pin itself was released only in response to a synchronisation pulse derived from a cam-and-pushrod arrangement on the aircraft's engine. It had a higher cyclic rate still than the MG15 – around 1200 rounds per minute (rpm) – and was frequently mounted in multiples (twins or quads) both in aircraft and on pedestals as a light AA gun. The MG131, also developed by Rheinmetall, but probably in Germany, rather than in Switzerland, also used the so-called Solothurn lock, together with a bolt accelerator similar to that incorporated in the MG13. Designed exclusively for use in aircraft, the MG131 was fired electrically, and thus used special ammunition; a variety of different trigger mechanisms, both mechanical and magnetic were developed, and the belt could feed from either side after some modification; it was the *Luftwaffe*'s standard machine gun throughout World

War II. As well as in Germany, the MG131 was manufactured in Czechoslovakia, at Brno, and after the war was over, an unsuccessful attempt was made there to produce it as a heavy machine gun for ground forces, for use in vehicles.

Aside from Rheinmetall, only one other German company attempted to produce an LMG in the interwar period, and that was – technically, anyway – a Swedish design, originated in the early 1930s by a Stockholm-based German national named Hans Lauf, which a Berlin manufacturer of brake parts for automobiles, Knorr-Bremse AG, acquired and put into production, apparently with little regard for its poor quality. The Knorr-Bremse *Modell 35* is by no stretch of the imagination a great machine gun. Its biggest failing was probably in the design of its safety catch which, if incorrectly applied, held the bolt at half-cock without engaging the trigger sear; releasing the safety catch subsequently caused the gun to fire a single round, which must have been extremely disconcerting, to say the least. Lauf's intention, it is said, had been to design a gun which was extremely cheap to produce, and in that, if in nothing else, he succeeded. Knorr-Bremse eventually sold a number to the *Waffen-SS*, which used them for training purposes and later issued them to 'foreign' SS Legions, which were always considered expendable anyway.

OTHER SWISS-MADE LMGS
Rheinmetall was not the only company in Switzerland active in the field during the period between the wars. At Waffenfabrik Bern, an officer named Fürrer also developed a light machine gun, usually known simply by his name but officially as the *Leichtes Maschinengewehr Modell 25*, using what was really nothing more than a copy of the Parabellum pistol action developed pre-World War I by Georg Luger at DWM in Berlin. Fürrer simply turned it on its side, so that the toggle broke to the left, rather than upwards (which meant that the 30-round box magazine was located horizontally on the right hand side of the receiver), and then engineered the gun to work on a variation of the differential principle, as employed by the Czech vz37/Besa and in the recoil-operated Browning guns, in order to attenuate the recoil to the point where virtually all its force was used up in cycling the action, and very little was transmitted to the firer. Fürrer achieved this by ensuring that the toggle joint which locked the breech-block to the barrel was remade – and the trigger sear tripped to fire the next round – while the assembly was still moving forward, which required sophisticated, precise engineering. The result was a gun which was markedly smooth in operation, but which was extremely expensive to produce. It was a commercial failure outside Switzerland in consequence, despite its high quality.

MG15

Calibre: 7.92mm Mauser
Weight: 12.7kg (28lb) (with stock and bipod)
Length: 1335mm (52.5in)
Barrel length: 595mm (23.5in)
Effective range: 1000m (3300ft) +

Configuration: magazine-fed, recoil-operated, air-cooled
Cyclic rate of fire: 850rpm
Muzzle velocity: 755mps (2480fps)
Country of Origin: Germany

Designers Kiraly (an expatriate Hungarian) and Ende, working at the Neuhausen-am-Rheinfalls factory of the best known of all Swiss arms manufacturers, Schweizerische Industrie-Gesellschaft (SIG) also produced a light machine gun in the late 1920s, the KE7. This too was recoil operated, though in this case the system was completely conventional and fired only when the relocked barrel and breech-block assembly had come to rest in battery. It was notable in particular for its weight – at under 8kg (17.25lb) it weighed even less than the BAR, and as a result, is said to have been rather difficult to control when firing bursts. Like the BAR, it fired from an open bolt, which did little to improve its controllability, and it was also cursed with a 20-round magazine, which adversely affected its performance. With much better light machine guns widely available, it is hardly surprising that the KE7 made no real inroads into the global market, despite being well made and attractively priced and available in a wide range of chamberings.

BRITISH LMGS
We observed earlier that machine gun design and development in the UK between the wars was almost non-

existent – almost, but not quite. At the Vickers machine gun factory at Crayford, where a much-reduced work force was busy refurbishing Class C guns left over from World War I, an attempt was made to produce a true LMG to replace the too-heavy Lewis gun. The design was the work of Frenchman Adolphe Berthier, who executed it in the early 1920s and sold the rights to it to Vickers in 1925. The gun was conventional – gas was tapped off the barrel around its mid-point and impinged upon the face of a piston operating in an under-slung cylinder, which in turn pushed on the breech-block, allowing it to tilt down at the rear and unlock from a recess in the roof of the receiver. It was magazine-fed from a top-mounted 'banana' box like that pioneered by the Danish Madsen, also employed on the Bren gun, which the Vickers-Berthier much resembled, and with which it was in direct competition. Had the Bren not been available, in fact, the Vickers-Berthier would almost certainly have been the LMG with which the British fought World War II (see below for an account of the very comprehensive selection procedure involved in the choice). As it was, it was adopted by the Indian Army (British-led and under British control, but effectively

■ABOVE: The best LMG of World War II was the British development of the Czech ZB vz26 – the Bren gun. This Mark 1 is shown in service in France in 1944 with the Durham Light Infantry.

managed from Delhi, not London) as the Gun, Machine, .303in Vickers-Berthier, Indian Mark 3 (the other marks were development models), and stayed in service there after Independence in 1947, and some were used for training purposes in the UK. It was a reliable and trouble-free weapon, and with a little extra development would probably have been the equal of the Bren.

AN EXHAUSTIVE TRIAL
In 1922, the British Army took a decision in principle that the Lewis gun should be replaced, and selected a number of LMG designs for consideration over a period of some years. The first tranche of trials included the BAR, the Madsen, the Beardmore-Farquhar, the Hotchkiss and the Lewis gun, and were inconclusive, but with the Browning emerging as the favourite, as it had, in fact, been all along. The Beardmore-Farquhar was actually designed during World War I, but didn't reach a point where it could be tested until the early 1920s. Its designer,

Farquhar, was also responsible for a bolt-action rifle which was tested against the SMLE, the standard British infantry arm, but was turned down. The Beardmore-Farquhar followed a rather unconventional design in which the gas-propelled piston compressed a spring which acted as a delaying device, and acted to unlock the breech only when the pressure in the chamber had fallen to an acceptable level; the action was notably smooth, the gun had a lower-than-normal cyclic rate and was very much lighter, as a result. However, two years later, it was definitively rejected, and over the three years which followed, the same fate befell

the Châtellerault, the Fürrer and a number of guns such as the McCrudden and the Erickson which never made an impact of any kind on what was by then quite an aggressive marketplace. On 30 October 1930, following a revision of the earlier decision to replace the Lewis gun – which saw it expanded to include the Vickers Class C, specifying that any gun selected must be able to fulfil the functions of both the British Army's then-standard machine guns – a set-piece comparative trial was set up, in which the BAR, the Madsen, the Vickers-Berthier, the KE7, the Darne and a newcomer from Czechoslovakia, the

■LEFT: A pan magazine was developed for the Bren to increase its capacity in the anti-aircraft role, usually in a twin mount. The magazine was available to the infantry, too, but proved unpopular.

ZB vz26, were set against each other. In the event, the Darne arrived too late to be tested and the Brno factory submitted an improved version of its gun, the ZB vz27; this was the only gun tested which was chambered for anything but the standard British .303in round. The report came down decisively in favour of the Czech gun, which was described in glowing terms: 'Excellent throughout. I doubt whether any other gun has ever passed through so many tests with us, giving so little trouble.' There had been 27 tests in all, and the notorious Enfield sand and mud tests and the definitive endurance test were still to come. The Vickers-Berthier passed too, being described as 'a promising gun, but requires further development and improvement in many details', and those

Bren Mark 1

Calibre: .303in
Weight: 10.25kg (22.5lb)
Length: 1150mm (45.25in)
Barrel length: 635mm (25in)
Effective range: 1000m (3300ft) +
**Configuration: magazine-fed, gas-
    operated, air-cooled**
Cyclic rate of fire: 500rpm
Muzzle velocity: 730mps (2400fps)
Country of Origin: United Kingdom

two went on to the final stage, which involved being fired, then buried (hot and befouled) in mud and sand for predetermined periods before being fired again, with only very superficial cleaning, followed by a 10,000-round endurance trial. Both passed, and were then submitted to further accuracy tests at a range of 457–2286m (500–2500yds) and a 30,000-round endurance test.

In the meantime, some detailed improvements had been made to both the finalists, as we may call them: the V-B was fitted with a heavier barrel, for example, and the Czech gun had been modified to accept rimmed .303in British service ammunition instead of the 7.92mm x 57 round for which it had been designed (though nothing as yet had been done to accomodate the cordite propellant the British employed, in place of the original nitro-cellulose, which had a quite different performance characteristic; this still remained to be done, and it is to the credit of the basic design that it was able to perform so well in the circumstances –

the characteristics of the two explosives are quite dissimilar, and this was one of the reasons why the Besa, when it was adopted, was left in the original chambering). Both passed these tests too, but the Czech gun, now re-designated the ZB vz30, proved superior; in the rather curiously phrased opinion of the examiners, it was 'of such outstanding design, workmanship and material as to warrant further serious consideration' (although one is left asking one's self how much more consideration could possibly have been thought necessary, after some six years and the most exhaustive battery of trials). Further modifications, including shortening the piston and cylinder by some 254mm (10in), as well as incorporating a new form of buffer and a refined gun, now known as the ZB vz32, were resubmitted.

There now seems to have been an element of 'just how good can we make this gun?' at work and no less than 25 very minor further modifications were subsequently made, and the gun was re-

designated again, as the ZB vz33. Two were supplied to Enfield, and a total of over 200,000 rounds was fired through each; 140,000 rounds were fired before the first component failure occurred. In April 1934 a further 50,000-round test firing against the latest Vickers-Berthier (the model selected by the Indian Army) confirmed that the Czech gun was superior, and it was finally selected as the British Army's new light machine gun. The lengthy development/approval process was finally justified by the end product, which is widely held to have been the best light machine gun ever produced. Much of the work in refining the gun actually took place at the British government's Royal Small Arms Factory at Enfield, to the north of London, and that is reflected in the name by which the gun was known thereafter – 'Br' for Brno, where it was conceived, and 'en' for Enfield, where the finishing touches were applied. In the event, the decision to adopt it to replace both the Vickers and the Lewis guns was rethought in 1937,

Bren Gun

Calibre: .303in
Weight: 10.25kg (22.5lb)
Length: 1150mm (45.25in)
Barrel length: 635mm (25in)
Effective range: 1000m (3300ft) +
Configuration: magazine-fed, gas-
 operated, air-cooled
Cyclic rate of fire: 500rpm
Muzzle velocity: 730mps (2400fps)
Country of Origin: United Kingdom

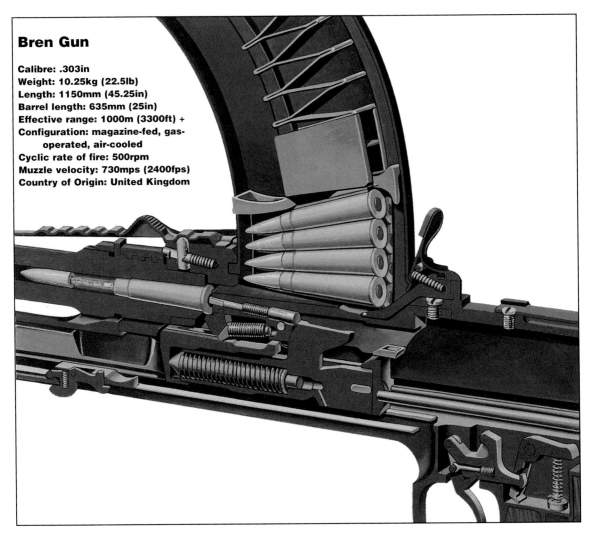

and the ZB vz53, which entered service as the Besa, was nominated as the replacement for the MMG; as we have seen, events were to force a different conclusion.

THE INCOMPARABLE BREN

The Bren gun was a paragon in the true sense of the word: a standard against which all others would be judged. It was a perfectly conventional gas-operated machine gun, the gas being tapped off the barrel 38cm (15in) before the muzzle (that is, either 25cm (10in) or 18cm (7.25in) from the chamber); the gun was produced with two different barrel lengths (see below). It passed through a simple regulator and into an underslung cylinder, where it impinged upon the head of a piston. This piston was driven

back by the gas pressure; the first 32mm (1.25in) of its travel was 'free', and resulted in a lag in the cycling of the action while the bullet left the barrel and the pressure therein – initially 2900kg/cm² (18.4 tons per sq.in) – dropped to a safe level. In fact, tests on the prototype gun revealed that the bullet had actually travelled 67.5cm (26.5in) from the muzzle when unlocking began, and just under 405cm (160in) by the time unlocking was completed. At that point, the piston head passed vents in the cylinder wall which allowed the propellant gases to escape to the atmosphere, and from that point on the piston travelled under its own acquired momentum.

The freedom of travel was the result of the post at the rear of the piston

■RIGHT: A beautifully-executed sectionalisation of the extremely accurate Bren Mark 2, with every one of the gun's component parts clearly visible.

assembly, which protruded up into the breech-block and subsequently drove it backwards, being located in a slot in the block, the length of which could be modified as desired during the gun's development process in order to 'fine tune' the action. The rear of this post was sharply undercut, and acted as a camming surface on the angled rear face of the slot in the breech-block, forcing it down, and the block out of engagement with the recess in the receiver roof which formed the lock itself; this motion resulted in primary extraction, which freed the empty case in the chamber. Now free to travel backwards, the breech-block first completed the extraction of the spent cartridge case, which dropped out of the gun through an elongated slot in the piston extension and through the bottom of the receiver, and then continued to compress the recoil spring housed in the buttstock. It was arrested in the out-of-battery position if the trigger were not still pressed or the selector was set to single shot as the gun fired from an open bolt. On its return journey into battery, the breech-block stripped a fresh round out of the top-mounted box magazine and guided it into the chamber under the pressure of the return spring. The final step was the piston post's driving the tail of the breech-block back up into the locking recess and jamming it there, whereupon the firing pin was re-aligned with the axis of the chamber and free to be driven forward by the blow from the piston post as it completed the last 32mm (1.25in) of its return travel, so that the entire

■RIGHT: Adapted for the rimless 7.62mm round, the Bren reverted to the straight-sided box magazine, this one in the hands of an Indian soldier during the war with Pakistan in 1971.

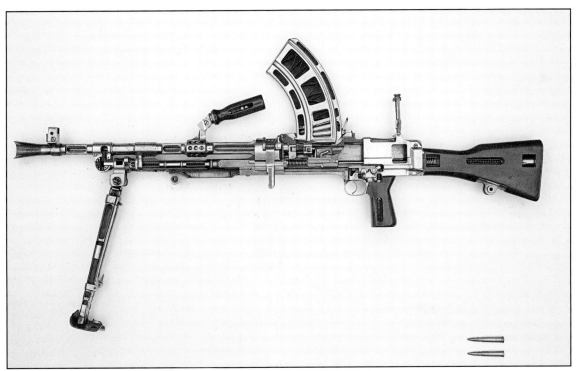

process could start all over again. The Bren was cocked conventionally, by means of a folding, non-reciprocating handle on the right of the receiver.

The complete cycle took a tenth of a second in the original guns, but the cyclic rate of production models was reduced from 600 rounds per minute (rpm) to 500rpm, and later to 480rpm. The actual theoretical rate of fire was something of the order of 120rpm – four magazines full. Standing orders were to change the barrel with every tenth magazine. That procedure was very simple indeed, thanks to the interrupted thread design of the barrel-locking mechanism. Raising the barrel catch turned the nut to which it was attached through 90 degrees, and allowed the barrel to be pulled out forwards, and a handle was provided for the purpose. A skilled Bren team (of two men) would have routinely made the change in a matter of seconds. The gun could also be set to fire single shots, the trigger sear in that case engaging in a bent on the underside of the piston and holding it off at the rear of its cycle stroke, leaving the breech open. In order to soften the shock of firing, the entire receiver and barrel/gas cylinder assembly was free to recoil for approximately 6.35mm (.25in) against a buffer at the head of the return spring in the butt. As a result, the gun was very accurate indeed, both in bursts and firing single shots, despite the drawbacks of the open bolt system in this respect (as discussed earlier). Early models were equipped

with a drum-type rear sight (and with a rear pistol grip which folded up against the buttstock when not in use), while most production guns had more conventional leaf sights.

PRODUCING THE BREN

The man who designed the ZB vz26, Vaclav Holek, started out as an apprentice machinist at the Zbrojovka factory in Brno, and rose to become a machine shop foreman. He had no formal training in gun design, but having developed an early fascination for the machine gun, he produced several of his own, not unnaturally using elements from existing guns as a starting point. The tilting block locking system he adopted for his most successful gun was certainly not an innovation – quite who first came up with the idea is unclear – but Holek, wittingly or not, applied it in such a way as to produce rather better results than had been achieved with it before. Perhaps he was purely lucky, perhaps he had an innate grasp of the ideal spatial relationship between the various components; we cannot know. But in any event, his design was good enough to be adopted for the newly emergent Czech Army, and from that starting point its reputation spread. The lengthy business of putting Holek's much-modified gun into production at the Royal Small Arms Factory began late in 1934 with the preliminary task of producing a set of master drawings calibrated in imperial units in place of the metric units

the Czechs had employed (an error in this calculation was to lead to the gun's magazine being unable to cope with its theoretical loading of 30 rounds; 28 was the practical limit). This was concluded in January 1935, and work could then begin on producing the tooling and the multitude of gauges – no less than 550 of them, each accurate to .0127mm (.0005in) necessary to the manufacture of the gun itself.

The first gun was finished in September 1937; 42 had been completed by the end of the year, and by the following July, production was running at 300 a week. By June 1940, when the British Army was driven out of continental Europe, more than 30,000 had been produced and issued, but after the escape from Dunkirk, the total number in British and Allied hands was in the region of 2300. By 1943, production at Enfield was running at 1000 guns a week, and plants in Canada and Australia were also producing Brens, though not at that sort of level; the former also produced them – for China – in the original 7.92mm chambering. The gun was equipped with a bipod, which could be folded back and up out of the way, its feet clipping each side of the gas cylinder, and a tripod was also available to allow the gun to be fired on fixed lines; it could be adapted to traverse, for use against aircraft. A 100-round capacity high-speed drum magazine was developed for use in that role, but it was seldom used because it was difficult to

Besal Mark 2

Calibre: .303in
Weight: 9.75kg (21.5lb)
Length: 1185mm (46.75in)
Barrel length: 560mm (22in)
Effective range: 1000m (3300ft)

Configuration: magazine-fed, gas-operated, air-cooled
Cyclic rate of fire: 600rpm
Muzzle velocity: 730mps (2400fps)
Country of Origin: United Kingdom

load and heavy and awkward to carry. The British Army adopted the gun in four types in .303in calibre, two with 63.5cm (25in) barrels, the other two with shorter, 56.5mm (22.5in) tubes; Mark 1s (of which comparatively few were produced) and 2s weighed over 10kg (22lb), while the shorter Mark 3s and 4s weighed just over 8.7kg (19lb). Just as the two sides in World War I had used Maxims against each other, so too did the British and the Germans face each other with Czech LMGs during World War II, the German Army having taken up the ZB vz26 and the ZB vz30 as the MG26(t) and MG30(t) respectively and issued them to reserve formations.

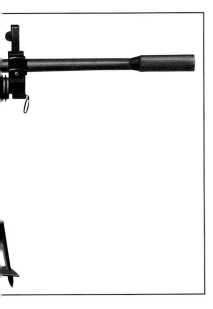

A LONG CAREER

The Bren gun was to stay in production until 1971, undergoing a major transformation in the early 1960s, after Britain, like the rest of NATO, adopted the rimless 7.62mm x 51 round in place of the old .303in cartridge which was by then almost 80 years old. The new Bren, now known as the L4, was easily distinguished from the old by the form of its magazine – a parallelepiped box, very similar to the original unit produced for the ZB vz26. Internally, there were other small modifications, most of them taken directly from the 7.92mm Brens which had been manufactured during World War II by Inglis in Canada. The conversion was straightforward – a Canadian-model breech-block with a differently profiled extractor was substituted, and the barrel, which of course contained the chamber, was replaced (and the new barrels were chrome-plated, extending their life very considerably and obviating the need to change them under normal operating conditions). The new magazines were exactly the same as the old in their locking mechanism, so that there was no need to modify the receiver at all. The L4A4, which was the version most widely issued (it was essentially a converted Bren Mark 3), had a barrel 53.5cm (21.125in) long, but weighed more than the short .303in guns at 9.5kg (21lb). With the adoption of the Bren, LMG development effectively stopped in the UK. There was an attempt made in the mid-1950s to update it to true GPMG status by converting it to belt-fed configuration, with the piston

■ABOVE: The final version of the pre-war Czech LMG, the ZGB vz33. It was the final submission to the British Army and thus the Bren's true precursor, chambered for the .303in rimmed round.

additionally driving the feed mechanism by means of a rotating vertical shaft, but in protracted trials the X11, as it was known, performed poorly under certain circumstances (notably at extreme elevation, when the energy available proved insufficient to lift the belt), and the project was abandoned in favour of the FN MAG, the development of which was already completed.

AN EXPEDIENT ALTERNATIVE

The British were more than happy with the Bren throughout the six years of World War II, but had a grave fear that production – it was manufactured in the UK only at Enfield – would be disrupted by an air raid, and took steps to develop an alternative capable of being manufactured by any half-way competent engineering shop, should the worst happen. The result was originally known as the Besal, and later, when the likelihood of confusion with the already-in-service Besa was pointed out, known as the Faulkener, after its designer at BSA. It looked something like a Bren – but then, so did many of the other LMGs of the day; a rifle-style buttstock and a pistol-grip, a top-mounted magazine and an underslung gas cylinder with a bipod mounted just abaft its front cap were their defining characteristics – but was very much simpler. The body and cylinder were simple pressings; the

Fucile Mitragliatore Breda Modello 30

Calibre: 6.5mm M95
Weight: 10.2kg (22.5lb)
Length: 1230mm (48.5in)
Barrel length: 520mm (20.5in)
Effective range: 1000m (3300ft)
**Configuration: magazine-fed, blowback-
      operated, air-cooled**
Cyclic rate of fire: 450rpm
Muzzle velocity: 610mps (2000fps)
Country of Origin: Italy

trigger group, which served to cock the gun in the manner of the Besa, was as simple as possible, and gave burst fire only, and the piston and breech-block were simple machinings, the former drilled to accommodate the recoil spring. It locked by means of two lugs which were forced by a camming ramp into recesses cut into the receiver. Despite its very basic character, the Faulkener performed surprisingly well; it was accurate to within acceptable limits, and stoppages were few. It was never put into production however, simply because manufacture of the Bren was never interrupted.

THE CZECH VZ 52

This was not the only post-war development of the original design, however, or even the most successful (and it is tempting to suggest that had RSAF really wanted to produce a GPMG based on the Bren, they would have done so; the belt-feed problem, for example, could certainly have been overcome by one means or another). In Czechoslovakia, a

much-modified (though essentially similar) version was to be produced as the Vz 52, and this time the belt-feed mechanism did work, thanks to considerable re-engineering. In the Vz 52, the gas was tapped off the barrel at a point much closer to the chamber – the bullet travelled fractionally under 18cm (7in) before the action started to cycle, which meant that the lag caused by the free movement of the piston post within the breech-block had to be that much longer. The breech-block was much smaller and lighter than that of the Bren, and the effect of this was to speed up the cyclic rate considerably, to 900 rounds per minute (rpm) in magazine fed form, and 1200rpm when feeding from a continuous-link belt (even though conventional wisdom has it that belt-feed systems have to overcome more friction in stripping a round out of the spring clip which holds it, than is encountered in stripping a round out of a magazine; however, no sound reason has ever been advanced for the Vz 52 seemingly setting this rule of thumb on its head). The belt-

feed mechanism was a German design, produced before World War II by Heinrich von Wimmersperg, and is considered to be a most effective and efficient one; it employed a simple bell crank moving in the horizontal plane, actuated by a roller at its base which ran in a groove machined into the side of the piston, the movement of the belt itself being controlled by two spring-loaded pawls.

LIGHTER LOADS

In detail, the Vz 52's locking system is closer to that of the Besa than it is to that of the Bren (though of course, the differences between all three are actually minimal). The ramp at the rear of the piston post has a square step cut in its front face, which locates with the breech-block and prevents it tending to rise on its way back to battery – this had long been identified as the only serious defect of the Bren design, and tended to produce unacceptable wear on the receiver roof after half a million or so rounds had been fired. The Vz 52's breech-block was locked

reduced power of the 7.62mm x 45 M52 cartridge in comparison to the 7.92mm and .303in rounds which the Besa and Bren chambered. The Czech M52 round was essentially an 'intermediate' round (that is, one which lay between the conventional rifle round and one a pistol might fire, in terms of its performance) and the only other ammunition for which the Vz 52 was to be chambered was another, the Russian 7.62mm x 39 M43 (in which case it was known as the Vz 52/57).

The gun was cocked by reciprocating the trigger group, exactly like the Besa, and barrel changing was accomplished in the same manner as with the Bren, but the quarter-turn movement of the nut was accomplished by the magazine port cover, rather than by a separate catch. The gun could fire either single shots or bursts, but unlike the Bren, a selector switch was not provided; instead, it had a 'double trigger' mechanism like that of the German MG13 and later guns. Pressure on the upper half simply released the trigger mechanism while pressure on the lower half performed this function too, but also engaged a trigger bar extension which disabled the hold-back function of the sear.

CLOSE TOLERANCES

The Vz 52 weighed just 8kg (17.5lb) 'clean', and one of the reasons why Ceskoslovenska Zbrojovka was able to keep the weight so low was by insisting on marginal material excess and very close manufacturing tolerances. The guns were universally held to be both difficult

■BELOW: The *Soviet Ruchnoy Pulemyot Dagtyareva* (RPD), the standard LMG of the Red Army and its Warsaw Pact allies from the mid-1950s until the RPK superseded it in the late 1970s.

into the receiver only at its rear end (and into the barrel extension at the front, as per the Besa), dispensing with the locking ribs which engaged with the receiver roof. This was possible due to the

■ABOVE: The first LMG Degtyarev designed was the DP, which appeared for the first time in 1928. It stayed in service for almost 20 years, despite some design deficiencies.

to strip (and not just because the parts were a tight push-fit, but because of design changes in the new model; the Bren and its Czech counterparts had been notably easy in this respect) and intolerant of less-than-ideal operating conditions; in other words, they behaved supremely well on the firing range, but could produce a very poor performance indeed under active service conditions. Where the less sophisticated Bren would have kept on firing, the Vz 52 was prone to regular stoppage. Some of this tendency was admittedly due to the ammunition, for the intermediate round had its drawbacks, chiefly its relatively low energy, and the Czech gun was certainly not alone in exhibiting these failings. A simplified version of the Vz 52, the Vz 59, was developed later for use in the general-purpose role.

OTHER EUROPEAN LMGS
Elsewhere in Europe, there were two attempts made in Italy to produce a workable LMG during the interwar period, both of them somewhat idiosyncratic. The more successful of the two was produced by Breda, which was by now well established in the sector, and adopted by the Italian Army as the *Fucile Mitragliatori Breda Modello 30* in 6.5mm calibre. It was essentially a re-vamp of a gun known as the Breda 5C, various of which various modifications had been

touted around since the mid-1920s, and was blowback-operated, which inevitably meant poor extraction and a reversion to cartridge oiling. It was a most peculiar-looking gun, too, its trigger group divorced from the receiver proper by a narrow tube in which the simple unlocked bolt reciprocated, with a box magazine mounted horizontally on the right hand side, not detachable, but was hinged at the front edge so that it could be loaded from rifle chargers, a most unhandy arrangement, and one which must have caused considerable anxiety in battle, because the process was not a rapid one. The barrel could be changed quickly, thanks to a simple locking collar, but was not provided with a handle. The other Italian LMG of the period was developed by Alfredo Scotti, most of whose work was done in collaboration with aircraft manufacturers. The system he developed and patented was a combination of standard gas actuation and blowback; gas tapped off the barrel was used to unlock the action, whereupon the residual pressure in the chamber threw the bolt back. The gun in its light form – it could be either belt- or drum-fed – was never a success, but the system eventually came to be used in larger-calibre machine guns.

In Finland, designer Aimo Lahti, who was rather better known for his sub-machine guns (see Chapter Four) also produced a workable LMG during the 1920s, this time a recoil-operated gun designated as the *Automaattikivaari Lahtisaloranto Malli 26* and known – at least outside Finland – as the Lahti m/26. We have come to regard recoil

operation as being rather outdated, and certainly it does not have the flexibility offered by gas actuation, but by careful engineering, Lahti used the principle to produce a true light gun – it weighed 8.6kg (19lb) unloaded – which was fed from either a 20-round box or from a drum very similar to that which he used for his SMG (a near-replica of which was also available for the Soviet RPK, see below), mounted on the underside of the receiver. It had a quick-release barrel, but the bolt had to be extracted in the process of changing it which, in the cold conditions which so often prevail close to the Arctic, made the procedure unnecessarily fiddly. It was adopted by the Finnish Army, and saw extensive use during the Winter War against the USSR in 1939–40, but was later superseded by Soviet weaponry. Lahti tried, unsuccessfully, to sell the gun in modified form as a weapon for aircraft observers, and supplied examples to the RAF for the trials which included the Darne, and which saw the Browning adopted. However, with a cyclic rate of just 500 rounds per minute (rpm), it was rather too pedestrian for the purpose.

A MEXICAN INNOVATION
As we shall see in due course, the operating principles of the selective-fire assault rifle and that of the LMG are essentially similar in character. The origins of both are generally traceable to Denmark, since the appearance of the original Madsen LMG was roughly contemporaneous with that of a self-loading rifle developed by Soren Bang, but in fact they have a rival, at least in

name, from a somewhat unlikely quarter: Mexico. In the early 1890s, artillery officer there named Manuel Mondragon had begun experimenting with designs for a self-loading rifle which utilised propellant gas tapped off the barrel by means of a 1mm- (.04in-) diameter hole situated some 165mm (6.5in) abaft the muzzle. In the short period between the projectile passing this port and exiting the barrel, gases at extremely high pressure (typically 3000 atmospheres and more, depending on the size of the propellant charge) passed through the port into a cylinder below the barrel and acted on the face of a piston; the piston was driven back, simultaneously compressing a coiled spring which surrounded its shaft and unlocking and driving back the bolt. The longitudinal movement was converted into rotation by a series of helical grooves in the bolt which acted on oval lugs on the cocking handle, located to the right of the receiver. The rearwards movement of the bolt extracted the spent case and cocked the action, and on its return stroke, gathered a new round and chambered it.

In an effort to make the piston work as efficiently as possible, its head was fitted with three copper sealing rings, and to make it as secure as possible, Mondragon incorporated no less than seven locking lugs, three at the front of the breech block and four at its rear.

Since there were no manufacturers in Mexico capable of producing such a complex article to the required tolerances, Mondragon turned to SIG in Switzerland, and in a show of patriotism, the Mexican Army 'adopted' the rifle (in a very limited sense indeed) as the rather grandiosely named *Fusil Porfirio Diaz Systema Mondragon, Modelo 1908* (Diaz being the country's president), and 4000 were ordered from Neuhausen. Only 400 had been delivered by 1911, at a cost of SFr160 each (approximately three times the cost of a conventional manually operated repeater rifle at the time), before the Mexicans realised the error of their ways and reneged; SIG was left with around 1000 completed rifles in its warehouse, and little prospect of ever making its money back. The company added a variety of extra refinements,

■ ABOVE: The DPM, a modernised model of the DP, its recoil spring moved to the rear of the bolt. The pan-type magazine was necessary due to the exaggerated taper of the 7.62mm rimmed round.

notably a fully automatic capability, in which role it could be fitted with a rather spindly bipod and a 20-round magazine (in place of the standard eight-round box). SIG tried to interest various countries' war departments, notably those in Berlin, London and Washington, in what was now, nominally at least, a light machine gun, but without any success.

Eventually, in 1915, when the German Army had discovered a requirement for a more flexible weapon than the Mauser 98 bolt-action rifle on the one hand and the heavy MG08 machine gun on the other to equip its fledgling air force (this, we may recall, was before the days of synchronising mechanisms which permitted fixed machine guns to fire through the arc of the propeller as developed by the Dutchman, Anton Fokker – see Chapter Five), someone remembered SIG's offer of Mondragons, and the entire batch was purchased, much, one may imagine, to the surprise and pleasure of the Swiss. A version of the over-complicated Tatarek and von Benkö 'snail' helical clockwork magazine, as developed for the long-barrelled 'artillery' version of the P08 Luger pistol (and later adopted for the Bergmann MP18/I sub-machine gun – see Chapter Four), was produced for the rifle, which upped the ammunition capacity to 30 rounds, and it was re-chambered for the 7mm x 57 Mauser cartridge; thus modified, and known now as the *Fleiger-Selbstladekarabiner Modell 1915*, (though it was actually 1917 by the time it was ready), it was issued to aircrew, on the strict understanding that each weapon must be checked by an experienced armourer before and after every mission. Even so, failures were commonplace. The Mondragon was not a success, but the basic principle was sound, and the system of tapping propellant gas off the barrel near the muzzle and using it to drive a piston which cycled the action was to be widely copied.

THE MENDOZA LMGS

The history of the Mondragon is a side-issue to the development of the LMG, although in fairness to its inventor one should say that his role has been somewhat neglected; however, it did much to establish the principle of an independent small arms industry in Mexico, thus serving as a stepping-stone to the work of the talented Rafael Mendoza, head of the design studio at Fabrica de Armas Nacionales, the Government arsenal, from the early 1930s onwards. The LMG which he produced in 1933, the *Fusil Ametrallador Mendoza Modello B*, chambered for the 7mm x 57 Mauser round, was a combination of the systems used by Lewis (the lock) and Hotchkiss (the gas cylinder and piston), assembled around a notably light receiver and mated to Mendoza's own feed system. The gun's cyclic rate of fire was low, which was to its advantage, though the limited capacity of the 20-round top-mounted box magazine was a drawback. Nonetheless, it was reliable, and cheap to produce; it stayed in service with the Mexican Army until roughly 1945, when it was superseded by a version chambered for the American .30in-06 round, but was otherwise essentially unchanged. That same round was also employed by a gun which was technically the successor to the *Modello 45*, although

RPK

Calibre: 7.62mm M1943
Weight: 4.75kg (10.5lb)
Length: 1040mm (41in)
Barrel length: 590mm (23.25in)
Effective range: 800m (2600ft)
Configuration: magazine-fed, gas-operated, air-cooled
Cyclic rate of fire: 600rpm
Muzzle velocity: 730mps (2400fps)
Country of Origin: Soviet Union

quite different in character, having been lightened to the point where it could almost be considered as an automatic rifle. The Modello RM2, as the newcomer was known when it appeared in the early 1960s, had one notable deficiency: a fixed barrel, the quick-change mechanisms of the earlier guns having been sacrificed in the interests of saving weight. Like the self-loading rifle the British Army adopted, the Belgian FN FAL, the RM2's buttstock was hinged behind the pistol grip, and locked into the receiver by a simple pin; thus, stripping the gun was a very simple operation indeed. It was an anachronism, however, appearing at a time when the assault rifle proper had taken over its role, and few were ever seen outside their country of origin.

THE SOVIET DEGTYAREVS

We noted in the previous chapter that Degtyarev produced a more-or-less successful light machine gun in the Soviet Union during the 1920s, using the locking system first devised by Friberg and perfected by Kjellman. The *Ruchnoy Pulemyot Degtyareva pakhotnyi*, usually known in the west simply as the DP, was a simple, unsophisticated design (one of

the criteria was that it could be manufactured by unskilled machine operators in simple workshops) and entirely conventional; the flaps which locked the bolt into position in the receiver were forced out by the profile of the firing pin, and unlocking was performed by a slide attached to the gas piston which forced the firing pin back, whereupon the bolt was free to begin its rearward travel. The gun fired from an open bolt (there was no provision for single shots, only bursts) and thus the bolt was held back by the trigger sear; releasing the trigger returned it to battery under the force of the recoil/return spring, picking up a 7.62mm x 54R round from the top-mounted 49-round pan magazine and chambering it in the process. The DP's main failing was in the feed path, due largely to the uncomfortable nature of the rimmed round, but there was nothing Degtyarev could do about that, though the magazines slight reluctance to feed properly was overcome by restricting its load to 47 rounds, whereupon it functioned quite happily. It was also found that the return spring, which was located under the barrel, lost its temper

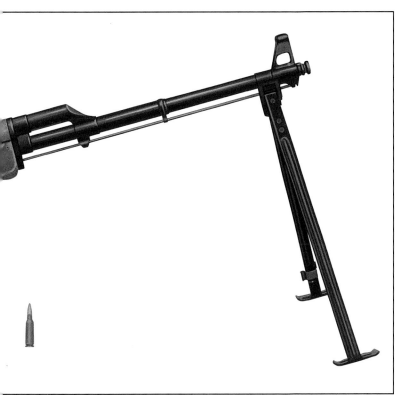

The light machine gun which superseded the Type 53 in China was home-produced and something of a hotchpotch, incorporating the feed mechanism of the Maxim, the bolt, piston and locking method of the Czech ZB vz26, the trigger mechanism of the DPM, the gas regulator of the RPD and the barrel changing method of the SGM. Anachronistically, it was chambered for the old 7.62mm rimmed round, but its belt allowed the individual rounds to be pushed out forwards, straight into the chamber, rather than extracted to the rear. In fact, the gun replaced not only the Type 53, but also the Type 58, a Chinese copy of the RP-46 (see Chapter Five), as the company support weapon; it could be fired from a bipod or a tripod.

A CHINESE PUZZLE
The light machine gun solved the problem of taking a meaningful capacity for producing sustained fire into the attack, but it was a stop-gap in the sense that it did not truly supersede the World War I-vintage medium machine gun, and could not be expected to produce true sustained fire over hours or days at a time, such as the Vickers, for example, certainly could and did; for example, on 24 August 1916 a Company of 10 British Vickers guns kept up a sustained support barrage for 12 hours, consuming 999,750 rounds of ammunition, one gun alone accounting for 120,000, an average of 167 rounds per minute (rpm); and during the crossing of the River Maas in February 1945 towards the end of World War II, one British machine-gun detachment fired a total of 850,000 rounds from its Vickers guns in a seven-hour period. The next step for the Chinese light machine gun was a design which would be light enough to go forward with the assault troops, but sturdy enough to be used in the true sustained fire role too – a general-purpose weapon which would effectively replace the two forms of rifle-calibre gun.

The quest for the Universal Machine Gun, the *Einheitsmaschinengewehr* as the Germans called it, began there during World War I, and a workable model was produced less than 20 years later, as we shall learn in Chapter 5. For now, we must return to the end of World War I, and turn our attention to the other end of the scale, to examine the way in which devastating portable firepower found its way into the hands of the individual fighting man in the form of the pistol-calibre sub-machine gun.

as it got hot, though by perforating the barrel casing, this tendency was also cured. There was a version manufactured for use in tanks, too, with a heavier barrel and a bigger-capacity magazine, and its wooden buttstock was replaced by a telescopic version. Perhaps the most significant shortcoming of the DP was its barrel mounting – the tube could be changed in the field, but the procedure was certainly not simple or straightforward. In 1940, a revised attachment was developed, which allowed the barrel to be changed much more quickly and easily (though it still required a spanner to turn the locking nut through the quarter-turn necessary to release it). In 1944, Shilin and others modified the gun slightly, moving the return spring to the rear of the action, where it operated in a cylindrical housing protruding from the back of the body, and providing a pistol grip since it was no longer feasible to hold the small of the butt in a cross-hand grip, as was usual with this and most other LMGs. This latter gun, known as the DPM (for 'modernized'), was also produced in huge numbers in the People's Republic of China as the Type 53.

A CLASSIC COMBINATION
The DPM was soon superseded by the not-entirely-successful belt-fed RPD, in the newly introduced 7.62mm 'intermediate' calibre chambering the short M1943 round, and that, in its turn, was replaced by an altogether more effective weapon, based on the turn-bolt design Mikhail Kalashnikov produced for the assault rifle which bore his name, the AK47 (see Chapter 5).

The new gun, known as the RPK (*Ruchnoy Pulemyot Kalashnikova*), was mechanically identical to the rifle it stood alongside, save in its safety catch and fire selector system and in the trigger mechanism, which was somewhat simplified. It even used the same 30-round capacity magazine, though an enlarged version holding 40 rounds and a complicated vertically mounted drum magazine holding 75 rounds were also available.

To improve its performance as an automatic in the support role, the barrel was heavier than that of the rifle, but it was non-replaceable, like that of the RPD. The wooden buttstock could be easily removed, and a folding bipod was fitted.

CHAPTER 4
THE MACHINE PISTOL – PORTABLE FIREPOWER

The new infantry assault tactics developed in the latter part of World War I called for a high degree of individual firepower at close range – a task to which the bolt-action rifle was not at all well suited and neither, really, were the new LMGs. Pistols were better in some ways, but they weren't particularly accurate, even at close quarters; what was needed was a new type of weapon, a small gun more like a pistol than a rifle, with a large-capacity magazine, which would continue to fire repeatedly while the user instinctively adjusted his aim; a machine gun in miniature, in fact.

The credit for developing the first practical sub-machine gun (SMG) or machine pistol (MP) – the two terms are quite interchangeable, and so, in British usage, was 'machine carbine' – is usually awarded to the creative pairing of Hugo Schmeisser, son of Louis, and Theodor Bergmann (the former developed the design, the latter put it into production), although in fact, the Italian Vilar Perosa, designed by Abiel Botel Revelli for Officine Vilar Perosa, and later manufactured by FIAT (and by GEC in Canada) has a better claim to primacy, since it appeared in 1915, while Marengoni's first design for Beretta, which used many elements of the Vilar

■ **LEFT: The Red Army realised that the machine pistol was a more effective weapon than the rifle in the hands of untrained troops, and produced them by the million during World War II.**

Perosa, may also have pre-empted the German claim, which rests on its effectiveness on the battlefield. But we shall return in due course for a closer look at these other weapons themselves, because to understand them and the genre they presaged we have first to consider briefly the development of 'automatic' (that is, self-loading) pistols in the 1890s, with particular regard to the ammunition they used, for it was the rounds developed for them which made the SMG possible.

THE 'AUTOMATIC' PISTOL
By the last decades of the nineteenth century, gunmaking had long been an industrial activity, and it comes as no surprise to see the workable innovations in new pistol design coming from the likes of Loewe (which was about to become DWM, and already had shares in Mauser), Steyr, Skoda and FN (which

MP18

Calibre: 9mm Parabellum
Weight: 4.2kg (9.25lb)
Length: 815mm (32in)
Barrel length: 195mm (7.75in)
Effective range: 70m (230ft)
Action: blowback
Cyclic rate of fire: 650rpm
Muzzle velocity: 395mps (1300fps)
Country of Origin: Germany

was also half Loewe-owned) in Europe, and Colt in the USA. The most important of this small band was definitely Loewe/DWM, for that company's design staff included Hugo Borchardt, who made the first really workable self-loading pistol with a removable box magazine, and Georg Luger, who developed Borchardt's design into the best-known pistol of the period, and, since it also controlled the activities of Mauser-Werke at Oberndorf-am-Neckar and the Feederle brothers, who were at work there on the pistol which was to become the C96.

Elsewhere, Theodor Bergmann, whom we last encountered developing an 'ordinary' machine gun in the company of Louis Schmeisser (without much real commercial success thanks to the predominance of Maxim's designs), also produced a series of workable self-loading pistols (Schmeisser designed them too), the first of them chambered for an entirely smooth cartridge – that is, without rim or cannelure – which Schmeisser also originated, and later, the same arrangement appeared in 'conventional' chamberings and with a

conventional extractor to replace the barely workable 'blow out' system which the first models employed.

NEW AMMUNITION

The form of the cartridge was a major problem. Before any of those self-loading, magazine-fed pistols could become a reality, their designers had to solve the perennial problem of coping mechanically with the unwieldy and obtrusive rim, which was still being used to seat the round and control the headspace, and which could be a positive nuisance when trying to feed rounds serially out of a box magazine.

Riflemakers like Vetterli, Lee, Mannlicher and Mauser had produced or incorporated box magazines into their manual repeater weapons during the previous decade, the 1880s, and some had adopted the solution presented by a Swiss, Rubin: rimless cartridges, in which a groove or cannelure allowed the extractor to grip the casing, while seating and headspace were achieved by overall profile and the thickness of the projectile's cartridge case (though the

development of the rimless round also had huge ramifications for belt-fed weapons as we have already noted).

Pistol designers had to go the same way, and soon developed appropriate rimless ammunition in calibres ranging from the diminutive 6.35mm up to .455in. Borchardt developed one such round, in 7.65mm calibre, which was eventually to become the Mauser 7.63mm; Luger, who came slightly later, developed the round which he called the Parabellum (a name long associated with DWM, as we may recall), which in its 9mm form, with a round-nosed bullet, was to become the most widely used chambering ever, not just for military pistols, but also for sub-machine guns.

The other modification made to the pistol ammunition of the day concerned the composition of the projectile itself. Previously, lead alone had been used, but the mechanical action was less kindly than finger and thumb, and it was found necessary to clad the projectile in a harder material to prevent it becoming damaged or impossibly distorted in the loading process; once again, pistol makers followed the practice adopted by riflemakers a decade earlier.

There was to be a sometimes bewildering variety of other pistol cartridges developed in similar calibres over the decades which followed; at least a dozen in 9mm, for example, often with more or less similar case lengths (a factor which led inevitably to confusion, since a gun designed for one round would sometimes chamber another, often with surprising results) and propellant charges varied from 200mg (3 grains) to around 400 mg (6 grains). We shall encounter some of these rounds specified for sub-machine guns, but they need not concern us more than in passing, as exceptions, for the vast majority of SMGs produced were chambered for the 9mm Parabellum cartridge.

By way of comparison, it is worth noting that the rifle ammunition of the day, roughly between 7mm and 8mm in calibre, was typically loaded with up to 10 times the charge of a pistol round – the British .303in ball round was loaded

with 2.46g (37 grains) of Cordite; the American .30in-06 with 3.3g (50 grains), German 7.92mm round with 3g (45 grains). They fired a projectile weighing around 11g (170 grains), while the 9mm NATO standard Parabellum round had a 400mg (6 grain) charge and an 8.25g (124 grain) projectile. The difference in energy produced by the two cartridges was thus enormous – the US .30in-06 round, for instance, produces almost 370mkp (2700ft/lb) of muzzle energy; the 9mm Parabellum round produces 51mkp (365ft/lb) – and that was to have a very profound effect on SMG design, for reasons we have already touched upon.

SIMPLIFIED ACTION

The heavier pistol cartridges – 7.63mm Mauser, 9mm Parabellum and .45in ACP (Automatic Colt Pistol), for example – were still powerful enough to require a mechanism to lock breech-block and barrel together until the pressure in the chamber dropped to a safe level. The Borchardt, Luger and Mauser pistols

were all conventional short-recoil designs, the lock being broken by the rearwards movement of the barrel and breech-block, and so were the designs Browning executed for FN and Colt to manufacture, the 9mm Grand Puissance and the .45in M1911 respectively. However, the breech-block of even a fairly heavy pistol, such as the Colt .45in, was still relatively light; when the sub-machine gun was proposed, its designers, with considerably more space available, could make that component much bigger, and therefore much heavier. By combining it with a stronger recoil spring, they were able to dispense with the locking mechanism, and rely on simple blowback action (much less complicated, cheaper to manufacture and easier to maintain), delaying it if they saw fit by any one of a

■ BELOW: The Bergmann MP18 'Muskete', constructed to very high standards, proved durable. Here, with the 'snail' magazine, it is in the hands of a Czech officer, circa 1936.

■ABOVE: The real successor to the MP18 was undoubtedly Hugo Schmeisser's MP28, seen here in the hands of an NCO of the Waffen-SS's *Totenkopf* Division.

variety of simple devices, this procedure becoming almost universal in the SMG.

THE MACHINE PISTOL

The history of the sub-machine gun divides, if not entirely neatly in terms of chronology, into two parts. The dividing line between Stage One, when the few SMGs manufactured met the sort of standards maintained during the nineteenth century, and Stage Two, when mass-production methods took over, is very clear and distinct in individual cases, but the transition did not occur simultaneously all over the world. The best we can say is that it had largely been completed sometime before the end of World War II.

The sub-machine guns of World War I, such few of them as there were, were characterised by their traditionalism. They were fabricated from steel forgings, machined to specification and finished by

hand, many of them to a very high standard, but there was only a slim chance that a part from one gun would be a perfect fit in another. They were slow to produce and expensive as a result.

Between the wars and more especially after 1939, mass-production techniques became the norm in the arms manufacturing industry as elsewhere, and everything changed. Now, the emphasis was on economy of effort and materials, and machining gave way to stamping and welding. In some instances, this transformation took place over a very short period indeed, and the resulting product was often unacceptable to men who had grown up with guns of a different era. The soldier's perception of necessity and the reality of the requirements of the situation were at odds, and it took some time for reality to triumph – the best example of that was probably to be found in the British Army with the appearance of the Sten gun, which was still routinely held in contempt by the men to whom it was issued when it was superseded in the mid-1950s, even though it had been in service for the best part of 15 years.

The gun Schmeisser and Bergmann produced as the MP18,I, the precursor of a line of very effective weapons, was 'traditional', and was to set the criteria for the entire sub-genre. It is unclear what was the significance of the suffix to the designation, and there is not even any uniformity in the way it is written – it also appears as 'MP18-I', 'MP18/I' and 'MP18.I', for example – but that only serves to confuse, and we will refer to it here simply as the MP18; there were not, as far as can be ascertained, two versions of it. Schmeisser's contract with Bergmann specified that the latter should hold any rights to designs the former produced, and the gun became known as the Bergmann MP18 or the Bergmann *Muskete* in consequence. As well as manufacturing it himself, Bergmann also granted a licence to SIG in Switzerland, where it was produced for export in the 1920s. Many Swiss-made MP18s went to Japan.

It was an entirely conventional weapon in execution – that is, its receiver and moving parts were forged roughly to shape and size and then machined out of the solid, and it had wooden furniture, in this case a one-piece butt and forestock,

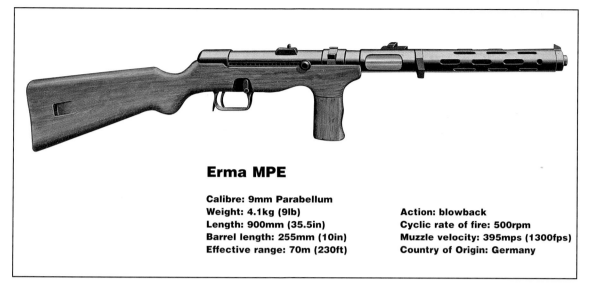

Erma MPE

Calibre: 9mm Parabellum
Weight: 4.1kg (9lb)
Length: 900mm (35.5in)
Barrel length: 255mm (10in)
Effective range: 70m (230ft)

Action: blowback
Cyclic rate of fire: 500rpm
Muzzle velocity: 395mps (1300fps)
Country of Origin: Germany

identical in form to the Mauser 98 rifle – and in operation, though since it played a central role in defining what 'conventional' meant in that context, that is perhaps something of an understatement! It was made up of just 34 parts ('counting the detached magazine but not the screws', as one detailed description of it says, rather fussily). The barrel and action were enclosed in a long casing tube, which was perforated with six rows of holes along the first part of its length, where it protected the 20cm- (8in-) long barrel, and was fixed into the forestock with a hinge at its midpoint, just below the (opposed) magazine and ejection ports. The action was no more than a cylindrical bolt or breech-block, which weighed 700g (25oz) and contained the firing pin within it. It had a simple spur-type cocking handle which protruded through a slot in the right hand side of the casing, and acted against a strong return spring located behind it in the tubular receiver.

THE BERGMANN MP18 'MUSKETE'

The magazine was mounted on the left hand side, with the ejection port opposite. It fired from the open bolt position, and no provision was made for single shots. Cocking it simply hauled the breech-block back and engaged it with the sear, against the compression of the recoil spring (at which point the action could be blocked, and the gun made safe, by hooking the cocking spur upwards into a notch provided for the purpose; this was

a commonly adopted method). Releasing the trigger depressed the sear and released the bolt in turn, and on its way forward into battery it stripped a round out of the magazine, chambered it and fired it. The pressure of the gas in the chamber and barrel first overcame the inertia in the breech-block, and then the resistance of the spring, and the action cycled, extracting and ejecting the spent casing in the process. As long as the trigger was pressed, it continued to repeat that cycle of events until the supply of ammunition was exhausted or a round misfed – not an uncommon occurrence at first. It was a simple as that.

Perhaps the Muskete's only technical deficiency was in its magazine – a complicated 32-round capacity clockwork 'snail' drum designed by Tatarek and von Benkö, originally for the long-barrelled 'artillery' model of Luger's Parabellum pistol. This was replaced eventually by a 'stick' magazine containing 20 rounds, just as Schmeisser had originally specified (the drum magazine had been the initiative of the German Army's all-powerful Rifle Testing Commission). Fired as one continuous burst, it took three and a half seconds to empty the 32-round magazine, a cyclic rate of around 500 rounds per minute (rpm). It must be observed that emptying the gun like that was a fairly futile exercise – few of the rounds would have been on target due to the tendency for the muzzle to rise and pull to the right – not a failing of Schmeisser's design, but of the entire SMG concept, and one which would

exercise designers from that point on. The MP18 entered service in 1917–1918, the last year of World War I, and in all likelihood no more than 30,000 were produced at Bergmann's Suhl factory. Perhaps half of those found their way into the hands of frontline troops, and there they were very effective indeed, allowing the stormtroopers much greater freedom of movement than they ever had with the Madsen, the MG08/15 or the captured Lewis guns they favoured, and further validating the 'von Hutier' tactics. After the war was over, the gun was extensively used by the police of the Weimar Republic in their increasingly futile attempts to maintain order within the shattered country.

SCHMEISSER'S MP28

After World War I ended, Hugo Schmeisser bought into another Suhl gunmaker, C.G. Haenel, and there he developed his SMG design further. The result, which became the MP28,II (the same comment on the suffix applies), was almost impossible to distinguish externally from its predecessor, but within the breech cylinder the firing pin and recoil spring were rather different. The latter, somewhat enlarged, was now mounted partially over the firing pin, where it fitted more securely, its forward movement being blocked by a collar.

Schmeisser also provided a selective fire capability, single shots being achieved by pushing aside a catch set into the trigger guard. He produced both 20- and 32-round capacity box magazines,

MP38

Calibre: 9mm Parabellum
Weight: 4.1kg (9lb)
Length: 630mm (24.75in) (stock
folded)
Barrel length: 245mm (9.75in)
Effective range: 70m (230ft)
Action: blowback
Cyclic rate of fire: 500rpm
Muzzle velocity: 395mps (1300fps)
Country of Origin: Germany

the cartridges in them staggered; he had tried to produce the larger magazine to hold 35 rounds, at the request of the Reichswehr's Inspectorate of Weapons and Equipment (successor to the Rifle Testing Commission) but found that 32 rounds were the most such a magazine would hold – the problem was the spring, of course – and at that there were still instances of misfeeding from time to time.

We may recall that the manufacture of automatic weapons was forbidden in Germany during that period, and Schmeisser transferred production of his new gun to the Pieper factory in Herstal, where it was produced for the Belgian Army, and for export to South America, Asia and other European countries. It was much in evidence during the Spanish Civil War, where it had a considerable influence, both on the outcome of individual firefights and on the mindset of those watching from afar, the most conservative elements amongst them still being far from convinced of the sub-machine gun's effectiveness as a weapon of war. The need for German

manufacturers to disguise the origins of their products disappeared in 1935, when Germany repudiated the Versailles Treaty, but Schmeisser was not the last to have to look abroad for his manufacturing base.

THE BERGMANN MP34
After Hugo Schmeisser left Theodor Bergmann Waffenbau AG, and even though the latter owned the rights to the MP18, the company attempted to develop an entirely new machine pistol, offering in 1932 a more complicated weapon which was known (perhaps to disguise its true nature; the ban on automatic weapons was still in force, of course, at least nominally) as the Bergmann Machine Carbine (BMk – *Bergmann Maschinenkarabiner*). Again, it was originally chambered for the 9mm Parabellum round, though examples were also produced in other chamberings, notably 7.63mm Mauser and .45in ACP. The gun has been described as both 'solid and reliable' and 'complicated and laborious', but seen in context, it was simply an artifact of its period –

'properly' made, by machining forgings, and with a hand-shaped wooden stock, once again resembling that of the Mauser 98 rifle and carbine suitably cut down.

It was an entirely conventional blowback weapon, but with a few features which set it apart from its rivals. Firstly, almost uniquely and somewhat curiously, its 20- or 32-round capacity 'stick' magazine was inserted from the right hand side of the action. Secondly, its cocking lever was located in the rear of the tubular receiver, and was – externally, at least – of the form of a rifle bolt; it had to be rotated through 90 degrees or thereabouts before it could be pulled to the rear to cock the action. If this was somewhat unexpected, and on the surface unduly complicated (the justification for it was twofold: there was no slot in which the cocking lever worked, to allow dust and dirt to find its way into the action, and the lever did not reciprocate with the bolt), it was actually even more complex in action, and required the breech-block or bolt to be made in two parts, the breech base and the breech cylinder. It seems likely that

■RIGHT: The German MP40 was the first 'modern' machine pistol, designed specifically for mass-production, and to be manufactured from metal and plastic.

Bergmann simply copied the entire mechanism from Finland, where Lahti had incorporated something very similar into his earlier 'Suomi' SMGs (see below). In the cocking process, raising the (external) bolt lever uncoupled the breech base from the receiver and coupled it with the breech cylinder, allowing the two to be withdrawn together; when the bolt lever was returned to the closed position, the breech cylinder, which contained the firing pin, was held to the rear by the trigger sear, against the pressure of the return spring. Releasing the trigger allowed it to return to battery, stripping a round out of the magazine and then firing it in the process. The trigger mechanism was actually more complicated than that, however, for like many other German automatic weapons of the period, the trigger itself was used to produce either single-shot or burst-fire,

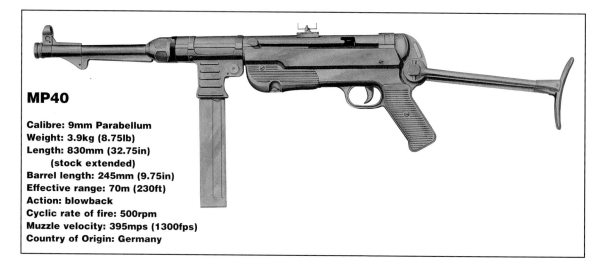

MP40

Calibre: 9mm Parabellum
Weight: 3.9kg (8.75lb)
Length: 830mm (32.75in)
(stock extended)
Barrel length: 245mm (9.75in)
Effective range: 70m (230ft)
Action: blowback
Cyclic rate of fire: 500rpm
Muzzle velocity: 395mps (1300fps)
Country of Origin: Germany

this time by means of either light or heavy pressure, a more satisfactory arrangement than the rocking trigger, since it allowed the soldier to go from firing single rounds to firing bursts with only the simplest, most instinctive action.

By dint of quite sophisticated engineering and design, the Bergmann MP34, as the weapon was known when it was first adopted by the Waffen SS in 1934, also circumvented a problem often encountered in simple blowback-operated weapons, whose firing pins are usually fixed within the breech-block, and protrude from it (or are simply a protrusion machined into the face of the bolt), an arrangement which introduced the risk of detonating a round as it is being chambered. The Bergmann design

■**BELOW: The Steyr-Solothurn S1-100 was German-designed and Swiss-made, and widely held to be one of the best of its kind. Machined from solid forgings, it was very expensive to produce.**

precluded this by holding off the firing pin by means of a small tipping lever which rested in the underside of the breech cylinder until the fresh cartridge had been driven fully home, and the breech was closed.

The MP34 was manufactured initially by Schultz and Larsen at Otterup in Denmark and later, when it had become the machine pistol of choice of the SS, by Carl Walther at Zella-Mehlis and by Junker and Ruh of Karlsruhe, who produced it in a simpler form as the MP35 during World War II. In all, some 40,000 are thought to have been produced, the vast majority for the SS in 9mm Parabellum chambering with 180mm (7in) barrels, some with barrels 15mm (.6in) longer, in the variant calibres.

THE 'STEYR-SOLOTHURN'

Confusingly, Rheinmetall also produced a sub-machine gun which was adopted by the German military as the MP34, but

this time, it was made in the Steyr factory in Austria, and as a result the suffix '(ö)' was added to the designation (ie, MP34(ö)). This weapon was developed at Solothurn as the S1-100, production being turned over to the other Rheinmetall subsidiary as soon as it was perfected; as a result it was widely known as the Steyr-Solothurn. Like the Bergmann MP34, it was produced in a variety of rival calibres to the 9mm Parabellum chambering in which it was most often made; it, too was offered with a variety of barrel lengths, the most common of which was 195mm (7.68in), and somewhat surprisingly, a tripod mount was also available.

If anything, the Steyr-Solothurn was even more complex than the Bergmann machine pistols, though it, too, was a simple blowback design. Like the Bergmann, it was largely machined from forgings, and had full wooden furniture. It, too, was capable of single-shot or sustained fire, the change being effected

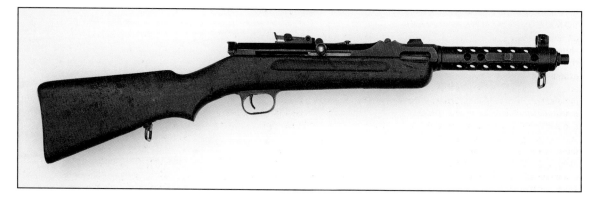

■LEFT: The MP40 was so widespread as to be almost a defining mark of World War II-vintage German soldiers – though these men are French, members of the Waffen-SS's 'Foreign Legions'.

developed a self-loading rifle chambered initially for the 'full-power' 7.9mm round and later modified it to accept an intermediate 7.62mm x 39 round; it was the appraisal of one of these prototype weapons, which fell into Soviet hands along with 20,000 rounds of ammunition in 1945, which led to the adoption of the intermediate round in the Soviet Union in the 1950s.

Vollmer perfected his machine pistol in 1930, having deleted the early side-mounted drum magazine (a legacy of his work on the MG08/15) in favour of a 32-round capacity box, switching from a lightweight, shrouded barrel to a heavier exposed barrel (the lightweight barrel and shroud, with its cooling slots, was later restored), and finally adding an important refinement to the action in the shape of a telescopic tube to house the return spring and stabilize its operation, a device which was to be found in one form or another in all subsequent World War II-era German SMGs and the many weapons which took them as their inspiration. Like the other weapons of its day it, too, was manufactured from parts machined out of the solid and had wooden furniture – in this case, incorporating a forward pistol grip.

Vollmer manufactured his machine pistol in very small numbers – an estimated less than 400 in all – in 7.63mm Mauser, 7.65mm Parabellum and 9mm Parabellum chamberings, before recognising that only significant economies of scale would allow it to become a viable proposition. He sold the manufacturing rights to Berthold Geipel GmbH, who put it into production at its plant in Erfurt, the Erfurter Maschinenfabrik, when it became known as the ERMA *Maschinenpistole* or EMP. Significant numbers were sold to both sides (Bolivia and Paraguay) during the Chaco War of 1932–35, and many more turned up in Spain. Significant numbers were issued to the *Wehrmacht*, too, before the arrival of the MP40. It could deliver single rounds or bursts, according to the position of the selector in a cut-out in the forestock above the trigger guard; safety was achieved, as in the MP18, by locking the cocking handle into a notch (the EMP fired from an open breech), but later a

by a slide switch on the left hand side of the forestock, just behind the port for the 32-round capacity magazine. Its barrel shroud was perforated with holes, rather than the slots of the MP34, and many examples had a lug for the attachment of an Austrian M95 bayonet on the right hand side. The Steyr-Solothurn was the machine pistol of choice of the German and Austrian police forces during World War II (though it was also issued to military personnel in significant numbers alongside the MP38 and MP40, see below), and it stayed in production until 1945 as a result.

THE ERMA MACHINE PISTOLS
The last of the 'old-fashioned' German machine pistols was actually developed between 1925 and 1930, by a second-rank (but by no means second-rate) weapons designer named Heinrich Vollmer, in co-operation with the Reichswehr's Inspectorate of Weapons and Equipment. Vollmer – who owned a machine shop in the small town of Biberach in southern Germany – had a variety of useful inventions to his name, including a beltless cartridge feed for the MG08/15, which failed to go into production only because it came too late. He later

Erma M58

Calibre: 9mm Parabellum
Weight: 3.1kg (6.8lb)
Length: 405mm (16in)
Barrel length: 190mm (7.5in)
Effective range: 70m (230ft)
Action: blowback
Cyclic rate of fire: 650rpm
Muzzle velocity: 395mps (1300fps)
Country of origin: Germany

secondary safety device was added, in the form of a lever on the right hand side of the receiver which blocked the movement of the breech-block independently. The barrel of the EMP was longer than that of its counterparts at 230mm (9in), and the gun overall was considerably longer, thanks to the longer receiver made necessary by the telescopic shroud.

THE NEW ERA
In Germany in the mid-1930s, there was a pronounced sense of urgency in the air, both to undo the results of World War I and to make up for the time lost in its dreadful aftermath. That urgency revealed itself clearly in the field of weapons development, in every particular from handguns to battleships, and much of the entire national output was devoted to re-arming, so it comes as something of a surprise to realise that it was actually 1938 before anyone's attention turned to making the machine pistol a more practical proposition, particularly when its original conception was so directly

linked with infantry tactics which had come close to winning World War I. Then, the experience gained by the German 'volunteers' during the Spanish Civil War combined with the newly defined needs of airborne forces and tank crews resulted in attention being re-focussed on personal automatic weapons.

None of the machine pistols described above lent itself to mass production. All were comparatively difficult, costly and slow to manufacture, and inevitably that meant appropriate companies were asked to develop proposals for more suitable designs. In the end, it was Erma (as we may call the company by way of shorthand) which was to come up with the answer, though not immediately, as we shall see.

THE MP38
Erma's starting position, not surprisingly, was the Vollmer-designed EMP, and indeed, many of the new weapon's features were taken straight from that gun, even though the two were quite

different in appearance. Essentially, the MP38, as the new weapon was designated when it was accepted by the Wehrmacht in August 1938, was the EMP with its wooden furniture replaced by metal and plastic, and with the magazine port rotated down through 90 degrees, so that both it and the 32-round capacity stick magazine to be inserted there did double duty as a forward pistol grip. Additionally, the buttstock, which was now fabricated from tubular steel, with a simple steel plate to serve as a pad for the shoulder, could be folded back to lie beneath the receiver. The cocking handle was moved to the left hand side, but retained the safety notch inherited from the Schmeisser design of two decades earlier.

Internally, too, the MP38 was clearly a development of the EMP, with the same simple blowback action and the telescoping breech case which extended to contain the return spring. There was no provision for single shots, but the weight of the breech-block and the strength of the spring combined to limit the gun's cyclic rate to 350–400 rounds per minute (rpm), and a practised gunman had little trouble in releasing the trigger fast enough to hold the action off after just one round had been fired. The MP38 lost the barrel shroud which Erma had re-fitted to the EMP, and was fitted with a heavier barrel, very similar to that with which the last of Vollmer's own guns had been equipped, and of the same length, 230mm (9in). It was made only in 9mm Parabellum calibre.

THE MP40

The MP38 was certainly somewhat easier to manufacture than the EMP, and was a rather superior weapon by virtue of the greater flexibility its ergonomic design gave it (the folding butt was to become a standard feature of the 'modern' SMG). If the gun had a major operational failing it was in the function of the single-column magazine. Curiously, its successor, the MP40, used the same unit, and at no time was any serious attempt made to develop it further, despite a tendency to misfeed. But in fact the new SMG was no cheaper or even quicker to produce than the EMP had been, because all the mechanical components, even the receiver, were still machined from forgings. Two years later, a major re-vamp of the design saw that basic fault corrected. Now all the mechanical components – save for the barrel and the breech-block – were produced from steel stampings, pressed into the required form and electro-welded where necessary, and could be mass-produced easily. A new

assembly methodology was introduced at the same time, and components were produced in many different locations for assembly at Erfurt, at Schmeisser's C.G. Haenel factory in Suhl and at Steyr. It has been estimated that something over a million MP40s, as the revamped machine pistol was designated, were produced in all.

Operationally, it was an almost exact copy of the MP38 (the differences were minor – the external form of the breech case, for example, and the magazine catch), and it functioned in exactly the same manner. It didn't last as long in the field, and one may imagine that the odd gun failed to function from time to time, but the principle held good, and the manufacturing philosophy was soon copied elsewhere; it was generally held in very high esteem by those who used it. The only major variant was the MP40/II, produced in 1943; this gun had a magazine housing modified to hold two magazines, which could be brought into action one after the other. Despite the welcome additional capacity, the gun was never particularly popular due to the extra weight – an extra 1kg. (2.2lb) over the 5kg (11lb) the standard gun weighed when loaded.

THE MP41

The MP38 and MP40 were known as 'Schmeissers' by Allied troops, quite inaccurately, for Louis was long dead and Hugo had had nothing whatsoever to do with the basic design, and became involved only when the revamped version went into production (it was he who

redesigned the magazine catch). He did, however, produce an unsuccessful variant of the gun with wooden furniture (once again, a cut-down version of the stock of the Mauser 98 rifle and carbine with which the majority of German infantrymen were still armed) and a lighter barrel. The gun went into limited production, and was designated the MP41, but it was not as practical as the metal-and-plastic MP40, and was never as popular. There is no record of it ever having been issued to Wehrmacht units, and the total production was quite small.

SINCEREST FORM OF FLATTERY?

The only other machine pistols produced in any numbers in Germany during World War II (though 'imported' SMGs, particularly Italian Berettas, were issued in considerable numbers) were, somewhat surprisingly, copies of the British Sten gun, of which more below. First came the MP3008, also known as the Gerät Neumünster (Neumünster Device), which was manufactured in Oberndorf, Suhl, Erfurt and elsewhere (and by engineering companies not otherwise known to have produced small arms, including 'local' engineering workshops). The MP3008 was somewhat modified from the original; the magazine was fixed to protrude downwards, instead of locking into a collar free to revolve through a quarter-turn as on the Sten (and the magazine itself was that developed for the MP38); some had a primitive pistol grip, while others had the crudest imaginable wooden buttstock – but the build quality, always a bone of contention

Konepistooli M/44

Calibre: 9mm Parabellum
Weight: 2.8kg (6.2lb)
Length: 825mm (32.5in) (stock extended)
Barrel length: 250mm (9.8in)
Effective range: 70m (230ft)
Action: blowback
Cyclic rate of fire: 650rpm
Muzzle velocity: 395mps (1300fps)
Country of Origin: Finland

with those who were issued with the Sten, was certainly not an improvement on the original, and if anything, many of the guns were even more poorly finished. This was a desperation weapon, clearly made to be handed out to anyone able to hold one and fire it, but in the event it came too late even for that, having been ordered into production in the Autumn of 1944. Most existing examples never left the factories and workshops where they were produced, and most were only assembled post-War.

FLATTERING TO DECEIVE?

The other German copy of the Sten – and this time it was an exact copy of the Mark II, down to the legend punched into the receiver, and so well executed that it was indistinguishable from the original – is more of a mystery; the reasons for it having been put into production by Mauser-Werke are lost and now quite incomprehensible. The most widely circulated theory – though theory is all it is – suggests that they were to be distributed to the few pro-German partisans in France (though there were actually few enough of those) who were to have come out of hiding after the Allied invasion, but this actually does nothing to explain why they were exact copies of the British weapon. Some 25,000 are recorded as being produced under conditions of great secrecy at Oberndorf (in just six weeks), and delivered to the *Wehrmacht*, but no absolutely authenticated Gerät Potsdam (Potsdam Device), as it was called, has ever been displayed. Perhaps this was because they were such good copies of the workaday Sten that they were truly undistinguishable from the real thing. One German authority suggests that the price paid for these weapons was enormous – RM1800 each, when a standard Mauser 98K rifle was costing RM56, which would suggest that they were required for a very special operation indeed. What exactly that could have been – or even might have been – is unknown, and the entire theory is frankly (to this author, at least) quite incredible.

POST-1945 GERMAN SMGS

Beaten into abject submission, her industrial base in ruins once more (and with the added burden of the country being split under two very different regimes, one of them intent, at least in the short term, on simply carrying off

anything that was in the remotest sense moveable), Germany therefore ceased to be a force in the arms world in 1945, but this time, the hiatus was to be relatively short-lived.

At least two important manufacturers – Erma and Walther – had been located in what became the Russian Zone, later the Communist German Democratic Republic (East Germany) and both were eventually to re-appear in the Federal Republic of West Germany. Erma was re-established at Dachau in Bavaria, in 1951, and between then and the mid-1960s, it was to produce a variety of new SMGs. Somewhat curiously, for the company had been a major force in the field pre-war, Erma now met with a complete lack of success. Though the machine pistols it produced in the period were universally well made, none were to be adopted by any nation's armed forces, and the company then changed direction, concentrating on sporting weapons. Walther, which relocated to Ulm, produced a single model of machine pistol in two variants which was to be adopted by police forces in various parts of the world. Mauser went on to produce two types of SMG, one of them originally developed at Erma, but the real success story was that of a group of ex-Mauser employees who established themselves in Oberndorf as Heckler & Koch and set a new *de facto* standard with their MP5 in its various guises.

THE ERMA PM9

The first product to come out of Erma's new factory was the French-designed SMG or PM9 (*pistole mitrailette, 9mm*). This was a most peculiar design incorporating a flywheel in place of a recoil spring, the advantage being a considerable reduction in overall length (it was just 640mm (25in) long with the stock extended, and weighed 2.5kg (5.5lb) unloaded). Like that of another French design of the same time, the MAT 49, its 32-round magazine could be folded forward to lie beneath the barrel and the skeleton stock could be folded back to lie alongside the receiver and barrel, making a very neat package indeed. In all likelihood, the first guns to use this innovation had appeared in Switzerland in the 1930s, produced by SIG; the unsuccessful Hotchkiss 'Universal' (see below), which also appeared in 1949, followed the same practice. The PM9 had a high cyclic rate – 750 rounds per minute (rpm) – but was said to have been

decidedly smooth in action. It was also decidedly expensive, however, since it required many precisely machined parts, and was never a commercial success as a result.

THE ERMA MPS

The PM9 had been the work of a designer named Louis Bonnet de Camillis, and he was also responsible for Erma's next attempt at getting back into the market, the MP56. This was a more conventional weapon but with one slightly unorthodox feature for its time: it had a wrap-around bolt, which as its name suggests was tubular in form, and fitted around the barrel and chamber, thus once again reducing the gun's overall length. Erma took it to prototype stage, but then decided that it was not a viable proposition.

The weapon's sponsor then took the design to Mauser, who produced it as the MP57. After another unsuccessful attempt at producing an unorthodox machine pistol – this time one which could fire an anti-tank grenade, necessitating operation from the closed bolt position – Erma attempted to follow very closely indeed the Federal Government's expressed requirements for a low-cost weapon, producing one in which the majority of parts were to be stamped out of a single sheet of steel in a single operation. In its operation, the MP58 returned to the telescoping mainspring housing used in the pre-war Erma MPs, and was largely immune to the intrusion of sand and dirt as a result. Though it seemed to be exactly what the *Bundeswehr* required, it was not adopted.

A refined version followed the MP58: the MP59, incorporating a hydraulic buffer which permitted the selection of a cyclic rate of 100–600 rounds per minute (rpm). Problems with the rate of wear of the buffer seals, though they were eventually solved, caused this project, too, to be shelved. Erma wasn't beaten yet, however – not quite – and immediately started to develop yet another new gun, the MP60. This was a return to orthodoxy, save that the barrel was entirely shrouded in a square-section extension of the receiver. In all, some 30 were hand-built and submitted to the *Bundeswehr* for field testing. Once again, despite the gun performing very well indeed, particularly in terms of its resistance to dirt, there was no official interest and the project was shelved. Erma had one last try, with what was essentially a modified MP60 incorporating a new type of safety mechanism and ambidextrous fire selector. Like its predecessor, the MP65 was very well finished and very robust, but it was no more successful. Erma finally gave up.

OVER TO ULM

Carl Walther Waffenfabrick, then located in Zella-Mehlis, was best known for the automatic pistols it developed in the inter-war period, the PP (*Polizei Pistole*) and PPK, chiefly in 7.65mm, and the P38 in 9mm Parabellum which replaced the Luger P08 as the German Army's regulation sidearm. In 1957, by now located in Ulm, the reconstructed company began manufacturing its very successful pistols once again, and soon branched out into other areas, one of which was a development programme which resulted in the MP-L and MP-K (for *Lang* and *Kurz*; long and short. The differences in length were in the barrel – 260mm (10.25in) and 173mm (6.8in) respectively).

The Walther MP was a purely conventional blowback weapon, save that it had an overhanging bolt which was located above the barrel and breech – an arrangement in principle not unlike that adopted for the Erma MP56 – which

allowed the receiver to be very short indeed (the MP-K, with its buttstock retracted, was just 380mm (15in) long; it was the precursor of an entire sub-genre of very small sub-machine guns which was to include the Czech Skorpion, the Israeli Mini-Uzi and the American Ingrams MAC-10, see below). It did have a number of refinements, however, for example the cocking handle did not normally reciprocate with the bolt, but could be reconnected with it, to clear a jammed round for instance, by pressing it inwards. The gun fired from an open bolt and used the principle of advanced primer ignition to reduce recoil forces. The Walther MP was never adopted as a regulation weapon, but was taken up by some police and Special Forces units.

Meanwhile, just down the road from the Walther factory, Anschutz, which was perhaps better known for its target rifles, was also embarking on the manufacture of a machine pistol, this time a re-vamp of a modification of a Finnish gun, the *Konepistooli* M/44, which was itself an almost direct copy of the Soviet PPS43. The drawings for this gun were taken by Willi Daugs, the manager of the Tikkakosi Arsenal where it was produced, when he fled to Spain at the end of World War II. He then worked with Ludwig Vorgrimler, one of the team which had

worked on the semi-rigid roller-locked breech (see below) at Mauser during the War. In the meantime Vorgrimler had gone to the *Centro des Estudios Tècnicos Materiales Speciales* in Madrid, where he had been responsible for the CETME M58 self-loading rifle (which was subsequently used as the basis for Heckler & Koch's G3 series of weapons so that the design finally came back home to Oberndorf). Daugs and Vorgrimler produced a modification to the design, and had it manufactured in Oviedo in Spain. The West German Customs Service bought 1000 of these guns, and sent some to Mauser, some to Sauer and some to Anschutz for further modification, aimed chiefly at making it easier and simpler to manufacture. The Anschutz proposals were found to be the most acceptable, and the gun was put into production at the company's factory in Ulm as the DUX MP59.

MAUSER'S SMGS

Mauser-Werke had been producing, first bolt-action rifles, then pistols and later self-loading rifles in Oberndorf am Neckar since taking over the Royal Württemberg Rifle Factory in the mid-1860s, but apart from the decidedly odd episode when it manufactured exact copies of British Sten Mk IIs for six

Dux Modell 59

Calibre: 9mm Parabellum
Weight: 3.5kg (7.7lb)
Length: 825mm (32.5in)
Barrel length: 250mm (9.75in)
Effective range: 70m (230ft)
Action: blowback
Cyclic rate of fire: 500rpm
Muzzle velocity: 395mps (1300fps)
Country of Origin: Germany/Spain

Heckler & Koch MP5A2/

Calibre: 9mm Parabellum
Weight: 2.55kg (5.6lb)
Length: 660mm (26in) (MP5A3, stock extended)
Barrel length: 225mm (8.85in)
Effective range: 70m (230ft)
Action: delayed blowback (locked bre
Cyclic rate of fire: 650rpm
Muzzle velocity: 395mps (1300fps)
Country of Origin: Germany

weeks in 1945, it was 1957 before the company began to produce a machine pistol, and then somewhat surprisingly, for one of its strengths was its design and development department, it was to be a gun conceived elsewhere. As we have noted above, the Mauser MP57 was actually the Camillis design produced in prototype form by Erma, the only major differences being the incorporation of an option to fire single shots and a forward pistol grip located right at the muzzle, which could be folded back under the barrel. Like the other design from the same source, the MP57 was somewhat unusual for its time in having its trigger group located forward of the breech, so that the 32-round capacity magazine was inserted through the pistol grip.

However, the MP57 was not a commercial success, and neither was the next attempt, the Model 60, designed this time by Ludwig Vorgrimler, who had by then returned from Spain. Like the Erma-Panzer, the Mauser Model 60 was designed to fire an anti-tank grenade, and operated from a closed bolt. It was somewhat unusual in using a concealed hammer to impact on the firing pin.

THE HECKLER & KOCH MP5

Far and away the most successful of the German machine pistols of this period, and the gun by which later developments were to be measured, was the Heckler &

Koch MP5. This was a significantly more sophisticated firearm than most of the genre, using the same semi-rigid roller locking system as the company employed for its G3 assault rifle, which Vorgrimler and his co-workers Illenberger and Jungermann, led by Wilhelm Stähle, had developed for the Third Reich in 1942–43 and the stillborn Mauser MKb machine carbine, chambered for the reduced-power 7.9mm *Pistolepatrone* ammunition (see above; also see below for references to the locking system developed earlier elsewhere, for the MG42 GPMG). Firing from a closed breech, and therefore without the preliminary movement of the breech-block in the receiver, which tends to throw the weapon off the line of aim even as the first round is fired, it was to prove much more accurate than competing designs, particularly in single-shot mode, and became very popular, particularly with police forces, as a result.

The roller locking system was a masterpiece. It had its origins in the mechanism of the MG42 general-purpose machine gun (see below), but was simpler and easier to manufacture. The genius of

its inventor, whoever he was, was to introduce a flat, arrow-shaped 'steering piece' through which the firing pin passed and which acted as a flexible link between the bolt head and the breech-block; gas pressure in the chamber acting on the empty cartridge case and pushed the bolt head and the 'steering piece' back against the pressure of a strong spring and allowed the locking rollers in the bolt body (which whilst in battery it jammed into recesses in the receiver wall) to retract into it, allowing the entire assembly to retire against the pressure of the recoil spring, and the action to cycle. The bolt was a complex machining on two tiers. The lower part contained the bolt proper, with the locking rollers, 'steering

piece' and firing pin, while the upper part, rigidly attached to it, operated within a secondary cylinder above the barrel, where it acted on the main recoil spring; the cocking piece was located above the barrel and acted on the upper portion of the bolt, the barrel and the cylinder in which the cocking mechanism was located being shrouded to form a forestock. This allowed the action to be cocked with the forehand, an altogether more convenient arrangement than was usual. Whether this arrangement constitutes a locking system or is 'merely' a refined delaying system is moot; it is perhaps significant that it is quite positive and strong enough to lock the breech of an assault rifle or a light

machine gun chambered for the full-power 7.62mm NATO round, a function it performs in the G3-series rifles and the HK13, -21 and -23-series light machine guns.

The MP5 shared a trigger and actuating mechanism with the rest of the 'family', too, employing a hammer. When the selector was set to automatic, the trigger was moved up physically, so that the nose of the sear was depressed sufficiently, on firing, to prevent it from re-engaging with the hammer. Setting the selector to single shot moved the trigger mechanism down sufficiently for the nose of the sear to re-engage the hammer, while setting it to safe lowered it so that the sear blocked the hammer

completely. A burst fire device was available, which allowed two, three or four rounds to be fired (the number had to be pre-determined when the device was fitted) when 'automatic' was selected; it worked by means of a simple ratchet which held the sear off the hammer until the desired number of rounds had been discharged.

MP5 VARIANTS
The MP5 SMG was available in two basic forms, though the difference between them was minimal. The MP5A2 was fitted with a rigid black plastic buttstock, while the A3 version was fitted with a telescoping metal stock, the two rigid arms of which slid along the receiver in

111

grooves machined there for the purpose when it was retracted. In fact, a simple locking pin secured both types of stock into the receiver, and could either be removed and one changed for the other, or alternatively, a simple receiver cap could be fitted. A silenced version, the MP5 SD, was also available, the integral sound suppressor consisting of a cylinder surrounding the barrel, which was drilled along its length. Propellant gas escaped into the cylinder via these vents and travelled around a helical path before escaping, losing much of its velocity in the process; the velocity of the emerging round was also reduced too, to below the speed of sound. A variant of the MP5, the HK 53 SMG, was chambered for the 5.56mm x 45 cartridge; it formed part of a modular family of weapons which also included two assault rifles and two machine guns, many parts of which were interchangeable; this was to be a common feature of the second-generation assault rifles, and one which we shall consider briefly in Chapter Five.

BRITISH SMGS
The British Army had no tactical requirement for the sub-machine gun during the interwar period. It classified

the genre as 'gangsters' weapons, and wanted nothing to do with them, even though many individuals had acquired considerable respect for them in 1918. It was to be 1940, when the realities of a new war (and a new type of war, come to that) had finally begun to hit home, before it changed its corporate mind, and turned first to the only accessible existing supplier, Auto Ordnance, requesting as many Thompson guns (qv) as it could deliver.

In fact, BSA had been producing Thompsons in the UK since 1926, and seems to have worked in close collaboration with the 'parent' company; some BSA-introduced modifications found their way into later Auto Ordnance products. By then, however, Auto Ordnance, having languished for years, had started to achieve sales in considerable quantities, and certainly couldn't provide for all the British Army's needs; Whitehall had to look elsewhere, and there was no time to lose. In a certain sense, coming late to a particular activity gives one an advantage over those who have been pioneers in the field, since one can learn from their mistakes at minimal cost, and essentially, that is what happened at the Royal Small Arms

Factory, where a design for a simple, no-frills sub-machine gun was hastily commissioned and quickly realised.

THE INFAMOUS STEN
Never has such an effective weapon of war ever been held in so little esteem by the men who employed it. The original Sten gun – the Machine Carbine, 9mm Sten, to give it its official designation, its name derived from the initials of the two men who were responsible for it, Major R.V. Sheppard, who was the project officer, and Mr H.J. Turpin, the designer, together with the 'En' of Enfield – was to become the standard sub-machine gun of all the British forces throughout World War II, and was to remain so for a good few years afterwards, despite being held in very little respect by the men to whom it was issued. They called it the Plumber's Delight and the Woolworth Special, after the mass-market chain store, and those were only some of its printable nicknames!

In essence, the Sten was a replica of the MP40 (though it resembled it hardly at all), and used the same distributed principle of manufacture, sub-components being produced in dozens of different locations, and shipped to the main

■LEFT: The Heckler & Koch MP5K (K for 'kurz': short), one of the new generation of miniature machine pistols popular with hostage-rescue teams and the like.

assembly centres (BSA's factories and Royal Ordnance Factories around the British Isles, as well as Enfield). The design was simple in the extreme, with no frills of any kind, only the unitary chamber and barrel, the breech-block and the magazine housing being anything other than pressings (and at that, the barrel in some models was a simple drawn steel tube). The action was simple blowback, with no form of retardation save the main recoil spring. It fired from an open bolt and was cocked by a handle operating in a slot in the tubular receiver, which could be lodged into a safety notch, physically preventing the breech-block from flying forward. A simple press-through selector allowing a choice of single shots or bursts worked by engaging or freeing a detent in the trigger mechanism, and on 'automatic', it operated at a cyclic rate of around 600 rounds per minute (rpm). It was crude and it was imperfect, but as history testifies, it was a successful weapon, despite the bloody-minded resistance of the soldiery to something which was so obviously a makeshift. It was manufactured in huge numbers – BSA alone produced 20,000 per month – and a similar number were turned out in Enfield, production continuing until well after the war was over.

In all, at least 11 different versions of the Sten were produced, though some of them never got beyond the experimental stage. The most widely issued was the Mk II, but by the end of World War II a very much better finished version, with wooden furniture and a forward pistol grip (which was subsequently removed; it was both more convenient and more practical to grip it by the magazine with the left hand) was being issued as the Mark V. Three silenced versions were produced in limited quantities, the best of which – and it was probably the best silenced SMG of the entire period – was the Mark IIS.

THE LANCHESTER SMG

The Sten was not the only British SMG, however; a much better weapon, in terms of its mechanism and finish, was issued to the Royal Navy. This was the Lanchester, and it returned (or more accurately, prefaced) the compliment the Germans paid to RSAF in that it was a direct copy of the MP28 produced by Hugo Schmeisser. The Lanchester, which was adopted in 1941, was manufactured by Sterling Arms, which was later to produce the successor to the Sten under its own name (see below). It differed from the MP28 chiefly in being fitted with the wooden furniture of the British standard rifle of World War I, the SMLE, together with its bayonet fixing lug, while the German original had featured the furniture of the Mauser 98K. Naturally enough, it was chambered for the 9mm Parabellum round (as, of course, were the Sten and the other British SMGs). Other points of departure from the original German design lay in the magazine housing, machined out of solid brass, and the receiver catch. The magazine supplied with the weapon was a copy of that which Schmeisser had designed, and clearly influenced Sheppard and Turpin, for the smaller-capacity box magazine they devised for the Sten had the same fitting, and could be employed with the Lanchester.

Somewhat curiously, the only major defect in the Sten's design lay in the magazine lips, and was thus attributable to Schmeisser; his considerable reputation was untarnished, however, probably because the connection was never made, though in fairness, the magazines he produced were much more robust in their construction, and deformities of the lips – the fault which plagued the Sten – were seldom, if ever, encountered.

QUALITY – A LUXURY

The contrast between the Sten and the Lanchester could not have been more marked; the latter was a high-quality arm, 'properly' built and finished, and a pleasure to handle. The soldiers and seamen to whom it was issued (and all those who could get their hands on one unofficially; it was a particular favourite of the irregulars who made up such units as the SAS), were universal in their praise for it, just as those who were issued with the Sten were universal in condemning its poor quality and poor finish. But the Sten was effective, and a caseful could be produced for every Lanchester made, both in terms of material cost and time, and therefore, in true terms, it was by far the better weapon, little as the troops could not bring themselves to believe it. Perhaps it could have been dressed up somewhat and perhaps it could have been rather more evenly finished, with the rough electro-welds ground down smooth, for example, but that would have made no difference to the gun's efficiency as a mass-produced weapon of war, but would only have pushed up the cost (from £2/10/00 (£2.50)) and slowed down the rate of production.

OTHER ALTERNATIVES

There were alternatives to the Sten and the Lanchester produced – but never fully developed and certainly never adopted – in Britain during World War II. The best of them was probably the Vesely or V42, named after its designer, an Hungarian expatriate who worked closely with BSA. By the time it was produced, differential recoil (advanced primer setback) had become the accepted method of smoothing out the action of an SMG, and the V42 was somewhat unusual in not adopting it. Instead it had a much larger than normal recoil spring, which was housed inside the buttstock, though there was a drawback of sorts to the arrangement, since it upped the cyclic rate to 700 rounds per minute (rpm). Another unusual feature – and this time it was an innovation – was a magazine which had two columns in tandem, the forward column being expended first. This allowed a capacity of 60 rounds without making the assembly impossibly cumbersome; there were problems with it initially, but it was eventually perfected, though never seems to have been employed since.

Vesely paid considerable attention, right from the outset, to the gun's 'manufacturability', as we may call it, and though it had a conventional appearance and was well finished (at least by contemporary standards), it employed pressings, stampings and simple machinings wherever possible, and was designed to be produced quickly by relatively unskilled workers. Even that, together with its superior performance, wasn't enough to see it ousting the Sten.

THE WELGUN

As well as producing the Sten in enormous quantities and working with Vesely to develop the V42, BSA also had a project of its own; to produce a small, lightweight SMG as an alternative to the Sten. The Welgun, as the weapon in question was known, used some Sten components – the magazine, barrel and mainspring – but co-located the latter two in order to reduce overall length, the spring now acting to pull the breech-block back into battery, rather than pushing it. There was no cocking handle, but instead the receiver had two large slots cut in its sides, which allowed the fingers and thumb of the left hand to grip the bolt itself and cycle it back and forwards (there was considerable concern expressed at the likelihood of this arrangement allowing mud and dirt in to jam the action). The magazine was located in the floor of the receiver, and fed upwards. The firing pin, unlike that of the Sten, which was fixed into the bolt face, was forced forward by a rocking bar pivoted inside the breech-block, which was in turn actuated by a plunger on the bolt face; this seemingly rather complex arrangement (at least in comparison to that of the Sten) allowed the incorporation of a mechanical safety catch which was certainly more sophisticated than that of most other SMGs of the period.

The Welgun's primary weakness lay in the positioning of the mainspring; surrounding the barrel as it did, it absorbed heat quickly, and was, in consequence, thought likely to fail in prolonged use. With its folding stock extended it was 700mm (27.5 in) long,

6.35cm (2.5in) shorter than the Sten, and unloaded it weighed the same as the established weapon at just over 3kg (6.5lb). Its cyclic rate of fire was comparable with that of the later Stens.

THE STERLING SMG

Sterling Arms stopped manufacturing the Lanchester SMG in 1942, by which time designer George Patchett had produced a prototype of a new lightweight machine pistol, rather better finished than the Sten, more sophisticated in operation and more robust though marginally lighter at 2.7kg (6lb) unloaded. Naturally, it was chambered for the 9mm Parabellum cartridge. Sterling began manufacturing it as the Patchett Mk 1 in 1944.

An improved version was introduced later that same year, known first as the Patchett Mk 2, then as the Sterling. The only significant change was to the form of the magazine; the early type had been straight, like that of the Sten (and was interchangeable with it) but the feed from the single column of 34 rounds was improved by curving it slightly. It was adopted by the British Army in 1953 as the Machine Carbine, 9mm Sterling, L2A1, and was to stay in service until into the 1990s, undergoing some very slight modification along the way. A version with an integral silencer, known as the L34A1, was also produced in small

quantities, for clandestine operations.

The Sterling used the advanced primer ignition system, the round being fired even as the bolt was still moving forwards; before, in fact, it was completely seated within the chamber. Over the next few milliseconds seating was completed and obturation was achieved, and almost immediately the pressure build-up behind the projectile, acting through the now empty cartridge case, overcame the force of the spring and the inertia of the bolt, brought it to a halt, and then sent it back against the recoil spring. In this way, the unwanted recoil force was minimised. Once clear of the chamber, the spent casing – held until now by the extractor claw in the bolt face – was ejected to the right by a simple fixed spur in the receiver wall. If the fire selector was set to single-shot or the trigger released, the bolt was then held back at the limit of its travel by the sear. When released again, it travelled forwards under the pressure of the spring, stripping a new round out of the magazine and starting the cycle all over again. Like the Sten, the Sterling's firing pin was fixed into the face of the bolt. The fire selector worked by means of a spring-loaded 'disconnector' acting on the sear; setting it to 'automatic' caused the disconnector to be removed from contact with the sear, permitting the action to

Sten Mark 2

Calibre: 9mm Parabellum
Weight: 2.95kg (6.5lb)
Length: 762mm (30in)
Barrel length: 195mm (7.75in)
Effective range: 70m (230ft)
Action: blowback
Cyclic rate of fire: 550rpm
Muzzle velocity: 395mps (1300fps)
Country of Origin: United Kingdom

■ **ABOVE: The Sten was almost universally derided by those using it, but that didn't always prevent it from being an effective close-quarters weapon.**

reciprocate freely for as long as the sear itself was held out of line. The safety mechanism also utilised the disconnector, locking it in such a way that the sear could not be released. The gun's cyclic rate was marginally slower than that of the Sten which it replaced, at 550 rounds per minute (rpm). The Sterling was to be the last sub-machine gun developed in the UK for mass production, being replaced in service by a 'bullpup' assault rifle, the SA80 (L85A1).

THE ITALIAN SMGS

At the start of this chapter, we cast some doubt on the status of the Bergmann MP18 as the first sub-machine gun, and suggested that the honour should go to a rival Italian design instead. This was the Vilar Perosa, certainly a very interesting weapon, at least from a design standpoint, though some authorities would not identify it as a sub-machine gun at all, but rather as a light machine gun which happened to be chambered for a relatively low-powered round, the 9mm Glisenti, developed for an automatic pistol which was first produced in 1905 and accepted by the Italian Army five years later. The round in question was almost identical in dimension to the German 9mm Parabellum, but gave a muzzle velocity some 20 per cent lower.

The Vilar Perosa SMG was, it is suggested, originally intended for use in aircraft as a flexibly mounted observer's weapon, and its characteristics and original form would seem to bear that out; it had an extremely high rate of fire, which is desirable in such a weapon but a positive disadvantage in a gun produced for the infantryman.

Its operative method was a straightforward delayed blowback: a lug on the breech-block ran in a track which performed a quarter-twist as the block was forced back by the gas pressure in the chamber and barrel. This caused the bolt to rotate through 90 degrees, thus retarding it (the turn performed no other function). At the end of the feed (ie, return) stroke, the track forced the breech-block to turn through 90 degrees again, of course, and only then could the striker emerge from its face and strike the cap to detonate the cartridge. This action took place while the breech block was still moving forward, and so the recoil was significantly reduced.

In its original form the VP, as the gun is normally known, was produced in pairs, two complete weapons joined side-by-side by means of a large collar which held both barrels and a connecting rod attached towards the rear of the tubular receivers. They were further joined by the

Sten Mark 5
(early production)

Calibre: 9mm Parabellum
Weight: 3.4kg (7.5lb)
Length: 445mm (17.5in)
Barrel length: 195mm (7.75in)
Effective range: 70m (230ft)

Action: blowback
Cyclic rate of fire: 550rpm
Muzzle velocity: 395mps (1300fps)
Country of Origin: United Kingdom

pair of spade grips, similar to that common in heavy belt-fed weapons, which they shared. Each had a separate cocking mechanism, though these were interlinked so that both guns were charged together. An individual trigger (though these were thumb-operated buttons, and placed side-by-side within the spade grips, so that they would normally be actuated together) and individual curved box magazines were set vertically above the receivers, which held 25 rounds each. Since the cyclic rate of fire of the gun was some 1200–1500rpm, the 50 rounds the pair held could be discharged in a single burst in around a single second.

The gun found occasional application as a vehicle-mounted weapon (in the side-car of a motorcycle combination, in some cases) but its characteristics and its physical form, and its lack of any sights, made it unpopular. Only after World War I was over, when it was produced as a conventional SMG, did the VP achieve

any real measure of popularity. It had a wooden stock and a pair of finger-operated triggers in line, the forward of which produced single shots and the rearward fully automatic fire (the cocking lever was transformed into a sleeve, which was cut away beneath, so that it slid around the trigger guard). The VP was issued to Italian infantrymen in the 1920s, and was still in use during World War II.

Even in its single form, the VP was a heavy and cumbersome weapon, weighing 4.1kg (9lb) with a full magazine, and 900mm (35.5in) long, even though the barrel had been reduced in length by 40mm (1.6in). When a young engineer named Tulio Marengoni joined the long-established family firm of Pietro Beretta SpA in 1918, his first task was to refine the weapon, and particularly to reduce its weight. He slimmed it down somewhat, replaced the trigger mechanism with one producing only fully automatic fire (it was the one developed for the

Mannlicher-Carcano carbine, the Italian Army's official rifle), beefed up the recoil spring to slow it down somewhat and produced what became known as the Beretta *Modello 1918*, which went into official service that year, and was still in use when World War II came to an end. More importantly, perhaps, it established Marengoni within the company, and Beretta as a manufacturer of machine pistols, though the pairing was not to reach maturity for another 20 years or so.

THE BERETTA *MODELLO 1938*
In the intervening period, Marengoni – by now Head of Research and Development – produced two self-loading carbines designed for police work and Beretta sold them widely, but by the mid-1930s, he had returned to machine pistols, and had begun to work on an all-new design. This was actually rather more complex than that of the VP or the *Modello 1918* but was certainly more reliable and operated at an altogether

which was located around the firing pin and held in place by a collar. Its rear end was enclosed in a tube which fitted into a recess in the end cap of the receiver. For the trigger mechanism, the designer reverted to the twin-trigger system the modified VP had used, the forward trigger producing single shots, the rear, fully automatic fire. There was a simple safety catch which locked the action by interruption.

Beretta produced the *Modello 1938* in three versions; the first had an integral folding bayonet, a perhaps over-complicated muzzle compensator and elongated slots in its barrel shroud. The second had round perforations in the shroud and a modified form of safety catch: the original was retained, but

and eventually exploited that by devising a more powerful loading still, known as the M38, which had the same dimension as the Parabellum (9mm x 19) but a heavier charge. The new round was different physically in having a 1mm (.04in) groove pressed into its case, two-thirds of the way up from the base, which allowed it to be identified visually or by feel in the dark. It produced a muzzle velocity of 420mps (1380fps) as opposed to the 365mps (1200fps) of the Parabellum and the 320mps (1050fps) of the Glisenti round.

In 1942, Marengoni modified the gun with the objective of making it lighter, simpler and cheaper to produce. He did away with the barrel shroud and shortened the barrel from 315mm

Sten Mark 2(S)

Calibre: 9mm Parabellum
Weight: 3.5kg (7.75lb)
Length: 908mm (35.75in)
Barrel length: 90mm (3.5in)
Effective range: 30m (100ft)

Action: blowback
Cyclic rate of fire: 450rpm
Muzzle velocity: 300mps (1000fps)
Country of Origin: United Kingdom

more realistic cyclic rate. The *Beretta Modello 1938* was to be the Italian Army's standard SMG from 1938 to 1960, and was issued in large numbers to German troops during World War II. It was also adopted by the Romanian Army, and was sold in significant quantities elsewhere. It was a simple blowback design with no retarding mechanism, though it incorporated a primary safety mechanism, in that only when the breech-block was returned to battery and the gun was ready to fire, the ejector stud came into contact with a camming surface which in turn forced the firing pin forward to impinge upon the cap and detonate the charge. The recoil spring was slim, and operated inside the bolt

supplemented by a sliding bar which blocked the action of the rear trigger, and prevented the gun from being fired in fully automatic mode. The third model had no bayonet, nor any provision for mounting one, and a simplified muzzle compensator. It was this variant which equipped the Wehrmacht and the Romanian Army; towards the end of its long life it was further modified with the fitting of a simpler but more secure cross-bolt safety, designed for a later model, the 38/49 (see below).

Marengoni turned away from the 9mm Glisenti round for the new gun, preferring to design it around the more powerful Parabellum cartridge, but he allowed a considerable safety margin,

(12.4in) to 215mm (8.4in), and used stampings in place of machinings for the receiver and magazine housing, by this means reducing the unloaded weight from 4.2kg (9.25lb) to 3.3kg (7.25lb). Shortening the barrel meant reducing the muzzle velocity, but only marginally, and this was a small price to pay for a weapon which was essentially meant for short-range work anyway.

The *Modello 38/42*, as the modified gun was known, was followed by the 38/44, with a shortened buttstock and a large-diameter recoil spring, and by the 38/49 or M4, with the cross-bolt safety. It sold widely in all its versions, the M4 staying in service with the Italian Army, *Carabinieri* para-military police and

Owen Mark 1

Calibre: 9mm Parabellum
Weight: 4.2kg (9.3lb)
Length: 815mm (32in)
Barrel length: 245mm (9.75in)
Effective range: 70m (230ft)
Action: blowback
Cyclic rate of fire: 700rpm
Muzzle velocity: 395mps (1300fps)
Country of Origin: Australia

civilian police forces until the 1960s, and it was also adopted by numerous foreign governments for military and civil use. Tulio Marengoni retired in 1960, but some time before that, the responsibility for the development of new SMGs had passed to Domenico Salza, whose first weapon was a modified M4 which appeared in 1953 and was fitted with a squeeze safety in the forestock, operated by the fingers of the left hand.

THE BERETTA MODEL 12

By this time, the Beretta SMGs were looking distinctly old-fashioned, thanks to the company's adherence to full-length wooden furniture (though the *Modello 38/49* had been available with both folding and telescoping metal buttstocks). This was clearly an area which needed attention, but when Salza's new designs appeared, it became clear that he had gone much further than just restructuring the gun externally along contemporary lines; he had produced an

entirely new weapon, much more compact thanks to the use of a wrap-around bolt, an innovation probably introduced in 1948 in the Czech CZ48, also known as the Samopal 23 (see below). The new gun was eventually launched onto the market in 1958 as the Model 12, and went into production the following year.

In appearance, the Model 12 was somewhat fanciful, with two sculpted pistol grips in black plastic almost at its extremities, the magazine housing between them, forward of the trigger guard, and joined by a large-diameter tube which was both receiver and barrel shroud, the large size being necessary to accommodate the tubular bolt which surrounded the barrel. The cocking handle was permanently attached towards its forward end, reciprocating in a slot on the left hand side of the shroud/receiver. The fire selector was a push-through type, and the safety mechanism was a duplex arrangement and a grip safety just below the trigger

guard which locked the bolt in either the open or the closed position, and had to be disengaged to allow the weapon to be cocked, together with a conventional safety catch positioned above it, which locked the grip safety and prevented it from disengaging.

Beretta had a virtual monopoly in the field of military small arms in Italy, since it supplied the armed services with pistols, rifles and machine guns, but in 1957, it was challenged by a newcomer, Luigi Franchi, also of Brescia. Franchi produced a sub-machine gun with a very strong resemblance to the Beretta Model 6, which had been produced on a limited basis and briefly, in 1954, as a step towards the development of the Model 12. The LF57 had the same overhung bolt – an intermediate step towards the wraparound bolt, and rather less stable in operation but going some way towards keeping the muzzle down when firing bursts and somewhat easier to manufacture – and the same grip safety

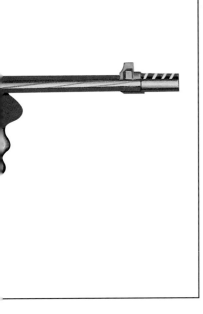

■RIGHT: Somewhat ungainly looking, with its top-mounted magazine, the Owen was nonetheless effective and popular, and was in Australian service from 1942 until the early 1960s.

located on the rear surface of the pistol grip. The Italian Navy equipped itself with the gun, but that was probably not enough to constitute a real success, and production ceased in the mid-1960s.

THE SPECTRE

During the 1970s and 1980s, Italy was to be plagued by terrorism on a massive scale from all points of the political spectrum and even from organised crime; at one point it seemed that every policeman – and policewoman – on the streets was armed with a sub-machine gun in addition to his or her personal sidearm, which was hardly surprising given that police officers were often the targets. This situation led to the development of the Spectre, a machine

pistol rather better adapted to the task of dealing with surprise attacks, a revolutionary double-action SMG with a unique four-column magazine containing 50 rounds of 9mm Parabellum ammunition. The Spectre was unusual in its appearance, too, since it was provided with both front- and rear-pistol grips, instead of the magazine housing doing double duty; this may have been a legacy of the Beretta Model 12, perhaps, but it is more likely that the magazine simply proved too large to be gripped comfortably, and was also located too far to the rear. It fired from a closed bolt, which allowed its designers to incorporate the sort of double action normally found in pistols or revolvers; the gun could be carried with the action

cocked and a round chambered but in complete safety, since the hammer, which actuated the firing pin, was not drawn back. This occurred when the first pressure on the trigger was taken up. A conventional safety catch was also fitted. The Spectre had a higher than usual cyclic rate of fire – some 850 rounds per minute (rpm). It had a folding stock, rather like that of the Uzi (qv) and its derivatives, and this stock lay flat along the top of the receiver/barrel shroud when not in use.

ACROSS THE ATLANTIC

Though Revelli and Schmeisser both produced sub-machine guns almost simultaneously and without, as far as we know, being acquainted with each other's

Patchett Mark 1

Calibre: 9mm Parabellum
Weight: 2.7kg (6lb)
Length: 685mm (27in) (stock
   extended)
Barrel length: 195mm (7.75in)
Effective range: 70m (230ft)
Action: blowback
Cyclic rate of fire: 550rpm
Muzzle velocity: 395mps (1300fps)
Country of Origin: United Kingdom

work, we can hardly conclude that the genre was 'an idea whose time has come' even though that is the basic thesis, since their objectives were clearly quite different.

To be able to draw that conclusion, we would need another factor, another inventor working along the same lines in isolation at the same time, and happily there was one, Brigadier-General John Tagliaferro Thompson. Thompson was a career Army officer, who had spent most of his life in the Ordnance Department. He had worked on the Springfield '03 and the .30in-06 cartridge, and had played a part in the adoption of the Colt .45 automatic pistol as the M1911. He retired in 1914, and became Chief Consulting Engineer for the Remington Arms Corporation; he set up two factories for Remington, to make rifles for the British and Russian Governments. But that wasn't his only occupation. In 1914, he conceived a design for a self-loading rifle; the following year, Commander John Blish (his name is also rendered as Bliss), late of the US Navy, collaborated with him on an improved version, which

incorporated a delaying system the latter had designed and patented in 1913. This was in the form of a phosphor-bronze wedge in the shape of an H, operating in an angled slot in the bolt. It worked as if by magic, but in fact by utilising the phenomenon of enhanced friction created when two different metals pass over each other; when both the wedge and the bolt were made in the same material, as they were initially, there was little retardation.

The Blish Hesitation Lock, as it was incorrectly known, was later discarded in the interests of economy, and the cyclic rate of fire of the Thompson gun went up from 600 rounds per minute (rpm) to over 800rpm in consequence (but see below). The self-loading rifle was not a success although BSA, Thompson's agent in the UK, did manufacture some, in .30in-06 calibre, and Thompson, operating as the Auto Ordnance Corporation, with offices in New York City, and now with further assistance from Thomas Eikhoff, turned his attention to what he called his 'Trench Broom', a hand-held 'sub-machine gun' (it was Thompson who coined the

phrase) chambered initially for the .45 ACP round which was the US Government standard.

THE TRENCH BROOM
In its first incarnation, the 'Trench Broom' was belt-fed, with an excessively high rate of fire – it is suggested over 1000 rounds per minute (rpm). It did not utilise the Blish Lock in its final form, the H-piece being made of steel. Later models, which used the bronze H-piece, were more manageable. It had no buttstock (though the boxlike receiver stretched back far beyond the trigger group, to accommodate the long recoil spring and buffer) and two pistol grips, the foregrip sculpted for the fingers, the rear incorporating a handguard, doubtless to offer some protection from the passage of the belt. By 1917, Thompson had switched over to conventional box magazines and did away with the handguard on the rear pistol grip, which was now also sculpted. The cocking lever worked in a slot in the upper surface of the receiver. The magazine was inserted from below,

Lanchester Mark 1

Calibre: 9mm Parabellum
Weight: 4.35kg (9.5lb)
Length: 850mm (33.5in)
Barrel length: 205mm (8in)
Effective range: 70m (230ft)
Action: blowback
Cyclic rate of fire: 600rpm
Muzzle velocity: 395mps (1300fps)
Country of Origin: United Kingdom

■**RIGHT: A very eclectic mix of guns –**
Lanchester machine pistols (centre),
Browning and Bren MGs, and Lee-
Enfield rifles – in Dutch hands during
the war of independence in Indonesia.

directly ahead of the trigger guard, and
spent cases were ejected through a port
on the right hand side of the receiver.
The forward pistol grip was attached not
to the barrel, but to a flat extension plate
which protruded from the front of the
receiver below it. Internally, the gun had
a fixed firing pin, and incorporated the
Hesitation Lock. It was otherwise an
unsophisticated design, though it worked
well enough. There was no provision for
the fitting of a buttstock, and there were
no sights. Later models had grooves
machined into the bottom plate of the
receiver, behind the rear pistol grip, into
which a buttstock could be fitted,
together with a simple post foresight and
a Lyman adjustable backsight.

In 1919, the first production model
Thompson guns appeared in a variety of
slightly different versions, though still in
very small numbers. It was this Model

1919 which Thompson demonstrated to
the US Army and Marine Corps at Camp
Perry in 1920, and met with considerable
enthusiasm but no orders. This was to be
an enduring feature of Thompson's
attempts to get his weapon adopted. In
fact, he read the situation wrongly, and
placed an order with Colts for the
manufacture of the parts to make 15,000
of what by now was the Model 1921; it
was to be 20 years before that supply of
parts was to be exhausted. This gives
some indication of the state of the market
for sub-machine guns in the USA at the

time, the efforts of the likes of Alphonse
Capone, 'Machine Gun' Jack McGurn, his
hireling trigger-man, 'Ma' Barker,
Charley 'Pretty Boy' Floyd, John Dillinger
and his associate 'Baby Face' Nelson
notwithstanding (not that reports of the
affection in which the Thompson gun was
held in underground circles were grossly
exaggerated, but simply that those circles
were never particularly big. BARs were
popular too, as we may recall).

As well as the 20-round stick
magazine, the Model 1921 was also
available with a 50- or 100-round drum

Remington-Thompson, which had a 16.2g (250 grain) projectile in place of the 11.66g (180 grain) bullet of the .45in ACP round, and achieved a muzzle velocity of 442 mps (1450fps) instead of 259mps (850fps), but this wasn't offered until two years later, when he assembled very few guns as the Model 1923. The Model 1927 – 'another attempt to use up Model 1921

magazine. Its barrel now had annular ribs to promote cooling, and could be fitted with a bayonet, a flash hider or a silencer which had been invented by Hiram Maxim's nephew. It was – nominally, at least – available in a variety of alternative chamberings, including 9mm Parabellum.

MASS-MARKETING THE TOMMY

Thompson tried everything he knew to create a market for his gun, but without any real success. He fitted 28 of them into the floor of an aircraft, facing downwards, and demonstrated the proto-gunship to the Air Corps, without success. Most of the guns jammed on spent cartridge cases, we are told, though it is difficult to imagine how that can have been the case; the alternative scenario, that the modified aircraft was impossibly heavy, doesn't stand scrutiny either; even with a full 100-round drum magazine, the gun weighed less than 44kg (20lb), and 1322kg (600lb) was not an impossible load for an aircraft of the period, by any means. If we look at the theoretical performance figures alone, the experiment deserved to succeed. Reckoning the Model 1921 to have a cyclic rate of 600 rounds per minute (rpm), 10 rounds per second, then firing

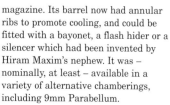

■ABOVE: The British Army issued SMGs to men for whom a rifle would have been an encumbrance, such as the Number Two of the GMPG group, as illustrated here.

all the guns simultaneously would have given a cyclic rate of 280 rounds per second – 10 seconds of fire with the 100-round magazine. At an airspeed of 290kph (180mph), the 10-second fusilade would have covered an area 800m (244ft) long and put 3.5 rounds into every linear metre.

Thompson went one step further and produced special ammunition loaded with birdshot, for use by law enforcement agencies, intended to 'allow serious occasions and disorders to be handled by officers of the law in the most humane manner possible'. He advertised in *Scientific American* (in those days not the learned journal it is today), suggesting that the Model 1921 was ideal 'for the protection of large estates, ranches and plantations' (the advertisement showed a rather fanciful cowboy in full rig, fighting off a band of desperadoes). He was more than willing to sell them to private individuals for unspecified purposes. He also developed – with Remington – a more powerful .45in round, known as the

parts', as one account says – was a semi-automatic variant. Al Capone bought three M1921s in 1926, perfectly legally, though they weren't the guns he personally used: McGurn and Fred Burke did his dirty work when they gunned down seven members of 'Bugs' Moran's rival gang, on St. Valentine's Day 1929, using guns supplied by Frank Thompson,

who had used one of them to kill his wife and her lover. With a degree of ironic justice, McGurn also met his death at the end, as it were, of a tommy gun, as the weapon was by then universally known.

THE TOMMY GUN GOES TO WAR

In 1928, the US Marine Corps bought a small number of guns for the

Expeditionary Force in Nicaragua and the US Cavalry soon followed suit, and ordered 400 identical guns which it designated the M1928A1, for armoured vehicle crewmen. But it was 1939 before Auto-Ordnance received a meaningful order, when the French Government purchased 3750 Model 1928s. And then, with Europe plunged into war once more,

Sterling Mark 1 (L2A1)

Calibre: 9mm Parabellum
Weight: 2.7kg (6lb)
Length: 685mm (27in) (stock extended)
Barrel length: 195mm (7.75in)

Effective range: 70m (230ft)
Action: blowback
Cyclic rate of fire: 550rpm
Muzzle velocity: 395mps (1300fps)
Country of Origin: United Kingdom

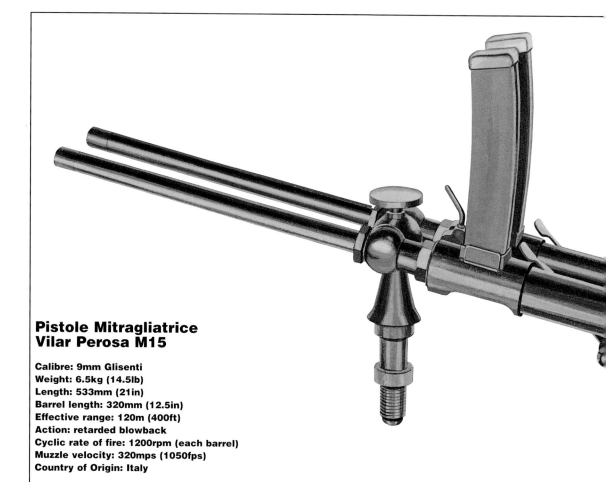

Pistole Mitragliatrice Vilar Perosa M15

Calibre: 9mm Glisenti
Weight: 6.5kg (14.5lb)
Length: 533mm (21in)
Barrel length: 320mm (12.5in)
Effective range: 120m (400ft)
Action: retarded blowback
Cyclic rate of fire: 1200rpm (each barrel)
Muzzle velocity: 320mps (1050fps)
Country of Origin: Italy

the flood gates opened. As we have noted, the British Government, post-Dunkirk (that is, after the end of June 1940), asked Auto Ordnance to supply as many guns as it could, and that order was passed on to the Savage Arms Company, a long-established arms manufacturer. The guns supplied, as the Model 1928A2, where stripped of their forward pistol grip and fitted with a straight below-the-barrel foregrip in its place. By now the annular cooling fins on the barrel had been deleted, and the buttstock had become fixed in place. The rate of fire was reduced by strengthening the recoil spring, and a muzzle compensator designed by a USMC Colonel named Richard Cutts, was fitted, which had four slots cut in its top face, and worked by diverting some of the propellant gases upwards to force the muzzle down, which

had been available as an option on the Model 1927. At this point the 100-round drum magazine, which had never been entirely satisfactory and was anyway judged to be far too heavy, was deleted, and a new 30-round capacity box magazine was introduced. This same model was also supplied to the US Army, but the requirements of mass manufacture soon saw it superseded by a simplified gun with the breech-block altered drastically. The Bliss Lock was deleted completely, turning the Thompson gun into a straightforward blowback-operated weapon, and, as we have noted, upping the cyclic rate of fire considerably. A floating firing pin was fitted, actuated by a hammer, and the cocking piece was moved to the right hand side of the receiver. The Cutts Compensator was deleted, drum

magazines, which were costly to produce, were abandoned entirely (and a simpler method of installing the box magazines devised), and the Lyman rear sight was replaced by a simple aperture. Later still, the floating firing pin and hammer were deleted, and replaced by a breech-block with a fixed firing pin in its face, very similar to the original, but that was the only meaningful difference between the M1 and the M1A1. In all, some 563,000 M1928As, 285,000 M1s and 540,000 M1A1s were produced (the US Government paying $209 each in 1939). The price which was reduced to just $44.85 including spares, magazine and cleaning kit, by 1945, when legislation controlling prices and profits had been introduced, and Thompson's 'Trench Broom' was the US Army and Marine Corps regulation sub-machine gun until

Moscheto Automatico Beretta (MAB) 38

Calibre: 9mm Parabellum
Weight: 4.2kg (9.25lb)
Length: 955mm (37.5in)
Barrel length: 320mm (12.5in)

Effective range: 120m (400ft)
Action: retarded blowback
Cyclic rate of fire: 600rpm
Muzzle velocity: 395mps (1300fps)
Country of Origin: Italy

■LEFT: Beretta machine pistols were virtually ubiquitous in Italy during World War II, as this picture, numbering several of these weapons, clearly illustrates.

it was replaced by the M3 'Grease Gun' in December 1942. It remained in full production until 1945, and even in the late 1990s was still available, though only in single-shot form.

THE TOMMY GUN'S RIVALS

Having finally adopted the sub-machine gun, the US Army and Marine Corps couldn't get enough of them. In order to supplement the flow of weapons from Auto Ordnance and Savage, they looked to other manufacturers who were offering similar guns, adopting three of them, the Reising Model 50/55, the United Defense M42 and the Hyde, which the Army designated the M2.

THE REISING

The Reising Model 50, manufactured by Harrington & Richardson, a long-established maker of revolvers, was a complex design, firing .45in ACP ammunition from a closed bolt. Its breech-block was cammed up into a recess in the receiver top, though that constituted a delay more than a lock. The mechanical train between trigger and firing pin was unnecessarily complicated. Some 100,000 were made between 1942 and 1945, mostly for the Marine Corps, but the Reising was never entirely successful or popular, since its shortcomings manifested themselves in a

Beretto Modello 12

Calibre: 9mm Parabellum
Weight: 3kg (6.5lb)
Length: 415mm (16.5in) (stock folded)
Barrel length: 205mm (8in)

Effective range: 120m (400ft)
Action: blowback
Cyclic rate of fire: 550rpm
Muzzle velocity: 395mps (1300fps)
Country of Origin: Italy

■RIGHT: The Beretta M12 was adopted by Italy's paramilitary and civilian police and by the country's armed services in the early 1960s. It was still in use almost four decades later.

tendency to jam if the weapon was not kept scrupulously clean. The Model 55 was essentially the same gun, but with the wooden buttstock replaced by a lightweight folding metal version, and no muzzle compensator.

THE UD M42
The UD M42 was designed before World War II, by Carl Swebilius who, we may recall, had re-designed the Colt M1895 'Potato Digger' and turned it into the Marlin M1918. It was available in .45in ACP calibre, but was actually intended to fire the 9mm Parabellum round, which made it unique in the USA at that time, and that may have contributed to, or even brought about, its being supplied almost exclusively to the the Americans' allies, and not to their own armed forces. The UD was an old-fashioned gun, manufactured largely from machined parts, and expensive as a result. It fired from the open bolt, the floating firing pin

Thompson Model 1928

Calibre: .45in ACP
Weight: 4.9kg (10.75lb)
Length: 860mm (33.75in)
Barrel length: 265mm (10.5in)
Effective range: 120m (400ft)

Action: retarded blowback
Cyclic rate of fire: 800rpm
Muzzle velocity: 265mps (870fps)
Country of Origin: United States

being actuated by a hammer, and its cocking piece was in the form of a slide, which did not reciprocate with the bolt, thus sealing off a potential entrance for dust and dirt. Some 15,000 were made in all, a few by High Standard, the majority by Marlin.

THE HYDE M2

The Hyde M2, though it was the only one of the trio to receive an official designation, was made only in very small quantities – some reports say less than 500 in all – apparently due to difficulty of manufacture. It was a simple blowback SMG with no retardation, relying on a heavy bolt and a strong recoil spring.

THE M3 'GREASE GUN'

None of these guns – not even the Thompson – was entirely suitable for the task at hand. They were expensive to manufacture, demanded careful maintenance and were heavy to carry. What was needed was something along the lines of the German MP38/40 or the British Sten, and the US Army's Ordnance Department set about creating just such a gun, commissioning George Hyde, who had produced the M2, to design it.

Hyde's first response was a lightweight all-metal blowback-operated gun with a selective fire capability, which was produced in small quantities as the Machine Pistol, T15. Testing proved it to be reliable in general, but somewhat over-complicated, so the selective fire capability was removed and the cyclic rate reduced to 400 rounds per minute (rpm), which meant that an experienced soldier could still get off single shots. Now known as the T20, it was tested extensively, and on 24 December 1942, it was officially adopted as the Sub-machine Gun Caliber .45in, M3.

There were production difficulties at first: the bolts were made by the Buffalo Arms Company, and the remainder of the gun by General Motors Corporation's Guide Lamp Division, which also produced the diminutive Liberator pistol, and there is a suspicion that co-ordination was not all that it might have been; only 85,000 were produced in the whole of the first year of manufacture, though that was corrected by 1944, by which time production was running at around 35,000 units per month.

Just like the Sten, it was designed with ease of manufacture, and not the soldiery's approval, in mind, and

predictably, the men to whom it was issued disliked and mistrusted it, as the sobriquet they awarded it demonstrates. Nonetheless, like the 'Plumber's Delight', the 'Grease Gun' was the right tool for the job, and cost something of the order of $30 to manufacture (something like three times the price of a Sten, we may note, though the two were of very similar quality).

Like the British SMG, it was welded and rivetted together from pressed components (the barrel was cold-swaged, and a simple press-fit). It was different from the Sten in one particular; the bolt was drilled longitudinally to take a pair of guide rods, around which the twin recoil springs were located, and this meant that less attention had to be paid to the fit of the breech-block within the receiver. The magazine was inserted from below, rather than from the side. It had a rather more sophisticated safety mechanism than the Sten, though that is actually saying very little; the cover over the cocking piece, located on the right hand side of the receiver and hinged along the centre line at the top, where the two halves of the receiver were welded together, acted as a safety. When closed, it locked the bolt in either the closed or open position, and thus had to be open before the gun would function, and needless to say, it also had to be open before the gun could be cocked, too.

THE 'IMPROVED' GREASE GUN

The US Army's Ordnance Department thought that the M3 was as simple as could be, but it was wrong. Troops training with the new gun in January 1944 reported problems with the cocking mechanism, and on investigation it was discovered that the entire retracting lever mechanism, the pawl which actuated it and the cocking lever itself were all redundant. All that was required was to drill a large-diameter blind hole in the breech-block itself, near the head, and the action could be cocked by inserting a finger and pulling back on the bolt (we may recall that the British Welgun, developed by BSA the previous year, had used the same method, and there may have been some transference). The gun thus modified was known as the M3A1, and some 15,000 were manufactured in 1945, when it was put into production at a cost of around $22 each. The M3A1 was still in service at the time of the Korean War in the early 1950s (and so was the M3) and manufacture was started up again then, at the Ithaca Gun Company,

which produced some 33,000 before the war was over. Like the Sten, the M3s had a recurring problem with their magazines, and that was never entirely solved even though the gun stayed in US service for some two decades.

THE INGRAM SMGS

Very few sub-machine guns were produced in the United States after World War II. Pistol makers Smith & Wesson produced one briefly, the Model 76, without any real success, and the only gun that really sold in any quantity was the Gordon Ingrams-designed MAC-10. Ingrams' first SMG was the M6, a Thompson M1928 lookalike with sharply raked-back sculpted pistol grips front and rear. Internally it was little more sophisticated than the Sten – a very simple open-bolt blowback mechanism. Its only novel feature was a trigger mechanism like that of the Bergmann MP34, which produced single shots when a light pressure was applied, and fully automatic fire when it was pressed all the way back. The Police Ordnance Company, with whom Ingrams was then associated, sold the gun to various police forces, the Cuban Navy and the Peruvian Army, which was quite surprising given that it appeared in the early 1950s, when

the arms market was flooded with rather better war-surplus weapons.

The Model 7 which followed was essentially similar, but fired from a closed breech. The Models 8 and 9 were improvements of the Model 6, but were not a commercial success. Ingrams later moved to the Military Armament Corporation, where in 1970 he produced a rather better design, the MAC-10, made entirely of steel pressings and extremely compact, due to the use of a wraparound bolt and a magazine, which held 30 rounds, and was located in the pistol grip. The inspiration for this SMG almost certainly came from the Beretta Model 6, and it was a development of a design which John Foote had earlier produced for the company. The gun was just 265mm (10.5in) long, and was light enough to be used with one hand. Because the centre of gravity was directly over the pistol grip, it was stable enough to allow that, too, though at full-auto, the muzzle rose alarmingly without anything to restrain it. The cocking lever was a

■RIGHT: Though it was only marginally practical, especially with the drum magazine, the Tommy gun was popular with those to whom it was issued, thanks perhaps to its cachet as 'the gun which made the Twenties roar'.

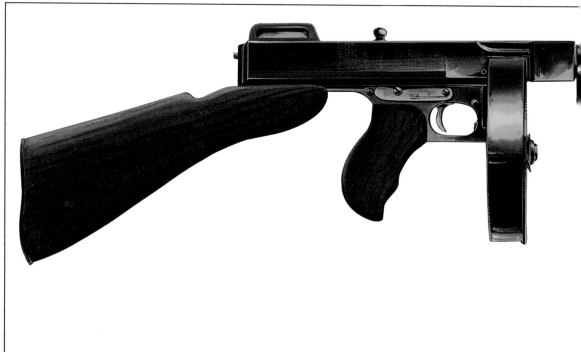

Thompson Model 1921

Calibre: .45in ACP
Weight: 4.9kg (10.75lb)
Length: 860mm (33.75in)
Barrel length: 265mm (10.5in)
Effective range: 120m (400ft)
Action: retarded blowback
Cyclic rate of fire: 800rpm
Muzzle velocity: 265mps (870fps)
Country of Origin: United States

small knurled cylinder located on the upper surface of the receiver; turning it locked the bolt and rendered the gun safe. The MAC-10 was available in both .45in ACP and 9mm Parabellum chamberings, and a lighter, smaller version, the MAC-11, was also produced, chambered for the much less powerful 9mm Short round. Both guns had a very high cyclic rate of fire – well over 1000 rounds per minute (rpm) – and a characteristic sound, something like an electric drill, as a result.

RUSSIAN SUB-MACHINE GUNS
One of the first successful self-loading rifles was produced in Russia as early as 1916, but the Bolshevik revolution in the following year put a stop to further developments for a decade. During the mid-1920s, a number of Soviet designers, including Tokarev, produced prototype machine pistols. In the mid-1930s an improved SLR, the Simonova, appeared, and at about the same time, Vasiliy Degtyarev, whose LMGs we have already examined in some detail, produced a design for an SMG, the *Pistolet-Pulemyot Degtyreva* or PPD34/38, chambered for

the light, high-velocity 1930-pattern 7.62mm pistol round developed for the Tokarev automatic. Internally it was almost identical to the Bergmann MP18 but with the firing pin machined into the face of the bolt and in outward appearance, it bore a distinct resemblance to the Schmeisser MP28 and particularly to the Lahti-designed Suomi (see below) of 1926, with a heavy barrel shroud perforated by slots and full-length wooden furniture, and a screw-off rear cap to the receiver, through which the recoil spring and bolt could be withdrawn. Like the Suomi it could accommodate a high-capacity drum magazine (the inspiration may have been down to Thompson). This was to become a standard feature of Soviet SMGs of the period, though in this first incarnation the Soviet version, like the Finnish, had a vertical extension which fitted into the receiver, a rather awkward feature which later versions lacked. Twenty-five-round box magazines were also produced. The blowback mechanism was straightforward, but of high quality; the entire weapon was machined from forgings and the barrel was chromed internally to prolong its life, which made it expensive to produce. Degtyarev produced a refined version in 1940. This had an improved bolt with a floating firing pin controlled by a lever in the bolt head which ensured that the mechanism was properly closed before the round was fired (there had been some instances of premature detonation in the earlier model) together with an improved drum magazine in which the feed lips fitted directly into the receiver. Many parts of the PPD40 were interchangeable with those of the earlier model, and the same manufacturing procedures were used throughout.

THE PPSH41

By the time Hitler's armies invaded Russia in June 1941, the Soviet Union had already fought a war in Europe, the so-called Winter War of 1939–40, against the Finns. Much of the action in that campaign had been at close quarters, and the sub-machine gun, which both sides used in large numbers, had been the most effective weapon. Thus, when faced with the necessity of arming an enormous People's Army to fight the Germans, it was a logical decision to commission a design for a machine pistol which could be manufactured cheaply and quickly, to replace the PPD40. The design chosen

was the work of Georgiy Shpagin, a career army officer who was later to rise to the rank of Lieutenant-General. It was extremely simple – a blowback-operated weapon with a wooden stock, with its receiver hinged at the extremity of the forestock, like the original Bergmann design, a feature which made field-stripping a very simple operation indeed. Once the locking latch was opened, the receiver and barrel tipped up, allowing the recoil spring and bolt to be withdrawn and giving easy access to the trigger mechanism. Its one refinement was the addition of a compensator which helped keep the muzzle down when firing bursts, a very desirable feature, since its cyclic rate was around 900 rounds per minute (rpm). It, too, used the 71-round drum magazine, though 35-round boxes were also produced. Unlike the PPD which it replaced, the PPSh used heavy-gauge steel stampings for the receiver and barrel shroud, though the bolt was still machined, albeit to a simplified design with a fixed firing pin in its face. The barrel was still internally chromed, however. The sub-machine gun was the Red Army's primary weapon, and it is estimated that well over five million

■LEFT: Even with the stick magazine, the Thompson was still only useful at close quarters, thanks to the ballistic characteristics of the .45in-calibre round for which it was chambered.

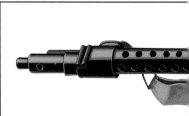

Type 100

Calibre: 8mm Nambu
Weight: 3.8kg (8.5lb)
Length: 890mm (35in)
Barrel length: 230mm (9in)
Effective range: 70m (230ft)
Action: blowback
Cyclic rate of fire: 400rpm
Muzzle velocity: 335mps (1100fps)
Country of origin: Japan

PPSh41s were produced between 1942 and 1945 and was later produced in many Soviet satellite and client states under a variety of different designations, and sometimes in a number of variants.

A very similar design was produced in Leningrad while the city was under siege in 1941–1944, as the PPS43 (the S stood for Sudarev, its designer), the chief distinction being in the gun's furniture. The PPS was made entirely of sheet steel, even to its distinctive muzzle brake and compensator, which was simply a strip of steel bent into a U and secured so as to support the muzzle in the jacket, the lower arm welded and the upper riveted, perforated in the centre to allow the bullet passage and on the upper surface to allow some of the propellant gas to escape upwards. It was fitted with a folding buttstock which rotated over the top of the barrel, the butt plate coming to rest behind the magazine, which was not interchangeable with that of the PPSh, though of similar form and capacity – a curved box, holding 35 rounds. In defiance of usual Soviet practice, which was to standardize on one type of weapon in each category, the PPS was later put into wider production, but modified somewhat (the fixed ejector was deleted, and the return spring guide rod was lengthened, so that as the bolt came back after firing, the spent round's rim caught on the rod and it was ejected that way). It is thought that around one million

were produced in all. Many were issued to armoured vehicle crewmen, it being rather less unwieldy than the PPSh inside a tank. It, too, was put into production in Soviet satellite states and also, in 9mm Parabellum chambering, in Finland, as the M/1944.

THE MODERN RUSSIAN SMGS
By the 1980s, sub-machine guns had rather fallen out of favour in military circles. The new breed of miniature-calibre assault rifles was effective in that role and in that of the infantryman's rifle at the same time, and were short enough to be convenient for vehicle crewmen, signallers and the like. The main exception, and the one area of military activity where they were still in demand, was in so-called Special Operations, which much of the time bordered on police work anyway. As a result, the number of new designs appearing on the market was considerably diminished – except in the Soviet Union. By the start of the 1990s, there were no less than six new SMGs being produced in Russia, two of them with innovative features, the others quite conventional according to the new model, and two of them designed and manufactured specifically for anti-crime operations, with 'red dot' laser sighting systems as standard. Of the innovations, one, the PP-90M, was quite remarkable: it folded up into a rectangular box, under 250mm (10in) long, and just 90mm

(3.5in) wide, with only the hook-shaped cocking lever, which protruded from the rear plate of the receiver, breaking its smooth shape. It weighed just over 1.6kg (3.25lb) with a full 30-round magazine, and was clearly not designed for military operations. It, like all other new ex-Soviet SMGs, was chambered for the 9mm x 18 round developed for the Makarov pistol, which produced a muzzle velocity of 350mps (1050fps), and was widely held to be underpowered as a result. It was considered to be the most powerful round that a simple, unlocked blowback pistol could handle safely, and was developed for just that purpose; during the 1980s an 'improved' version with a muzzle velocity of 470mps (1540fps) appeared, and some, at least, of the new Russian guns – specifically, those developed for military rather than police, use – were available chambered for that round as an alternative. The most interesting of these was perhaps the 'Bizon', which had a novel type of magazine – a helical-feed cylinder – which lay under the barrel and receiver (and was of a size to be comfortable as a foregrip) and held 50 rounds. As if a half-dozen SMGs weren't enough, Russia also developed what it called a 'miniature assault rifle', the Vikhr, chambered for the improved 9mm Soviet round, which was not an assault rifle at all. Confusingly, a shortened version of the true assault rifle, the AKS74U, chambered for the much higher

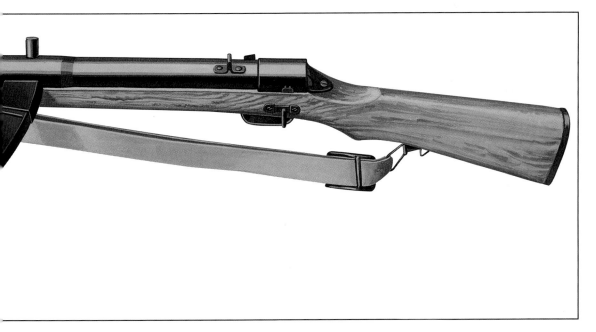

Reising Model 55

Calibre: .45in ACP
Weight: 2.9kg (6.25lb)
Length: 790mm (31in) (stock
    extended)
Barrel length: 265mm (10.5in)

Effective range: 120m (400ft)
Action: 'semi-locked' blowback
Cyclic rate of fire: 550rpm
Muzzle velocity: 265mps (870fps)
Country of Origin: United States

powered 5.45 x 39 cartridge (but also available in 5.56 and the old 7.62mm chamberings) was also produced, and referred to in official literature as a sub-machine gun.

FRENCH SUB-MACHINE GUNS

The first machine pistol produced in France was the MAS35, manufactured at the State Arms Factory at St Etienne in very limited numbers, more as a design exercise than as a gun intended to go into series production. This led to the development of the first regulation SMG, the MAS38, chambered for the somewhat underpowered 7.65mm Long pistol cartridge, which, like the Russian 7.62mm pistol round, fired a light projectile at high velocity. It came to be quite highly regarded as a weapon in its own right, though the round it fired was always somewhat suspect. Its most unusual feature was the alignment (or, more precisely, the non-alignment) of the receiver and bolt with the barrel – the two met at an angle of approximately 8 degrees, the bolt face being machined appropriately. This permitted the buttstock, which was in line with the axis of the barrel, to be at a similar angle to the line of force of the bolt; in combination with the relatively low power of the ammunition, this made for a controllable, accurate gun which was generally popular with those who used it. The same principle was to be employed in

other machine pistols developed more recently. In other respects, the MAS38 was quite conventional. It was machined from the solid but with considerable attention paid to removing as much metal as possible. That, and the lack of a forestock (the forehand gripped the magazine) kept the unloaded weight down to considerably less than that of the all-steel Sten Mark II, at just 2.85kg (6.25lb). Had the MAS38 been produced in the more usual 9mm Parabellum chambering, it would perhaps have been a commercial success after World War II. It stayed in production until 1949, and was then superseded by a much more conventional 'new model' SMG produced at the State Arms Factory at Tulle, the MAT49.

MAT49 & 'UNIVERSAL' HOTCHKISS

In addition to the MAS35, the French Army also employed Thompson guns imported from the USA, and following the fall of France in 1940, Free French forces were also armed with Stens. Having three different SMGs employing three different types of ammunition side by side was a logistical mess, of course, and France adopted the 9mm Parabellum cartridge for its new machine pistol, developed in 1948 and put into production the following year. The MAT49 was an entirely conventional design employing metal stampings wherever possible, with a short, square-

section boxlike receiver, extendible metal skeleton stock, plastic-clad rear pistol grip with a squeeze safety and a foregrip fashioned around the magazine housing. That last item was the only out-of-the-ordinary feature of the gun, since it pivoted at the front and lay flat under the barrel when not in use. The magazine itself was copied from that of the Sten; this had its advantages, of course, but it also meant sharing the weaknesses of the design, and the consequent stoppages due to misfeeding. We have already noted that the rather curious PM9 which Erma put into production also had this feature, and so did the private-venture Hotchkiss 'Universal' SMG, produced that same year initially, and somewhat unusually, as a single-shot self-loading weapon without a burst fire capability, for police use. It is impossible to say for sure which gun pioneered the folding magazine. In contrast to the MAT49, the Hotchkiss 'Universal' had a tubular receiver and a tubular metal extending stock, which telescoped to half its length and was then folded to lie under the receiver, the butt plate behind the magazine housing and helping to form a rather more substantial grip there. The barrel was semi-telescopic, too, and when closed up, the entire gun was only just over 440mm (17in) long. All this rather fanciful effort to reduce its overall length made for a complicated manufacturing procedure (it would have been much simpler to have

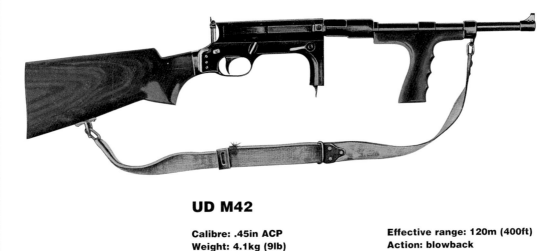

UD M42

Calibre: .45in ACP
Weight: 4.1kg (9lb)
Length: 820mm (32.25in)
Barrel length: 280mm (11in)

Effective range: 120m (400ft)
Action: blowback
Cyclic rate of fire: 700rpm
Muzzle velocity: 265mps (870fps)
Country of Origin: United States

followed the Italian example, and incorporate an overhanging or wraparound bolt, though internally the gun was quite conventional), and it was not competitive in price as a result. Those who used it also found it difficult to maintain to the required standard in the field. It went out of production in the 1950s.

CZECH MACHINE PISTOLS

We have seen how the old-established arms manufacturers of Bohemia played a minor role in the development of the machine gun before World War I, and how their successors in what was to become Czechoslovakia played a more prominent part in the development of light machine guns during the interwar years. During that same period, the first Czech sub-machine gun was produced, to a design executed by the Koucky brothers, Josef and Frantisek, and known as the ZK383. It was an entirely conventional weapon of its period, but endowed with a number of unusual features. Firstly, it was fitted with a bipod as standard; secondly, it had a quick-change barrel, and thirdly the breech-block had a removable 170g (6oz) weight; taking it out upped the cyclic rate from 500 to 700 rounds per minute (rpm). It was issued to the Bulgarian Army and to some German units, and was said still to have remained in service until 1960. The Koucky brothers also produced two

new weapons in 1948; the ZK466 was very similar to the American M3, but with a magazine housing which hinged to lie under the barrel, like the French guns of the same period, while the ZK467 fired from a closed breech and had a semi-wraparound bolt, a feature which may have influenced later Czech designs. All the Koucky guns were produced in 9mm Parabellum chambering. After World War II, the most talented of Ceskoslovenska Zbrojovka's designers, Vaclav Holek, also turned his attention to sub-machine guns, and produced the Samopal VZ 23 (also known as the CZ48a), which was just as revolutionary and was to be as important an influence as the Bren had been 20 years earlier. As we noted above, when discussing the antecedents of the Beretta Model 12, the VZ 23 (it was actually one of a range of four almost identical guns). It was chambered for the 9mm Parabellum cartridge, while the VZ 24 (CZ48b) was chambered for the Soviet 7.62mm M1930 round. Both had wooden buttstocks. The VZ 25 and VZ 26 were the same guns with folding metal buttstocks. The chief difference between the two models lay in their magazines, the 7.65mm-calibre guns having a 32-round capacity box, those of the 9mm guns having either 24- or 40-round capacity. The VZ23 displayed three somewhat novel features. Firstly, its bolt was hollowed out, and lay around the breech and the rear portion of the barrel,

allowing a great reduction in the overall length of the gun while maintaining its weight – an important consideration in keeping its cyclic rate of fire down to a manageable level – and at the same time transferring that weight forward and giving it considerably greater stability when firing bursts in consequence. Secondly, Holek located the magazine in the pistol grip, which went a long way towards putting the centre of gravity directly above the firer's trigger hand, with important further consequences for the gun's stability as well as for its ability to come directly to a natural point of aim. Thirdly, he introduced a wedge-shaped two-column magazine which proved to be very much more reliable than any other form. There is some disagreement about the origins of this type of magazine. In the same year, 1948, the Swedish State Arms Factory, Carl Gustav Stads Gvarfaktori, introduced a similar type of magazine for its existing MP45; it is unclear whether one copied the other, or whether it was simply another display of the synchronicity we have noted previously. Frankly, Carl Gustav already had something of a reputation for plagiarism, and the MP45 was an otherwise undistinguished design. The weapon was more satisfactory in the original 9mm Parabellum chambering than in the slightly later 7.62mm form, if only because the ammunition had more satisfactory characteristics. Nonetheless,

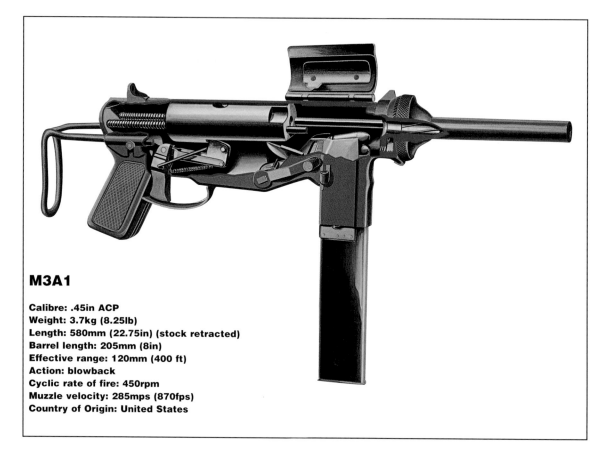

M3A1

Calibre: .45in ACP
Weight: 3.7kg (8.25lb)
Length: 580mm (22.75in) (stock retracted)
Barrel length: 205mm (8in)
Effective range: 120mm (400 ft)
Action: blowback
Cyclic rate of fire: 450rpm
Muzzle velocity: 285mps (870fps)
Country of Origin: United States

the VZ 23/25 was superseded in Czech Army service (the only place it was adopted) by the VZ 24/26 by 1952. The only concession made by their Soviet overlords was to permit the Czechs to use a more powerful loading of the 7.62mm round, known as the *naboj 48*; that in itself defeated the stated purpose of maintaining uniformity throughout the Warsaw Pact armies, since it was rather too powerful to be used comfortably in the other weapons chambered for the original M1930 cartridge, particularly the Tokarev pistol.

THE SKORPION

We noted at the start of this chapter that the terms 'machine pistol' and 'sub-machine gun' were interchangeable, and until the 1960s, that was certainly the case (freaks such as the fully automatic

■LEFT: The M3 and M3A1 were made in huge numbers during World War II, and many were still in service two and three decades later, in particular amongst 'irregular' US clients.

versions of the Mauser C96 pistol, the notorious *Schnellfeur-selbstladepistole*, and of the Spanish Star Model A and the later Stechkin notwithstanding). Sometime around the middle of the decade, however, that changed, with the introduction of miniature SMGs which could be operated comfortably – if not particularly accurately – with one hand. The genre includes the Walther MP(K), the MAC-10 and (more realistically) the MAC-11 and the Mini-Uzi, but the prototype was the Czech Skorpion, produced in a variety of different calibres, some more effective in the role than others. The Skorpion is somewhat difficult to classify. It was apparently first produced for armoured vehicle crew members, and that seems realistic given the limited space available inside tanks and other armoured vehicles, but almost at once found a home in the hands of the terrorist groups which were coming into being even as it became available. Later it was to find an even warmer welcome in the ranks of the so-called narco-terrorists and other successors to Al Capone and his ilk, or at least, so the cinema would have one believe. For all that, the Skorpion was an authentic sub-machine gun, with a high cyclic rate – around 850 rounds per minute (rpm) – and a barrel short enough – just 112mm (4.4in) – to ensure that despite the advantages of its wraparound bolt, those rounds would go almost anywhere. In that respect, it was a truly fearsome weapon. The rate of fire was, of course, the product of a light bolt and a relatively weak recoil spring – there was no room to increase either –

and would actually have been far worse were it not for the presence of a cunning retarder device located in the butt. This is essentially a spring-loaded weight which is driven downwards as the bolt reciprocates. The bolt is then held back by a trip-catch which is released only by the return of the weight to the top of its travel. As one expert put it, with his tongue perhaps in his cheek: 'It might be expected that this action would make itself felt to the firer, but it is in fact masked by the general recoil and [muzzle] climb.' The original Skorpion, the Model 61, was chambered for the Soviet 7.62mm pistol cartridge; the Model 64 was chambered, like the MAC-11, for the 9mm Short cartridge, and was probably the best of them; the Model 65 was chambered for the rather odd 9mm Soviet cartridge, developed for the Makarov pistol, and the Model 68 was chambered for the 9mm Parabellum round, and was in consequence rather a handful in more ways than one.

MINOR SMGS

Before and just after World War II, sub-machine guns were produced in many more countries than those we have covered here in detail: in some of them, their manufacture constituted a large part of the national arms industry, LMGs and medium machine guns and even rifles and pistols (all of which were considerably more complicated to produce than the 'second generation' sub-machine guns like the Sten or the American M3), being procured elsewhere. Some of the guns in question were simple,

straightforward copies, legitimate or otherwise, of models designed and developed elsewhere, others were home-grown; the simplistic nature of the sub-machine gun inevitably meant that many 'new' guns closely resembled existing designs, and all had at least some elements which had been seen before. There were to be useful innovations made, however, and some of them came from rather unexpected places.

ARGENTINIAN SMGS

Argentina, which had no real arms industry before World War II, was a good example. Argentina had a large Italian immigrant community. It is therefore not surprising that the Beretta Model 38 most clearly influenced the design of the first indigenous SMG, manufactured by Halcon from 1943, though it had features which were entirely its own: the barrel was unusual in being finned with annular rings from muzzle to receiver, and being fitted with a large and very distinctive muzzle brake/compensator and a bayonet lug. The below-receiver magazine housing was sculpted into a pistol grip, and the comb of the buttstock was so exaggerated that it, too, formed a pistol grip. Like the Beretta, its receiver end cap screwed off to allow the recoil spring and the bolt to be removed for cleaning. It was chambered for both the American .45in ACP round and the 9mm Parabellum, and 17- and 30-round box magazines were available. In 1946, a lightened version appeared, the wooden buttstock swopped for a skeleton metal version almost identical to that fitted to

Ingrams Model 10, silenced

Calibre: .45in ACP
Weight: 2.85kg (6.25lb)
Length: 265mm (10.5in)
Barrel length: 145mm (5.75in)
Effective range: 70m (230ft)
Action: blowback
Cyclic rate of fire: 1150rpm
Muzzle velocity: 285mps (870fps)
Country of Origin: United States

the American M3, and the complex compensator exchanged for one very similar to that which Cutts produced for the Thompson. A much simplified version, produced from steel stampings and with a very distinctive curved 40-round magazine, was produced in 1957 and was revamped three years later, in 9mm calibre only.

One might be forgiven for thinking that a single manufacturer of machine pistols would probably have been enough to serve the needs of a country such as Argentina, whose population at the end of World War II was scarcely more than 15 million and whose economy was largely agrarian, but that was not the case – there were not one, but three! In addition to the two manufacturers Halcon in Buenos Aires and Domingo Matheu in Rosario, Armas y Equipos in Cordoba also commenced manufacturing SMGs in the

five years after the War ended. In fact, it can be seen that Matheu's PAM1 and PAM2 was clearly derived from the American M3, though it was slightly shorter and somewhat lighter, and chambered for the 9mm Parabellum round only. A worthwhile addition was a second safety mechanism which worked via the trigger. These were the first 'second generation' SMGs produced in Argentina.

A later development, the PM3, was a much more refined weapon. Introduced in the mid-1970s, it had some features in common with the Uzi – an enlarged plastic forestock with the cocking handle adjacent to it, on the left hand side, and the trigger group moved forwards so that the magazine could be inserted into the pistol grip. It was produced in two forms: with a fixed plastic buttstock like that of the Heckler & Koch MP5, and an

■ABOVE: The PPD, designed by Degtyarev in 1938, was the Soviet Union's first effective machine pistol, but was expensive to manufacture, and was soon replaced by the PPSh41.

extendible wire stock exactly like that of the earlier models. It had a wraparound bolt, which allowed the overall length of the version with a retractable butt to be reduced to 525mm (20.5in), even though the barrel was 290mm (11.5in) long. Armas y Equipos produced its first machine pistol in 1952, and this was a local design, the work of Miguel E. Manzo Sal, whose initials gave it its name, the

■BELOW: The PPS43 was produced in Leningrad while the city was under siege. It was the only Soviet machine pistol of its period not to be fitted with a drum magazine.

PPSh41

Calibre: 7.62mm M1930
Weight: 3.6kg (8lb)
Length: 840mm (33in)
Barrel length: 265mm (10.5in)
Effective range: 120m (400ft)
Action: blowback
Cyclic rate of fire 900rpm
Muzzle velocity: 490mps (1600fps)
Country of Origin: Soviet Union

■LEFT: The PPSh41 was produced in enormous numbers – certainly more than five million between 1941 and the end of World War II. It was crudely made, but reliable and effective.

MEMS. It was a conventional enough blowback design, using advanced primer ignition to reduce recoil, and the overall arrangement owed something to the German MP40; the barrel was easily changed, being retained in the receiver by a large knurled nut which bore on a flange. The MEMS design was successively refined through the 1950s, 1960s and 1970s (including the introduction of a new system of rifling the barrel and a new trigger actuation and fire selection mechanism, both of them patented). In its last incarnation as the M75 it used a wedge-shaped two-column magazine, which held 40 rounds of 9mm Parabellum ammunition; the magazine had to be removed before the folding wire buttstock, which was pivoted just above the pistol grip, could be stowed or deployed, since in the stowed position, the butt plate lay beneath the barrel. It could accept either a bayonet or a grenade launcher. By the 1970s, machine pistols from Argentina were in use not only in their country of origin, but throughout South America.

Among the other countries whose arms manufacturers have produced sub-machine guns – and the list is a long one – half a dozen stand out, usually, but not always, by reason of their having produced just one significant weapon. Belgium was well-known for the quality

ABOVE: The MAT49 was in service with the French Army throughout most of its wars in Indo-China and Algeria. Its only serious weakness was its single-column magazine.

of its firearms even before the establishment of Fabrique Nationale d'Armes de Guerre (FN) in Herstal, to manufacture Mauser rifles in 1889, and later was to produce three interesting machine pistols: the over-complicated RAN, which thought it was a complete weapons system but was not, and never really made it past the prototype stage; the Vigneron M2, which was much less ambitious and rather more successful as a result (it was adopted by the Belgian Army, and a close copy was also produced in Portugal and Luxembourg); and in recent years, the FN P90, one of the very few attempts made to produce an all-new sub-machine gun adapted to modern needs.

FN P90 - THE BULLPUP SMG

The P90 was the first weapon to be chambered for FN's new 'sub-intermediate' round, the SS190 in 5.7mm calibre, which offered much better stopping power than the near-ubiquitous 9mm with only two-thirds the recoil. In essence, the FN P90 did for the sub-machine gun what the Steyr AUG or the FN MAS did for the assault rifle, and, consequently, it was different from any machine pistol ever seen before. To start with, it was a bullpup design, with the breech a long way behind the trigger group, which permitted a much longer barrel than was usual in a weapon which was actually shorter overall. Its magazine, which was made of transparent plastic, lay along the top of the receiver and barrel, and the 50 rounds contained within were at right angles, cross-wise, to the breech, and turned through 90 degrees as part of the loading procedure. A laser target

designator, housed below the barrel just ahead of the combined trigger guard and foregrip, replaced conventional sights, though unmagnified optical sights with a tritium niobate illuminated reticule, for use in low-light conditions, were also fitted. With the exception of the bolt, with its twin guide rods, and the barrel, virtually the whole gun was made from plastic, formed by injection moulding. All the components were produced as self-contained modules, which were interchangeable.

Loaded with 50 rounds the gun weighed just over 3kg (6.5lb) and had a cyclic rate of fire of 900 rounds per minute (rpm) in bursts. At a range of 50m (54.7yds), an experience shooter could put each shot of a 10-round burst into a 200mm (8in) circle – the sort of performance reckoned absolutely impossible with any other machine pistol at that time. The P90 went some way towards revalidating the entire SMG

Samopal M25

Calibre: 9mm Parabellum
Weight: 3kg (6.75lb)
Length: 685mm (27in)
Barrel length: 285mm (11.25in)
Effective range: 120m (400ft)
Action: blowback
Cyclic rate of fire: 600rpm
Muzzle velocity: 395mps (1300fps)
Country of Origin: Czechoslovakia

concept at a point in history when it seemed as if its days as an effective battlefield weapon might just be drawing to a close.

MADSEN SMGS

We last encountered Danish machine guns before World War I, when the Madsen *Let Maskingevaer* was a pioneering light machine gun. The original manufacturers, Dansk Rekylriffel Syndikat AS, turned into Dansk Industri Syndikat AS (DISA) sometime between the two world wars, but continued to manufacture the LMG, in refined form (and did so until the 1950s, when it switched over to the production of a GPMG, the Madsen-Saetter (see below). It also put a series of sub-machine guns, with some novel features, into production from 1945.

Its first machine pistol looked distinctly old-fashioned when it appeared that year, for it had a wooden stock. It

was of conventional blowback design, but its breech-block was attached to a slide, rather than a cocking piece, and that slide extended forwards over the barrel and wrapped around it to form a serrated grip. It contained the recoil spring, which also surrounded the barrel; the gun was cocked by pulling back on the slide with an action reminiscent of that employed in a pump shotgun. The following year, 1946, DASI produced an entirely new design, the keynote of which was accessibility to the moving parts. This was achieved by the simple expedient of making the body of the gun – its receiver, magazine holder, barrel bearing and pistol grip – in symmetrical halves, one pivoted around a pin in the receiver's rear plate and the other vertically in line with it at the rear of the base of the pistol grip; the skeleton buttstock was also attached by these same pins, and could be locked in place or swung around to lie along the right hand side of the

body. The barrel was a push-fit into the bearing, and located by a massive external knurled nut which also served to lock the two halves of the body together. Thus, cleaning and maintaining the gun was very simple indeed.

This basic system was retained when refinements of the M/46 were introduced, in 1950 and then in 1953, the main difference between them and the original being in the design of the magazine; early models were straight, later models were curved to produce a more even feed path for the 9mm Parabellum rounds for which all of them were chambered.

FINLAND'S LAHTI

We have already referred, almost in passing, to a pair of SMGs produced in Finland, the second of which was an influential design and was extensively copied, at least in one important particular. The guns – the *Konepistooli* M/26 and M/31, both known as the

■LEFT: Like the British Army, the Swedish routinely issued machine pistols – in this case M/45s – to assist the men of its armoured fighting vehicle crews.

a protective sleeve pierced with slots. It had an entirely conventional unretarded blowback action, though it was cocked by means of a piece resembling a rifle bolt, virtually identical to the one later employed by Bergmann in his MP34, described above.

However, the most important feature of the M/31 was its magazine, and that was something Lahti himself copied and refined, taking as his starting point that developed for the Thompson. This was a 71-round capacity drum magazine which, though it weighed almost 2.5kg (5.5lb) when loaded, was so located, near the gun's natural centre of gravity, that it didn't unbalance the weapon at all. Shpagin copied it line for line when he produced the PPSh-41.

Such was the quality and reliability of the M/31 that it remained in service with the Finnish Army until long after World War II. In peacetime there was little need for such a large store of ammunition, however, and surviving examples were modified to take the double-column wedge magazine as manufactured by Carl Gustav in neighbouring Sweden, which reduced the weight of the loaded weapon considerably.

Suomi, which is the Finns' name for their country – were the work of Aimo Johannes Lahti, who was in charge of design at the State Arsenal at Sakara, known as Oy Tikkakoski. The M/26 is variously described as having been chambered for the 7.63 Mauser round and for the 7.65 Parabellum; it had a large recoil buffer at the rear of the receiver, and a sharply curved box magazine to accommodate the severely bottle-necked cartridges. Comparatively few were produced, largely, one suspects, because the rounds for which the gun

was chambered were not particularly satisfactory; their ballistic performance was acceptable, but their form made them difficult to feed. In 1931, Lahti produced a revised model, this time chambered for the reliable 9mm Parabellum cartridge. The M/31 was to become a considerable success, and was later also put into production by Husqvarna in Sweden and Hispano-Suiza in Switzerland. It was a product of its times; its metal parts were machined out of the solid or forged, and it had wooden furniture, with a long barrel shrouded in

Carl Gustav M/45

Calibre: 9mm Parabellum
Weight: 3.45kg (7.5lb)
Length: 805mm (31.75in) (stock extended)
Barrel length: 205mm (8in)
Effective range: 120m (400ft)
Action: blowback
Cyclic rate of fire: 600rpm
Muzzle velocity: 395mps (1300fps)
Country of Origin: Sweden

Samopal 62 'Skorpion'

Calibre: 7.65mm
Weight: 1.3kg (2.75lb)
Length: 270mm (10.7in) (stock folded)
Barrel length: 115mm (4.5in)
Effective range: 50m (160ft)
Action: blowback
Cyclic rate of fire: 700rpm
Muzzle velocity: 295mps (975fps)
Country of Origin: Czechoslovakia

ISRAELI MACHINE PISTOLS

The history of arms' manufacture in modern Israel actually predates the foundation of the state in 1948. Armed resistance groups such as the Hagganah were making crude copies of Stens (if that is not stretching the imagination too far) before independence, and doing somewhat bizarre things with them, such as ganging four together to serve as an expedient weapon against low-flying aircraft. Soon after independence, the nascent Israeli arms industry began trying to produce something more refined, and in 1951 it unveiled its undisputed masterpiece, the Uzi.

The gun was the work of Major Uziel Gal of the Israeli Army, though it owes a very considerable debt to designs produced in Czechoslovakia. This included both Havel's Models 23-26 and the Koucky brothers' ZK 476, particularly the form of its bolt, which was wrapped around the barrel to bring the weapon's centre of gravity forward (a factor enhanced by placing the trigger group forward in the receiver and inserting the magazine through the pistol grip). Much of the barrel was shrouded within the receiver, of course, but the muzzle protruded, surrounded by the knurled locking nut which located and retained it in a bearing tube and permitted it to be changed easily. The lower portion of the forward part of the receiver was fitted with a plastic handgrip, as was the pistol

grip to the rear. Here a grip safety catch was located but the main safety lock formed part of the fire selector mechanism; both of them acted on the trigger bar directly, though independently of each other. The Uzi SMG, chambered for the 9mm Parabellum round, with a cyclic rate of fire of 550 rounds per minute (rpm), and its recoil diminished by use of primer set-back, proved popular with customers abroad, and Israeli Military Industries, which originally manufactured it, soon found difficulty in keeping up with demand. During the 1960s, a licence to produce the gun was acquired by FN in Belgium, and many were subsequently manufactured there. Later in that decade, a reduced-size version of the gun, known as the Mini-Uzi, was also produced, to rival the Ingrams MAC-10 and MAC-11 and the Skorpion. It was small and light enough to be operated with one hand, but like the others of its type, was wildly inaccurate, due to its high cyclic rate of fire and ultra-short barrel.

SPANISH SMGS

Thanks to its unenviable history of political unrest, insurrection and civil war during the 1930s, Spain was to become known as a testing place for new weapons and tactics, the rebel nationalists under General Francisco Franco being supported by both Nazi Germany and Italy, and their opponents

being aided by the Soviet Union. Both these groups of backers needed to find out if the new weapons they were developing were actually capable of functioning satisfactorily under real combat conditions. They tested everything from bombers, fighter-bombers and fighters to tanks and artillery pieces, but at least as important were the machine guns, both LMGs and GPMGs, as well as sub-machine guns and machine pistols, which they introduced. The German MP28s and MP34s, the Italian Beretta M18s, and the Soviet PPDs weren't the only SMGs in use in Spain, however, and the Government forces in particular produced their own weapons, using the long-established resources of the Basque and Catalan gunsmiths.

The earliest Spanish SMG was probably the Star S135, produced by Bonifacio Echeverria in Eibar in the Basque country and chambered for the 9mm Largo round originally developed by Bergmann for his first-generation self-loading pistols, which was rather lower-powered than the 9mm Parabellum but which had a loyal following in Spain. The S135 was a most complicated weapon, actually developed from a self-loading rifle design, with its blowback action delayed by a cam on the breech-block engaging in a recess in the receiver. It had a hold-open device which held the bolt back when the magazine was empty

(more often encountered in self-loading rifles and pistols than in sub-machine guns), and an almost unique feature – a cyclic rate which could be switched between about 300–700 rounds per minute (rpm). Despite being unnecessarily complicated, the weapon functioned well. It was tested by both the American and British Armies, though rejected as being impractical to manufacture because its construction being 'traditional'. The Labora SMG, produced in Cataluña during the last part of the civil war, was also chambered for the 9mm Largo round. It was, at first sight, a complete anomoly. At a time when one might have expected to find a very rough and ready expedient weapon being manufactured, one is confronted instead by a beautifully crafted object, made entirely by machining components out of the solid, with a difficult-to-produce annular fluted barrel and solid wooden furniture. The reason for that was quite simple, however; in Nationalist Spain at that time, there was a dearth of

■LEFT: Since its introduction in the early 1950s, the Israeli Uzi has achieved world-wide popularity, and as a consequence has sold in huge numbers.

Uzi

Calibre: 9mm Parabellum
Weight: 3.5kg (7.6lb)
Length: 635mm (25in) (stock extended)
Barrel length: 260mm (10.25in)
Effective range: 120m (400ft)
Action: blowback
Cyclic rate of fire: 600rpm
Muzzle velocity: 395mps (1300fps)
Country of Origin: Israel

Mini-Uzi

Calibre: 9mm Parabellum
Weight: 2kg (4.4lb)
Length: 305mm (12in)
Barrel length: 125mm (5in)
Effective range: 50m (160ft)

Action: blowback
Cyclic rate of fire: 600rpm
Muzzle velocity: 395mps (1300fps)
Country of Origin: Israel

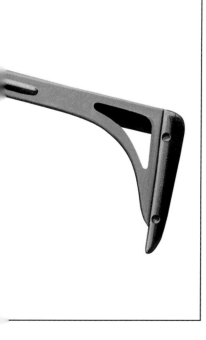

machine shops, but plenty of artisan gunsmiths with traditional tools. In its design, however, the Labora was uncomplicated – a simple unretarded blowback action, but with a rapid rate of fire thanks to a strong recoil spring being matched with a light bolt. The Spanish civil war finished just before World War II began, and during the course of that larger conflict, Spain, now under the control of Franco's right-wing Nationalist government, stayed determinedly neutral, despite Hitler's pressures. The country was largely in ruins and it was not until the mid-1940s that the arms industry, in particular, got on its feet again. Echeverria SA was one of the first companies to recover, and as early as 1944 began producing a copy of the German MP40 (with some improvements of its own added), as the Z45. One of the refinements which the company introduced was a bolt lock, which prevented accidental discharge should the weapon be dropped vertically on its butt (a not uncommon occurrence), but

perhaps more important than that refinement was a new trigger mechanism akin to that found in the Bergmann MP34, which produced single rounds under light pressure and bursts when pulled right back. The Z45 was also the first SMG to make use of a fluted chamber to ease extraction, a feature more commonly found on rifle-calibre and heavier weapons. It was available with either a folding metal stock or a fixed wooden butt. While it was certainly an improvement over the original MP40, the Z45 could not compete with more modern designs, and was probably not built later than 1950. It, too, was produced in 9mm Largo calibre, for the Spanish police and armed forces, but also in 9mm Parabellum for export purposes.

SWISS SUB-MACHINE GUNS
We have already noted how during the interwar period, German arms manufacturers turned to Switzerland to manufacture their weapons, but following the repatriation of German efforts after

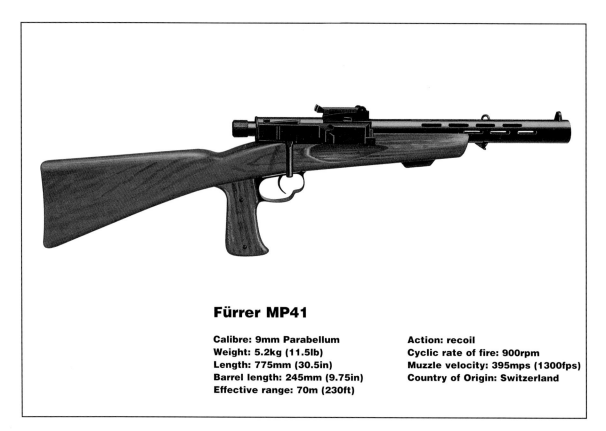

Fürrer MP41

Calibre: 9mm Parabellum
Weight: 5.2kg (11.5lb)
Length: 775mm (30.5in)
Barrel length: 245mm (9.75in)
Effective range: 70m (230ft)

Action: recoil
Cyclic rate of fire: 900rpm
Muzzle velocity: 395mps (1300fps)
Country of Origin: Switzerland

Hitler threw off the yoke of the Versailles Treaty, Swiss arms makers continued to produce military weapons both for their own citizen army and for export (though it was 1940 before they became entirely serious about it). Waffenfabrik Bern and Schweizerische Industrie Gesellschaft (SIG) were then the most important producers of sub-machine guns, but as we have seen, Hispano-Suiza, better known in the context of weapons manufacture as makers of aircraft cannon, also joined in, producing the Finnish M/31 under licence. That came about in 1943, as a result of the failure of the other two main players to actually produce the weapons they had offered to the Swiss Army in competition in 1940. The SIG contender, later offered elsewhere as the MP41, was a development of a pair of more or less unsuccessful guns produced during the 1930s, the MK33 and the MK37, the former a delayed blowback design, the latter with the retardation removed. The SIG MP41, chambered, like the others, for 9mm Parabellum rounds, and with a simple undelayed blowback action, had an annular ribbed barrel and a wooden

forestock, wooden pistol grip and wooden buttstock mated to a receiver milled from forged steel; it was heavy and unattractive, and its best feature was probably the manner in which the recoil spring and breech-block could be extracted, which was appropriated from the Beretta M1938. The Swiss Army turned it down, and accepted instead an impossibly complex design from Waffenfabrik Bern, known as the Fürrer after its designer. The Fürrer was a real anachronism, for it was a short recoil-operated locked-breech design, similar in nature to the Maxim and Vickers guns (and the Mauser and Luger self-loading pistols, of course), the toggle of which broke sideways. Quite why it was chosen over the graceless but straightforward SIG MP41 is impossible to understand, but it was, and entered service as the MP41/44. It appears that less than 5000 were delivered, for it proved all but impossible (and certainly impossibly expensive) to manufacture in the required quantities, and the Swiss Army, in panic, turned to Hispano-Suiza, which had negotiated rights to the Suomi, and

acquired its machine pistols from them instead. The MP43/44, as the Finnish gun was known in Switzerland, remained in service until 1948, when it was replaced in first line units by the SIG MP48.

THE SIG MP48 AND MP310

The MP48 was essentially an updated MP41, its wooden furniture and expensive ribbed barrel deleted, and its manufacturing process brought up to date. In fact, in that latter, SIG went a step further than any of its contemporaries, using precision casting – then in its infancy – instead of stamping or machining; such components have the precise dimensions of machining and are even cheaper than the former. It had a collapsible wire buttstock, which slid into tubes below the receiver when not in use, and reinstated the forwards-folding magazine. That latter feature was retained when the MP310 was launched in 1953. SIG fitted no other form of safety device to its SMGs, claiming that the positive discontinuity of the feed path which occured as the magazine was folded up to lie under the barrel was the

■RIGHT: Fabrique Nationale hoped that its P90 5.7mm machine pistol, largely made from plastic injection mouldings, introduced in the mid-1990s, would be the shape of things to come.

best form of security possible (though had that prevented a chambered round from being fired by accident is doubtable). The magazine housing was closed off by a retractable shutter when the magazine was folded. The only real advance the MP310 featured was its two-stage trigger, like that of the Suomi and the Bergmann MP34.

THE MACHINE PISTOL'S FUTURE?

In many circles, the question had become redundant by the 1980s. With the introduction of miniature-calibre bullpup assault rifles, which were little bigger or heavier than most SMGs and provided both fully automatic fire and the accuracy of a conventional rifle over ranges of up to about 500m (547yds), the need for small fully automatic weapons, particularly on the battlefield proper, had apparently evaporated. The 9mm Parabellum round, by then virtually ubiquitous outside the Soviet bloc, was perceived to be of only very limited value in military operations – though it was ideal for police work, where the limitation of collateral damage was a more important consideration, and the use of military ammunition, which could easily penetrate masonry walls and come out the other side with its lethal force intact, was impossible to countenance. It was generally agreed that the 'conventional' 9mm SMGs had a role to play in anti-terrorist operations, but as we have noted, these usually share more characteristics with police work than military combat, and the former's rules quite properly apply. As we shall see in the final chapter, abbreviated versions of the new assault rifles, often organised into 'families' of weapons and including general-purpose and light machine guns, were to take over almost completely from the SMG on the battlefield, leaving it in the hands of the Special Forces and paramilitary police, barely a man's natural lifetime after it had first been devised.

■RIGHT: The Spanish Star Model Z-70 – an entirely conventional pressed-steel gun, designed with an eye to cheap production, which is both easy to maintain and repair.

CHAPTER 5
THE MODERN MACHINE GUN

As we have seen, by the time of World War II, automatic weapons had become established in four categories: heavy, medium and light machine guns and machine pistols. Medium- and light guns used the same rifle ammunition, and the distinction between them had already started to blur – and in one celebrated case had already disappeared entirely – however, the SMG was still very much in a class of its own, perceived as an attractive and effective alternative to the rifle in close combat. The HMG was a singular weapon, too, and was to go through that conflict virtually unchanged.

Self-loading rifles were already in widespread use by 1939, and were to become universal soon after the end of the war which began that year, but they were still chambered for ammunition which was lethal out to 1829m (2000yds) or 2743m (3000yds), and that was entirely unnecessary (and truth to tell, had been so since the start of World War I), for the nature of combat and the distances at which most engagements were fought had been reduced to something very much less – less than 914m (1000yds) certainly, and probably half that. The first-generation self-loading rifles were as heavy, if not heavier, than the bolt-action weapons they replaced, and the weight of a desirable amount of ammunition – say 200 rounds – had not changed at all (at least, not outside the Soviet bloc, where a so-called 'intermediate' round had been adopted along with the new generation of

■**LEFT: The German MG34, when mounted on the MG-Lafette 34 tripod, and fitted with tangential sights, was effective out to its maximum range of over 3000m (9842ft).**

weapons). They had, however, shown that they could replace the light machine gun as an expedient support weapon to 'shoot in' an assault at close range, even if the British Army steadfastly refused to embrace the concept, and kept its first-generation SLRs without a burst fire capability. And then the miniature calibres arrived – 5.56mm in the West and 5.45mm in the Warsaw Pact group and its allies and clients – and with them, miniature rifles. They were to make the sub-machine gun redundant as a battlefield weapon, as we have observed (though that was a lengthy process), and to change the character of the basic infantry weapon too. Very soon, we would have 'families' of infantry weapons, all sharing a common core (the receiver and trigger group), with the other components swapped and switched around, and they would stretch from sustained-fire support weapons on the one hand, through light machine guns, assault rifles and carbines to sub-machine guns on the other. The true general-purpose automatic weapon had arrived, at long last. Somewhat surprisingly, the concept did not prove entirely popular, and its developers had to settle, instead, for having produced a new and more flexible support weapon.

EINHEITSMASCHINENGEWEHR

We first came across the concept as far back as 1916, when we were looking at the search for alternatives to the German Maxim, the MG08. The Erfurt Arsenal came up with a gun based on the adjustable Vickers 1901-pattern lock; it was lighter than the MG08, which used the original lock, but the main difference between it and the older gun was conceptual; it was designed from the outset to be just as much at home employed on a simple bipod, like the lightened MG08/15, or on a tripod in the sustained-fire role. It never got beyond the prototype stage, and almost certainly never saw combat, but it was the shape, figuratively, if not literally, of things to come.

THE MG34

Promising though the MG16 appears to have been, it would have been entirely impractical for Germany to have attempted to put it into production, and the Versailles Treaty which ended World War I forbade her such developments; we must therefore look way ahead to see the concept finally realised. In 1932 a development programme got under way in Germany, aimed at producing a completely new class of automatic weapon, both more flexible in action and more adaptable to the needs of mechanised warfare – the *Einheitsmaschinengewehr* brought up to date. At that time, both Rheinmetall and Mauser-Werke were involved in developing air-cooled light machine guns, and though neither projects went far enough to satisfy the Army, both included promising new elements. The Rheinmetall project gun was the Steyr-Solothurn S2-200. It was a production model of the so-called Söda machine gun, designed at Rheinmetall's Sömmerda factory by Louis Stange, and then passed to Solothurn in Switzerland for development and to Steyr in Austria for production.

Mauser at Oberndorf am Necker was simultaneously working up a design by Ernst Altenburger for a light machine

gun of similar capabilities to the S2-200, known as the LMG32. This was the first time Mauser had been involved in the development of a machine gun and Altenburger's design had certain very interesting basic features, but was generally unsatisfactory. With a ruthlessness which many other procurement authorities singularly failed to display around that period, the German Army ordered Rheinmetall's Louis Stange to manage the project at Rheinmetall's Dusseldorf factory, under the overall direction of Major (Dipl. Ing.) Ritter von Weber, making use of the bolt-locking procedure and barrel-changing method developed by Altenburger at

■RIGHT: The MG34 was routinely used to equip tanks and other vehicles, as well as being a light anti-aircraft gun, frequently in twin mountings, such as those shown here.

MG34

Calibre: 7.92mm
Weight: 12.1kg (26.75lb)
Length: 1220mm (48in)
Barrel length: 625mm (24.75in)
Effective range: 3000m (10,000ft)

Configuration: belt- or drum-fed,
short recoil operation
Cyclic rate of fire: 900rpm
Muzzle velocity: 800mps (2650fps)
Country of Origin: Germany

Oberndorf. This has given rise to considerable confusion, and some authorities persist in stating that the MG34 which eventually resulted was a Mauser design. It was not; it was a Rheinmetall-developed composite which used some Mauser features, for which Mauser-Werke AG later received a royalty payment from Rheinmetall-Borsig, as the former became in 1936.

A MODULAR APPROACH

The essence of the entire project was a systematic approach to the problems of providing a single gun capable of acting as either a light- or heavy machine gun (that is, as an individual weapon in the assault mode, or as a crew-served, sustained-fire weapon in the support mode) without compromising either, and to that end the accessories and even the ammunition feed method were modularised.

Experience with the MG08/15 had proved that an LMG in the assault role could not be belt-fed, and so the *Doppeltrommel 15* 75-round saddle-drum developed for the MG15 was employed, feeding rounds from different sides alternately to preserve balanced weight distribution. The *Patronentrommel 34*, as it was known in the context of the MG34, remained in service until perhaps 1940. It was not a simple device, and the gunner needed a selection of tools to load and unload it. It also required the belt-feed cover and cartridge-feed block to be

temporarily removed from the gun. More straightforward was the 50-round belt contained in a single drum, the *Gurttrommel 34*, mounted on the left-hand side of the receiver and positioned against the feed block by a simple hook and latch. It was feasible to fire the 12kg (26.5lb) gun from the hip, with the help of a sling, but more common to employ the built-in bipod, which could be located either close to the muzzle or further to the rear, near the receiver. The former was preferred, since it was more stable and hence more accurate. A lightweight tripod, the *Dreifuss 34* was also available in the LMG role, but for sustained fire, the *Lafette 34* tripod, which supported the gun in a sprung cradle, was essential. The *Lafette 34* was considered a masterpiece of design, combining low integral weight – just 21kg (46lb) – with the highest degree of stability, adjustability and flexibility. Only standard belt-feed could be used with the tripod, but that was hardly a drawback in the sustained-fire role. Belts were of 50-round capacity (so as to fit the belt-drum) but could be linked together.

For use in a vehicle the buttstock could be readily detached, and a ball-mount fitting over the barrel's protective shroud and located with a pintle could be installed. Single- and double-pedestal mounts for anti-aircraft fire were available, and in the latter case, it was a relatively simple matter to change one gun over to feed from the right hand side,

and install a central ammunition-belt box. Optical sights for both direct and indirect fire were available; they were mounted on the *Lafette* tripod, not on the gun itself, and were good out to 3000m (3300yds) in direct-fire mode and 500m (547yds) more in indirect mode. This was one of the few instances of the MG34 being fractionally less capable than its predecessors, though of course it fired the same round. Permanent metal sights consisted of a blade foresight and a notched rear sight, adjustable up to 2000m (2188yds).

QUICK-CHANGE BARREL

The gun's designers fixed on a fairly conservative 250 rounds as being the desirable interval between barrel changes; they could afford to keep the period low because the procedure was simple and straightforward, if a little unusual at first impression. With the action cocked and the bolt held to the rear, and the safety lever to 'safe', the receiver latch below the rear sight was depressed and the entire receiver rotated clockwise around an offset axial pin, through almost 180 degrees. Then, as the rear of the gun was lowered, the entire barrel simply slid out backwards, to be caught – at least in training – by a crew member wearing an asbestos glove. A cold barrel was inserted, located at the muzzle within a bearing tube which was part of the recoil booster/flash hider and formed a permanent part of the barrel sleeve,

■RIGHT: Despite its capabilities, the MG34 was designed to be extremely transportable, and could easily be carried by one man, even in the most difficult conditions.

and the receiver was returned to the operating position. When the gun was mounted on the heavy tripod, the procedure was essentially the same, save that the barrel jacket was rotated anti-clockwise instead, and the exposed barrel hooked out with anything handy (an ammunition belt tab served) as the gun could not then be tipped down. Each gun was supplied with two spare barrels, the hot one being cooled after use by any expedient means. It was quite acceptable to plunge it into cold water.

THE MOST COMPLEX LOCK – EVER
The action of the MG34 was the most complex and complicated ever seen in a machine gun up to that time or since, and that, combined with the very fine manufacturing tolerances necessary, was its chief failing. In a sense, it was like an artillery piece in miniature, employing a locking system first used 70 years previously. It was operated by a short-recoil action, the barrel moving backwards approximately 2cm (.75in), unlocking the bolt head within the first 1.5cm (.56in) before being stopped by the barrel buffer. A short locking collar was attached to the barrel, cut away through

Solothurn MG 30

Calibre: 7.92mm
Weight: 7.7kg (17lb)
Length: 1175mm (46.25in)
Barrel length: 595mm (23.5in)
Effective range: 2000m (6600ft)+

Configuration: magazine fed,
   short recoil operation
Cyclic rate of fire: 500rpm
Muzzle velocity: 800mps (2650fps)
Country of Origin: Germany/
Switzerland

■RIGHT: The Rheinmetall MG15 was originally mounted in aircraft; this one, ironically, came from a crashed German bomber, and was later used to bring down another.

two opposed 90-degree arcs; the two quarter-circles left had interrupted threads cut into them. The collar had a pair of lugs on its outside; these travelled in slots in the receiver and prevented the barrel itself rotating. A pair of cams extended to the rear from the locking collar and had two functions: they locked and unlocked the bolt head, and also contributed to the rearward acceleration of the bolt assembly. The bolt assembly was in two parts: head and body. The body reciprocated within the receiver, guided by a pair of simple lateral lugs. On its lower surface was a third lug which engaged with the trigger mechanism (or not as the case may be) and on its upper, a pair of studs which drove the belt-feed mechanism. The rear of the bolt provided the surface against which the pressure of the mainspring acted. The body had a drilling from front to back to accommodate the tubular rear portion of the head, leaving the head capable of some independent rotation around its axis, which coincided with that of the barrel. The shoulder of the bolt head featured interrupted threads machined to mesh with those in the locking collar, the engagement being

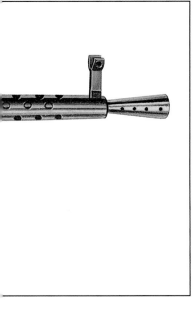

secured by rotating the bolt head through a quarter turn. This was brought about by two pairs of rollers mounted on two extended studs on the head itself, which acted against paired cams on the rear of the barrel collar, the inner pair locking the bolt head and the outer pair reversing that process during recoil. The rollers did not lock or unlock the bolt head themselves; they merely acted on the bolt head to turn it through 90 degrees and thus free it from, or engage it with, the interrupted threads in the locking collar. The face of the bolt head was machined to receive the cartridge case, and contained the simple mechanisms of both the extractor and the ejector. The extension tube to the rear of the bolt head contained the firing pin and its associated spring. The assembly was cocked during the unlocking of the bolt head, and held by a pivoting lever on the right side of the bolt head. When the locking process was complete, the tail of that lever contacted an inclined surface on the bolt body, releasing the firing pin. Acceleration of the bolt assembly, after unlocking was complete and the barrel was on its way forward again, was achieved by means of interaction between the bolt head rollers and a system of cams, both on the barrel collar and in the

receiver. And all that happened at least 15 times every second!

A HIGH RATE OF FIRE

The early MG34s utilised the same rocking trigger found on the MG13, pressing on the lower automatic trigger half and resulting in a cyclic rate of about 900 rounds per minute (rpm). The actual rate varied considerably between one gun and the next, and the spring-loaded *Patronentrommel* drum produced a distinctly faster rate of fire than a belt. Specially modified versions produced cyclic rates of up to 1650rpm, but at the price of unacceptable wear to moving parts. A short-lived lightweight variant, the MG34/41 was adapted to fire at 1200rpm, and was tested in action on the Eastern Front but it was not adopted, for by that time the MG42 project was nearing completion.

The MG34 was far from perfect, but it was undeniably successful. From its basic principle sprang a succession of even more proficient general-purpose designs, starting with the MG42 and leading to the post-World War II MG3. The MG34 was undoubtedly an excellent weapon, both in terms of quality and performance, but it was, also undeniably, a product of its time, and that meant that practically

MG42

Calibre: 7.92mm
Weight: 11.5kg
Length: 1220mm (48in)
Barrel length: 535mm (21in)
Effective range: 3000m (10,000ft) +

Configuration: belt-fed, short recoil
 operation
Cyclic rate of fire: 1200rpm
Muzzle velocity: 800mps (2650fps)
Country of Origin: Germany

speaking it was both over-specified and over-engineered. More critically, it was also over-complicated and that was its crucial failing. As early as 1935, the German authorities had begun to doubt its ultimate serviceability (or, more accurately, the ability of the five factories responsible for assembling it to produce enough of the guns to satisfy demand) and eventually, in February 1937, three companies – Grossfuss of Doblen, Rheinmetall-Borsig of Sömmerda and Stubgen of Erfurt – were asked for proposals for a new gun to replace it, specifying that accessories from the MG34 must be interchangeable, an aim which was imperfectly achieved, largely because of the different method of changing barrels eventually adopted.

A MOST UNLIKELY SOURCE
The least likely of the three contenders, the Paul Kurt Johannes Grossfuss Metall- und Lackierwarenfabrik, which had no previous experience of weapons manufacture at all (the company's main product line was sheet-metal lanterns), submitted a demonstration model, consisting of only two receiver side-walls and a novel breech-locking mechanism – which can be described as the rotating bolt-head and locking cams of the MG34 redesigned to operate on a flat plane – on 26 October 1937, and a working example in April 1938. Its barrel-changing method was unacceptable, as was its receiver

construction, but its roller-locked breech mechanism (reportedly the work of one Dr Ing. Gruner, who had no more experience of weapons design than the company for which he worked; see above for references to the same design being produced at Mauser-Werke by the team led by Wilhelm Stähle; but bear in mind that Stähle claimed to have come up with the idea in December 1942, by which time the MG42 was actually in service) was clearly an inspired piece of design, both simple and relatively insensitive to dirt and dust. As a result, the proposals of the other two would-be manufacturers were eliminated then and there, and work on the MG39/41, as it was soon to be designated, went ahead at full speed. By late 1941, large-scale field trials were underway with around 1500 of the new guns, and after favourable reports all round, it was adopted as the MG42 early the following year. The gun first saw action in North Africa in May 1942.

MG42 PRODUCTION
We cannot be sure of the full extent of wartime production – many of the records pertaining to it were destroyed – but a total of around 400,000 units seems to be a fair approximation. Component parts of the gun were made in factories all over the Reich, final assembly being carried out in a number of locations, including the Maget and Mauser-Werke plants in Berlin and by Steyr-Daimler-Puch, as

well as by Grossfuss. It was to become, in the words of one expert, 'one of the greatest of the great weapons of World War II [and] proved its effectiveness alike in the burning sands of Africa and the frozen steppes of Russia'. The MG42 never went completely out of use after 1945, for guns recovered from the *Wehrmacht* and the Waffen-SS were re-issued widely (to the re-established German Army, for example, which had to purchase them from other countries), but it did go out of production in Germany and worse still, from a would-be manufacturer's point of view, the master drawings of it went missing. The fact that the MG42 went into production in Yugoslavia as the Model 53 soon after the end of World War II perhaps gives a clue as to their whereabouts.

In the process of recreating the drawings from an existing gun, Rheinmetall made a few detailed changes and added more later, but adhered very strictly to the basic operating procedure. The most important changes concerned the bolt group. Firstly, there was the need to prevent improper field assembly: the original components could be assembled with the bolt head and the bolt housing inverted in relation to one another; the gun would seemingly go together correctly but would not function. A simple change prevented that. The second was the addition of a bolt catch inside the bolt housing to prevent (very

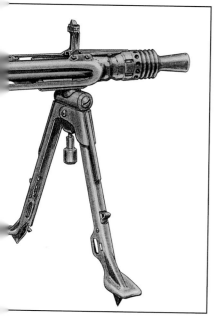

uncommon) premature unlocking, about the only operating fault of any magnitude identified in the original design. The improvement had been contemplated as early as 1944, and may have been put into effect; the records in question have been lost (but see the SIG 710, below). Conversion to 7.62mm NATO chambering apart, the most important new modification – and it was not applied to all variants – allowed the operator to alter the gun's rate of fire by changing the bolt and buffer: the V550 bolt, at 550g (20oz) and the Type N buffer produced a fire-rate of between 1150 and 1350 rounds per minute (rpm), depending on the condition of the gun and the ammunition used, while the V950 bolt 950g (33.5oz) and Type R buffer gave a more economical cyclic rate of between 750 and 950rpm.

A NEW VERSION

The remodelled gun went into production as the MG42/58, and the new German Army promptly redesignated it MG1. From that time on, it has been variously described as the MG42/59 (by Rheinmetall), and MG2 and then MG3 (by the Bundeswehr), which added sub-designators (-A1, -A2 and so on) as further detailed changes were made. As well as at Rheinmetall's factory in Dusseldorf, production of one or other version was established in Iran, Italy, Pakistan, Spain and Turkey. A very

similar gun, itself developed directly from the original MG42, was produced in Switzerland by the Federal Arms Factory at Bern, and adopted by the Swiss Army as the MG51 in 7.5mm x 54 Swiss calibre, while Hispano-Suiza and SIG also produced versions.

The latter's MG710 in 7.62mm NATO calibre was an unsuccessful competitor for the British Army's GPMG contract which went to the FN MAG (see below), but was probably the best of the MG42 developments. At the end of World War II, Allied intelligence officers routinely interrogated senior staff from Germany's arms manufacturers, and heard reports of a gun known as the MG45 from the directors of research of both Mauser-Werke and Grossfuss. They could find no trace of the gun itself, however, nor of the drawings for it. In 1961, SIG unveiled the 710-3 GPMG, which tallied 'in nearly all respects with the known details of the

ABOVE: The MG42 machine gun is widely held to have been the best weapon of its type in use during World War II: light in weight, very reliable and providing devastating firepower.

MG45', as one authoritative source says, carefully. Working backwards from the muzzle, as it were, the SIG 710-3 had a much-improved method of locating and attaching its barrel, which gave it the quickest and simplest changing procedure of any of the GPMGs – one simply pushed in on the barrel release catch on the right of the shroud, near to the point at which it met the receiver, and then lifted the barrel up and out to the rear. The fore sight was fixed to the barrel casing shroud, not to the barrel itself, and thus the gun stayed in zero. Chamber flutes were introduced, to aid case ejection, and the roller-locking system was further refined, slowing the

■ ABOVE: Some 50 years after the introduction of the MG42, its successor, the MG3, which was virtually unaltered save for its calibre, was still in service with the German Army.

cyclic rate to 550 rounds per minute (rpm) in the process.

Despite the all-round excellence of the MG1/MG3, elsewhere in Germany Heckler & Koch GmbH – which was later to be acquired by the British Royal Ordnance plc, successor to the Royal Small Arms Factory, and by then moved from Enfield to Nottingham – continued to work on the StG45 design. This design also formed the basis of the French AAT 52 (see below) in collaboration with designers from the Spanish Government's *Centro de Estudios Tècnicos de Materiales Especiales*, CETME, which we have already encountered when discussing the Heckler & Koch machine pistols. The first fruit of this collaboration was to be the *Fusil d'Assalto Modello 58*, which later evolved into the G3 assault rifle accepted for the Bundeswehr, but neither CETME nor Heckler & Koch were finished with the design yet. In succession, they produced the HK 11, a magazine-fed LMG (essentially, a G3

with an exchangeable barrel) firing the 7.62mm NATO round; the HK 12, a similar LMG chambered for the Soviet 7.62mm short cartridge; and the HK 13, chambered for the 5.56mm x 45 round which was to become the new *de facto* NATO standard. They also produced belt-fed variants of these guns (the designation has a 2 in place of the original 1, hence HK 21, HK 22 and HK 23) which are supplied with tripods for sustained-firing. Experts generally rate these guns as inferior even to the M60 (see below), though the magazine-fed versions had been entirely acceptable; this only goes to highlight the real and essential differences between light machine guns and those actually intended for use in the sustained-fire role. CETME also experimented with the locking device of the unfinished variant of the original MG42 design, and produced an experimental gun known as the Mauser-CETME light machine gun (in 7.62mm NATO chambering) and the CETME-SPAM (Special Purpose Assault Machine gun which was also known as the AMELI, an acronym of the Spanish for light machine gun, *ametrallador ligera*), which was chambered for the 5.56mm round.

THE JIMPY

One nation which did not adopt a a development of the MG42 as its first-generation GPMG was Britain, pressing though the need was to find a new sustained-fire weapon to replace the Vickers guns. Instead, the British looked to the same source as for their self-loading rifles, and adopted a design produced in the Herstal-lez-Liège factory of Fabrique Nationale, which, despite twice in three decades having been the victim of enemy occupation, had never looked back since first arriving at an understanding with John Browning in 1900. In the light of that long involvement with Browning, it comes as no surprise that the MAG (*Mitrailleuse d'Appui Générale*, sometimes rendered as *Mitrailleur a Gaz*) was similar to that of the BAR which Browning had devised during World War I. The British were to adopt it as the L7 General-Purpose Machine Gun in 1957, and British soldiers promptly christened it the Jimpy. FN inverted the bolt this time around and placed the locking shoulder in the floor of the receiver, in order to locate a roller on what was now the upper surface and use it to drive the belt advance mechanism. They added the ammunition feed path designed for the MG42 and finished up with a gun weighing in at a fraction over 10kg (22lb). This was equally at home stripped down in the LMG role; when its butt was removed, fitted with a tangential sight and mounted on a tripod for use in indirect/sustained-fire mode or as a vehicle- or helicopter-mounted gun.

CHANGING BARRELS

The barrel was locked into the body of the Belgian gun by means of an interrupted thread, and could be exchanged in a matter of seconds by simply turning the carrying handle through 90 degrees, releasing a catch and lifting the barrel and gas regulator free of the body and cylinder, exactly in the manner of the Bren gun. It was not necessary to unload the gun in order to change the barrel – cocking it and making it safe (the safety was a very positive push-through plunger). The gas regulator was adjustable, more gas being progressively fed into the actuating cylinder either to compensate for the build-up of deposits or to regulate the gun's cyclic rate, which was thus variable between 600 and 1000 rounds per minute (rpm) in a clean gun. Heavy barrels with partial stellite coatings like that used in the M60 (see below) were tested for use in the sustained-fire role but rather surprisingly were not adopted, due to manufacturing difficulties. There were also enough detailed differences between

the GPMGs manufactured by Royal Ordnance, the successors to the Royal Small Arms Factory, and the MAGs made by FN Nouvelle (likewise the succesors to Fabrique National d'Armes de Guerre and by now owned by the French government's arms supply conglomerate GIAT), to render parts for the two guns non- interchangeable.

Experts consider the MAG/GPMG to have been the best of the third-generation medium machine guns, outstripping the German M3 (and the other MG42 derivatives), the Heckler & Koch HK21, the Swiss SIG 710 and the French AAT 52, as well as the much over-rated American M60 and the Russian PK (*Pulemyot Kalashnikova*) series. In terms of market penetration, which is probably a good indicator of both its popularity and its efficacy, it was more widely disseminated than even its British predecessor, the Vickers gun, and was purchased by some 75 national governments. Forty years after its introduction it was still in production in India, Israel, Sweden and the USA, as well as in Belgium and Britain.

THE PIG

To pass from a great gun to one which, in its original form at least, was little better than mediocre, we need look no further than NATO's most powerful member. A great deal of rubbish has been written in praise of the M60 machine gun, mostly by contrasting it only with the M1919

Browning it replaced in the US Army's inventory, and ignoring its modern peers. It was never the great gun these descriptions alleged it to be, and, in its early form, was barely usable in combat; the sobriquet the soldiers themselves gave it – The Pig – says it all. The gun's early defects had little or nothing to do with its basic design, which was a sound adaptation of the one first seen in the German FG42 assault rifle (see below) with the addition of the belt advance mechanism from the contemporary MG42; rather, it was the detailed arrangement of the gun's furnishings that were poorly thought out.

This is not to say that the M60 in its original form was flawed through and through; some aspects of the gun were excellent – the stellite lining, for example, in the first 15cm (6in) of the barrel (the remainder was chromed), which permitted the gun to continue firing without causing lasting damage even when it was glowing red hot. Stellite is a patented nonferrous amalgam of cobalt, chromium, molybdenum and tungsten, bound together by a polymer and was developed by the Haynes Stellite Corporation; it represented an important step forward in firearms metallurgy. One very rigorous test, which took place at Fort Benning, Georgia, in 1967, saw a standard off-the-shelf M60 fire a 50m (164ft) belt of ammunition in a single burst; the barrel became red-white hot and each of the last few hundred rounds

MG3

Calibre: 7.62mm NATO
Weight: 11.5kg
Length: 1220mm (48in)
Barrel length: 535mm (21in)
Effective range: 3000m (10,000ft) +

Configuration: belt-fed, short recoil operation
Cyclic rate of fire: 750–1350rpm, selectable
Muzzle velocity: 825mps (2700fps)
Country of Origin: Germany

FN MAG
(Mitrailleuse d'Appui Générale)

Calibre: 7.62mm NATO
Weight: 10.15kg (22.25lb)
Length: 1250mm (49.25in)
Barrel length: 545mm (21.5in)
Effective range: 3000m (10,000ft)+

Configuration: belt-fed, gas
   operated
Cyclic rate of fire: 850rpm
Muzzle velocity: 825mps (2700fps)
Country of Origin: Belgium

fired caused showers of sparks to radiate from its outer surface. On later examination, the gun was found to be substantially undamaged.

UNWIELDY PROCEDURES
The gun's critics would say that the inordinate strength and resistance to distortion of the barrel liner was probably just as well, since changing the barrel of the early M60 was not the sort of task to be undertaken in combat. Firstly, there was no barrel handle (the carrying handle, which in any event proved too flimsy for its purpose, was receiver-mounted) which meant that the Number 2 had to grasp the barrel itself, using the asbestos mitten thoughtfully provided (at considerable expense) in the gun's spares kit and almost invariably mislaid, and secondly, the bipod on which the gun rested was integral with the barrel (as was the forward portion of the gas cylinder). Consequently, while the changeover was accomplished, the gun either had to be held up in the air, which was hardly wise on tactical grounds, or laid on the ground, with all the attendant risk that dirt and debris would foul the ammunition feed mechanism and even

the receiver itself. This poor piece of functional design (a result of wanting to get the bipod as far forward as possible, for reasons of stability) was also present in the French AAT 52 and the Russian PM, though overall, the latter gun was rated as easier to use and more reliable than the M60 by the American infantrymen who test-fired it.

The M60 had a long development history, the first steps toward replacing the aging Browning M1919 having been taken in 1944, when engineers at the Springfield Armoury mated the ammunition feed system of the MG42 with the action of the FG42 to produce an experimental gun known eventually as the T44, retaining the 7.92mm x 57 chambering of the originals. However, the new gun was to have no user-adjustable means of regulating gas flow – an unusual solution to a problem which plagued the designers of gas-operated guns from the outset. The gas passages of such a gun rapidly become fouled with the by-products of combustion, and it is normally necessary to introduce a regulator to compensate, allowing more gas into the actuating cylinder as the system became constricted. The FG42

dispensed with this necessity through a form of demand regulation known as the constant pressure system: the gas enters the cylinder through a drilling connecting it with the bore but via a second drilling in the long hollow head of the piston within. When sufficient pressure has been built up to overcome inertia (this occurs in a matter of milliseconds, during the interval between the round clearing the bore drilling and leaving the muzzle), the piston is pushed backwards to begin the actuating stroke, the first effect of which is to move the drilling in the piston head out of alignment with the one from the bore into the cylinder, shutting off the gas supply. In theory, such a system is foolproof, but in practice it is not dirt- and dust-proof, and this aspect of the M60 proved to be extremely sensitive to contamination by foreign bodies.

These (and other) drawbacks aside, the T44 was passed to the Bridge Tool and Die Company for development, a long process which saw many modifications to little real benefit. Eventually, a version known as the T161E3 was produced, chambered for the 7.62mm x 51 NATO cartridge, and it was this gun which became the M60, being authorised for issue in 1959. As if to add insult to injury, the M60 in its basic form cost over four times as much as its rather better contemporary, the MG42/59, when it was finally adopted. It saw action throughout the Vietnam War and, as a result of shortcomings observed in combat, no less than 12 major modifications (including a complete redesign of the gun's front end) were necessary to turn it into a practical infantry weapon, but before the modified gun (known as the M60E1) could be brought into general service, the entire concept of the 7.62mm-calibre infantry machine gun came under review by the US Army and was rejected, whereupon the M60 was phased out, from 1986, in favour of a switch to 5.56mm calibre and the Squad Automatic Weapon (SAW).

The M60 stayed in service as a tripod-mounted fire-support weapon in a number of variants designed for fixed or flexible mounting in vehicles and helicopters. The US Marine Corps, which had always considered its role to be rather different from that of the US Army, adopted the Echo variant, but in a version developed privately by one of the M60's civilian constructors, Saco Defense: the M60E3, which was lightened by almost 2kg (4.4lb). Saco also produced a heavy-barrel version of their modified

■BELOW: The British Army routinely employs the FN MAG (Mitrailleuse d'Appui Générale) as the GPMG L7. In the sustained fire role it is tripod-mounted.

■ABOVE: The GPMG is equally at home in the light machine gun role, when it employs its integral bipod. Weighing little over 10kg (22lb), in service it is easily portable.

gun, which incorporated all the desirable features of the abandoned M60E1 together with a further set of improvements, including provision of a forward pistol grip, notionally to make the gun more manageable as an assault weapon.

THE IMPROVED M60

In terms of performance in the field, the most significant modification incorporated into the M60E3 rectified a howling design fault in its predecessor. Originally, the M60's foresight was a simple blade, with no protection and no provision for adjustment; thus the gun had to be re-zeroed at the rear sights whenever the barrel was changed. Naturally enough, few gun teams ever bothered to do so (and it is a safe bet that none did under fire) and accepted the consequent loss of accuracy, even though that effectively invalidated the gun as a long-range fire-support weapon. The M60E3 barrels produced by Saco had foresights adjustable for both windage and elevation, so that all barrels allocated to a particular gun body could be pre-zeroed together with it; that eliminated this source of inaccuracy, at least. Needless to say, M60E3 barrels were not interchangeable with those of early-model M60s.

Unsurprisingly, considering its overall poor performance, export customers for the M60 were relatively few in number and were restricted to those client states of the US Government who received weaponry at well below its par value, such as South Korea and Taiwan, though Australia also procured small numbers. The Taiwanese, who began manufacturing the gun themselves in 1968 as the Type 57, later switched to a modified FN MAG designated the Type 74, even though they had to pay the market price for it.

OTHER GPMGS
The Belgian MAG, that is the various models of revamped MG42 and the M60, had a virtual monopoly of the market for general-purpose machine guns outside the Soviet bloc, the People's Republic of China and their client states. That didn't prevent other manufacturers from trying to penetrate it, but few succeeded outside their own countries. Ceskoslovenska Zbrojovka could be guaranteed to produce a design, even though it was equally sure that the strength of the Soviet Union's grip on its satellites would force it to use unsuitable ammunition; in Denmark, DISA produced the Madsen-Saetter; the French inevitably went their own way, with the unorthodox, blowback-action AAT 52; and the Japanese designer Kawamura Masaya produced a series of weapons, post-war, culminating in the Model 62. The Soviet Union produced the RP-46, which was essentially just a belt-fed DPM. Both the People's Republic of China and North Korea copied it precisely, and later replaced it with the PK series.

THE CZECH VZ 59
The Vz 59 was essentially an update of the successful and reliable Vz 52, somewhat simplified and certainly easier to manufacture. It was produced in two versions: with a conventional trigger group for employment by infantry units; and with a solenoid in place of its trigger, for armoured vehicles. Both light and heavy barrels, with or without an integral bipod, were available. The gun was originally chambered for the awkward Soviet 9.62 x 54R round, but it was later made available in 7.62 x 51 NATO chambering. It did not use the

integral belt-or-magazine dual feed system of the Vz 52, but belts only – an open-pocket non-disintegrating type. This allowed the Soviet rimmed rounds to be pushed through, not extracted to the rear as in the PK and others, and so considerably simplified the ammunition feed procedure.

THE MADSEN-SAETTER
By the 1950s, the Madsen LMG was certainly both obsolete and obsolescent, and the Danish manufacturers began looking round for a replacement. Unfortunately, the gun which resulted was not of the same quality of design as its predecessor, though the build quality was high. It had a major weakness: the action was locked by two lugs which were forced out of the bolt body into recesses in the receiver walls, but unfortunately it was possible to leave out the all-important lugs when reassembling the gun after cleaning it. Worse still, it could be fired in that condition.

THE FRENCH AAT 52
Only in absolute extremis have the French armed forces ever been equipped with weapons designed or manufactured outside France itself – notable exceptions occurred during World War I, when Darne manufactured Lewis guns under licence at St Etienne, and the state arsenal at Châtellerault manufactured some thousands of air-cooled Vickers guns, and also during World War II, when the Free French Army and Air Force had no resources of their own. With World War II over, France soon reverted to her policy of self-sufficiency, and produced, in quick succession, a new sub-machine gun, the MAT 49; a new self-loading rifle, the MAS 49, which used a rather idiosyncratic method of gas operation which dispensed with a conventional piston and cylinder, the gases acting directly on the bolt-face instead, with all the problems that caused in terms of fouling; and three years later, the *Arme Automatique Transformable, Modèle '52*. Usually known as the AAT 52, this was a general-purpose machine gun which, like the M60, drew heavily on German experience, the action this time being derived from the unfinished StG45 self-loading assault rifle Mauser-Werke was developing when the War came to an end, which was chambered for the reduced-power *kurz* round. The ammunition handling method was, once again, a

Heckler & Koch HK21

Calibre: 7.62mm NATO
Weight: 6.6kg
Length: 1015mm (40in)
Barrel length: 450mm (17.75in)
Effective range: 2000m (6600ft)
Configuration: drum- or belt-fed,
**   delayed blowback operation**
Cyclic rate of fire: 750rpm
Muzzle velocity: 825mps (2700fps)
Country of Origin: Germany

modified version of that developed for the MG 42.

There have to be doubts as to the applicability of the assault rifle's action at this level (and we may recall those expressed about the quality of the belt-fed Heckler & Koch weapons, above). Unusually for a modern general-purpose machine gun – or even an LMG, come to that – the AAT 52 used a delayed two-stage blowback action which frankly would have been more at home in a weapon using a less powerful cartridge than either the 7.5mm x 54 M1929, for which it was originally chambered, or the 7.62mm NATO round for which it was modified in the 1960s, despite France's partial departure from NATO. Most experts agree that it was operating at the very limits of the safe capability of its action, and it is certainly true that headspace adjustment (the clearance between the bolt-head and the rear face of the chamber) was critical; even when it was correctly adjusted, the AAT 52 tended to split its cartridge cases,

resulting in frequent jams. Nonetheless, it was also available with a heavy barrel for use, tripod-mounted, in the sustained-fire role. When the original 7.5mm version was superseded in French service by the new version firing 7.62mm NATO ammunition, it was redesignated the AAT 52/mle NF-1.

JAPANESE GPMGS
Dr Kawamura must have been a very busy man. He was managing director of NTK, which was forcibly hived off from its parent, the Japan Special Steel Company in 1946, to become a major manufacturer of agricultural tractors. When the Japanese Self-Defence Force came into being, NTK bid successfully for a contract to repair its automatic weapons, and in 1956 was asked to design a new GPMG. This appeared as the Model 5M, a conventional gas-operated, air-cooled machine gun in US .30in-06 calibre, the strongest feature of which was the easy switch-over of the belt feed from one side to the other. It

came with light and heavy barrels (both with annular cooling fins), and a substantial tripod was produced for it. The buttstock could be replaced by twin spade grips which incorporated a thumb trigger. In LMG form, the debt it owed to the pre-war Model 99 was clear. However, Kawamura's next effort was less successful. The Model 7M was a curious gun, with its gas cylinder – reduced to a very narrow, short tube – placed above the barrel, and the long piston acting on the breech-block exposed. The Model 7M never made it past prototype stage. The Model 9M, subsequently redesignated as the Model 62 when it was accepted into service in 1962, was much more successful, however. Now, the gas actuation arrangement was again orthodox, but the locking system was unusual; it incorporated a tilting block, which the head of the bolt pushed up into a recess in the piston extension, whereupon two wing lugs moved into recesses in the receiver walls and were locked there by the rearwards action of

the piston extension. Its method of extracting empty cases was somewhat odd, too; most firearms have a spring-loaded hook of some kind incorporated into the bolt face, which locates either on the rim or in the cannelure; the Model 9M, however, had a spring-loaded plunger in the lower face of the chamber, which was forced up into the cannelure as the round was chambered. As the front end of the bolt was brought back down into line, a fixed ejector hook in the upper part of the bolt face was forced down into the cannelure, gripping the case as it was forced to the rear and extracting it. It was thus a fairly complex gun, but soon acquired a reputation for accuracy and reliability.

COMMUNIST-BLOC GPMGS
The first dual-purpose gun (it wasn't really a true GPMG, but it was a solid step in the right direction) to come out of the Soviet Union, the RP-46, was a hastily conceived conversion of the Degtyarev-designed DPM, with its drum

M60

Calibre: 7.62mm NATO
Weight: 10.4kg (23lb)
Length: 1110mm (43.75in)
Barrel length: 645mm (25.5in)
Effective range: 3000m (10,000ft)

Configuration: belt-fed, gas
**   operated**
Cyclic rate of fire: 600rpm
Muzzle velocity: 800mps(2700fps)
Country of Origin: United States

magazine replaced by the two-stage belt feed, made necessary by the continuing use of rimmed cartridge cases. It worked well enough, and had the decided advantage that when the belt feed was an encumbrance – in the final phase of an assault, for example – it could be quickly replaced with a drum magazine. In the early 1950s it was superseded by the PK (*Pulemyot Kalashnikova*), which used the locking method designed by Mikhail Kalashnikov, described below. Like the RP-46 and all other Soviet medium machine guns, it used the 7.62mm x 54R M1891 round, the intermediate 7.62mm M43 round being considered insufficiently powerful, together with the closed-loop belt, and

that meant that it required a two-stage ammunition feed as developed for the RP-46 without substantial modification. The feed mechanism was located above the receiver, and withdrew a round from the belt on the rearwards stroke of the breech-block, dropped it down into the plane of the barrel, and then chambered it on the return stroke. This was a throwback to the original system Maxim had employed 80 years before. The barrel could be changed, but the procedure was by no means as quick or easy as in some of its contemporaries, since it required the gun to be unloaded and the feed cover to be lifted right up in order for the barrel to be released. The somewhat oddly designed buttstock could be

removed. A sustained fire version was little more than the basic gun equipped with a heavy barrel and mounted on a substantial tripod, which could be adapted for use in the anti-aircraft role.

which bears his name was surely the small-arms success story of the latter part of the twentieth century, not just in terms of global diffusion (though it would certainly win that contest by a walkover), but also in respect of its wholly appropriate technology. Specified for the reduced-power 7.62mm x 39 M1934 round, the AK (*Avtomat Kalashnikova*), the AKM (*AK Modernizirovanni*) and the AKMS (*AKM Skladyvayushchimsya* 'folding stock') became the standard infantry small arms, not just for the armed forces of ex-Soviet Union members and the old Warsaw Pact nations, but for

■ **BELOW: The US Army and US Marine Corps rely on the M60 machine gun for fire support at squad level. After a poor initial showing, it became an acceptable weapon.**

they did retain the capacity for automatic fire, and were quite comfortable and controllable in that role, the AK and AKM (a lightened, more easily manufactured version) fall outside the scope of this work, though the shortened AKMS, which largely replaced the sub-machine gun in the old eastern bloc, equally falls within it, such are the vagaries of modern weapons classification. For our purposes, it is the gas-management system and the two-part rotating bolt action Kalashnikov conceived that are of primary interest, since they were also employed in the RPK (*Ruchnoy Pulemyot Kalashnikova*) light machine gun and in the general-purpose PK (*Pulemyot Kalashnikova*) which, as we have seen, were actually distinctly different guns, despite the similarity of their names.

THE KALASHNIKOV ACTION

The action Mikhail Kalashnikov designed was simple enough. Gas was drawn off the barrel near the muzzle into the superimposed cylinder and propelled the piston and bolt carrier – the two were integral – through just over 8.5mm (.34in), during which time the gas pressure in the chamber dropped to a safe level. Excess gas passing into the cylinder was vented off at this point through a series of small holes drilled in the wall; there was no gas regulator. A slot in the bolt carrier engaged a stud on the bolt, and the rearwards motion was translated into a rotation through 35 degrees, releasing the locking lugs. There was no primary extraction during rotation and unlocking, but instead an oversized extractor claw was fitted in the bolt head and the interior of the chamber was fluted. The bolt, carrier and piston were now free to continue on their way, extracting the spent case, which was thrown out of the port on the right hand side of the receiver when it passed over the ejector built into the guide rail, cocking the hammer and compressing the return spring. The bolt was brought to a halt by its impact with the rear of the receiver. Relocking was accomplished in the last 8.5mm (.34in) of the bolt carrier's travel by a simple reversal of the unlocking process, and the bolt carrier and piston then continued forwards for some 5mm (.2in) to eliminate any chance of partially releasing the bolt should the carrier rebound on hitting the stop. The cocking handle formed part of the bolt carrier, and reciprocated with it.

THE AK AND PK SERIES

The action M.T. Kalashnikov designed (in 1947, while on convalescent leave from the Red Army) for the series of Soviet assault rifles and sub-machine guns much of the Communist world, including the People's Republic of China, North Korea and Vietnam, as well as the weapons of choice for guerrilla fighters the world over. Strictly speaking, though

AAT M'52
(Arme Automatique
Transformable)

Calibre: 7.62mm NATO
Weight: 9.9kg (21.75lb)
Length: 990mm (39in)
Barrel length: 490mm (19.3in)
**   (light); 595mm (23.5in)**
**   (heavy)**
Effective range: 3000m (10,000ft) +
Configuration: belt-fed, delayed
**   blowback operated**
Cyclic rate of fire: 700rpm
Muzzle velocity: 800mps (2700fps)
Country of Origin: France

However, there was no hold-open device to indicate that the magazine was empty and this is held to be the AK's most serious shortcoming. The 30-round curved magazine could not be recharged on the weapon, but had to be removed. The AK was a selective-fire weapon, single-shot or automatic fire being selected by a long change lever mounted on the right hand side of the receiver, behind the ejector port and directly above the trigger guard, which also acted as the safety catch, blocking the trigger and physically preventing the bolt face from coming back past the head of the top cartridge in the magazine (the design of the change lever has also been heavily criticised). The AKM was fitted with a cyclic rate of fire reducer, though it was complicated in design and only very marginally effective, relying on inertia during the cycle.

The differences between the AK and the AKM were substantial, but not immediately obvious. The forged and machined receiver of the former was replaced by a 1mm (.03in)-thick steel pressing, formed into a U-shape and

rivetted to inserts which comprised the locking recess, the barrel bearing and the front and rear blocks. This meant a considerable saving in weight – from 4.3kg (9.6lb) to 3.15kg (6.9lb) could be achieved, and the folding-stock version became somewhat lighter again. The rotating-bolt action which Kalashnikov designed also found its way into the light machine gun, the *Ruchnoy Pulemyot Kalashnikova* or RPK, which conveniently used the same magazine as the rifle, and into the rather different belt-fed PK, which was chambered for the old, long 7.62mm x 54R M1891 round. When the new miniature 5.45mm x 39 round was introduced in the late 1970s, the powers-that-were in Moscow sensibly decided not to try to fix something which was patently not broken, and simply converted the action of the existing automatic weapons to the new cartridge,

producing in the process the AK-74 (and variants; the AKS-74 was actually rather more common), as well as the RPK-74 LMG.

THE AMERICAN ANSWER
The US Army employed two generations of self-loading rifle – the MI and the only slightly modified M14 – in .30in-06 chambering, but by the mid-1950s interest had turned to a smaller, lighter round. This development was largely due to the work of one man, a retired US Marine named Eugene Stoner, who had joined the Armalite Corporation as Chief Engineer in 1954. Stoner had already started work on a new military self-loader which eventually became known as the AR-10, chambered for the 7.62mm NATO cartridge. It dispensed with the gas cylinder and piston and instead, like contemporary French designs, allowed the propellant gas to act directly on the bolt carrier. Its most important component was the multi-lug front-locking rotating bolt which was subsequently used in the AR-15 rifle as well as in semi-automatic shotguns. It also appeared in the Model 63 multi-purpose weapon which Eugene Stoner was to develop after he parted company with Armalite (and in Armalite's later AR-18 and a variety of later derivative designs, including the British SA-80 and Austrian AUG bullpup weapons systems); it was certainly his most important contribution to the design of modern firearms, though it was not entirely original. In fact, its design owes much to the work of Melvin Johnson two decades earlier; Johnson had produced an SLR and an LMG, both which were adopted in small numbers.

THE STONER ACTION
The Stoner action worked by channelling gas from the barrel vent two-thirds of the way between breech and muzzle through a stainless steel tube above the barrel into a space within the cylindrical shell of the bolt carrier, forcing it back. After 3mm (.125in) of free travel, during which the gas pressure in the chamber fell to a safe level, a camming slot in the internal wall of the carrier located with a pin on the bolt, causing it to rotate clockwise through 22.5 degrees around its axis, so that the seven locking lugs on the bolt head were aligned with the seven grooves cut in the barrel extension (there was a slot which housed the extractor where the eighth lug would have been). The

carrier then drew the bolt to the rear to start the operating cycle. There was no primary extraction, and re-locking was a mirror-image of the unlocking process, assisted by a coiled spring housed in the butt.

THE AR-15/M16 RIFLE
Much of the physical form of the new rifle – its straight-through profile, which carried the axis of the barrel directly to the butt, and its combined rear sight/carrying handle – was copied directly from the AR-10, as of course were the gas system, the multi-lug rotating bolt and the trigger and safety mechanisms. The AR-15 was simply scaled down from the earlier weapon to meet the requirements issued by the US Army's Infantry Board for a rifle which was not to exceed 2.72kg (6lb). In fact the AR-15 never achieved this, and an early M16 with a loaded 20-round magazine and a sling actually weighed almost 3.65kg (8lb) when loaded, with a selective fire capability and similar ballistic characteristics to the M1 rifle out to 457m (1500ft). On the face of it, this seemed a tall order, but in fact the only serious problem facing Stoner and his team was the non-availability of suitable ammunition.

A NEW CALIBRE
The choice finally fell on the .222in Remington 'sporting' round with a 3.56g (55 grain) bullet, which achieved a muzzle velocity of 920mps (308fps); however, it dropped 840mm (33in) in 400m (438yds) and developed only half the kinetic energy of the M2 .30in-06 round, which dropped 595mm (23.5in) over the same distance. Armalite turned to the Sierra Bullet Company to develop a new projectile, and the result was a boat-tailed design, which not only had more efficient aerodynamics, but also displayed a tendency to tumble on impact, negating criticism of its poor hitting power. The cartridge case was lengthened slightly to allow a greater propellant charge, which upped the muzzle velocity to 990mps (3249fps). The redefined round became the .222in Special (and in military circles the M109) until Remington launched a similar round as the .222in Magnum, whereupon it became the .223in Remington.

It is suggested that it would have been more sensible for Armalite to have developed a new round entirely, in something like 6.6mm calibre, with a projectile of between 5.2g–5.8g (80–90 grains) instead of adopting the .222in round with which Stoner had previously experimented, and a glance at the characteristics of a cartridge which falls within those parameters is instructive. The .257in Winchester Magnum, for example, with a 5.64g (87 grain) bullet produced a muzzle velocity of 1166mps (3827fps), almost identical kinetic energy to the .30in-06 round, and dropped less than 200mm (8in) at 400m (438yds). Eventually, and after very considerable political wrangling, the US military fell into line with the rest of NATO, which had in the meantime accepted a 5.56mm x 45 round of exactly identical form but with much improved ballistic characteristics, developed by FN in Belgium and known as the SS109.

THE ASSAULT RIFLE GROWS UP

The adoption of the 5.56mm x 45, (and later, by the then Soviet bloc, of the similar 5.45mm) round for military use was to have lasting ramifications for the further development of the general-purpose machine gun. We have already

PK
(Pulemyot Kalashnikova)

Calibre: 7.62mm M91
Weight: 8.9kg (19.75lb)
Length: 1195mm (47in)
Barrel length: 660mm (26in)
Effective range: 2000m (6600ft) +
Configuration: belt-fed, gas operated
Cyclic rate of fire: 700rpm
Muzzle velocity: 800mps (2700fps)
Country of Origin: Soviet Union

■LEFT: The PK family of machine guns are gas-operated, rotary bolt locked, belt-fed machine guns. The ammunition is fed by non-disintegrating metallic belts.

noted how important it is for infantry assault and support weapons to use the same ammunition, and the necessity for that certainly did not diminish with the adoption of a much smaller round. Instead, it led to the development of a new generation of still more flexible GPMGs and the sort of weapons system 'families' we touched on earlier. Eugene Stoner was one of the development's most ardent proponents. Like most designers of self-loading rifles, Stoner believed that the weapon could supplant – or at least

gun and a sustained-fire machine gun. They all shared a common receiver, and the variations were in the different barrels, the butt stocks, the ammunition feed mechanisms and the choice of box magazines or belts. Both the US Navy and the US Marine Corps put the M63 through comprehensive battle testing in Vietnam, and liked it, but no order was forthcoming.

THE BELGIAN MINIMI

There seems to have been a general reluctance to accept wholly the concept of the modular weapons system, but less resistance to the introduction of more flexible general-purpose machine guns, with interchangeable magazine or belt feed, in the new smaller calibre. First on the scene with such a weapon was FN, which had already produced its own 5.56mm assault rifle, the CAL. The new Belgian machine gun came to be called the Minimi, and by the Americans, whose army also adopted it, the M249 Squad Automatic Weapon. The FN Minimi prototypes were produced during 1974, and they aroused considerable interest. However, the development process went slowly, even for the notoriously conservative weapons industry, and it was 1982 before volume production began. That said, it is worth noting that the Minimi came to the commercial market as a properly developed design, finished and complete in every sense – a telling contrast to the M60, for example. It was light enough, in theory anyway, at slightly under 7kg (15.5lb) 'dry', to function as an assault weapon, and with that in mind, was equipped from the outset to accommodate both conventional box magazines (it accepted FN's own and those from the M16) and belted ammunition. The latter was either fed free or was contained in a lightweight plastic box. There was no modification necessary to switch between belt and magazine. The Minimi came equipped with a conventional rigid skeleton stock, or with an even lighter extendible version, and the quick-change barrel, which utilised a system much akin to that of the MAG, was available in two lengths. Its kinship with the MAG was also manifest in the tripod and accessory sights used in the sustained-fire role.

The Minimi, slightly modified to meet US production methods, was adopted for the US armed forces the same year it went into series production. The US Government made an initial order for

supplement – the light machine gun in the role of support weapon at the squad level, and he developed a heavy-barrelled version of the AR-10, fitted with a bipod. He then went on to produce a more basic conversion to belt-fed ammunition, at which point he developed a quick-change barrel and a traversing tripod, too. He had no takers for his expedient LMG, nor for the 'carbine' version, with its shortened barrel, but that didn't stop him producing prototypes of the AR-15 in the two configurations, and here he had rather more success. Colt's put the short barrelled version into production as the Commando – with a further refinement, a telescoping butt stock – and saw it used extensively in Vietnam and afterwards by US Special Forces, and the magazine- and belt-fed LMG was manufactured as

the Colt Automatic Rifle (an obvious though unacknowledged homage to John Browning), but with poor results.

SYSTEM 63

Stoner was actually more committed to the multi-purpose/multi-role weapon than most designers, as his next offering was to show. System 63, as the family of weapons was originally known, was designed after Stoner left Armalite, and was produced by Cadillac Gage, which was better known for its light armoured vehicles. Not entirely surprisingly, it used the Stoner action, but this time with a conventional gas cylinder and piston, in order to minimise fouling. It comprised 15 assemblies in all, and could be made up in five forms: as a sub-machine gun, a carbine, an assault rifle, a light machine

■ LEFT: Stoner's M63 was a brave
attempt to create a modular infantry
weapons system encompassing SMG,
assault rifle, LMG and sustained-fire
machine gun.

to use the more powerful round,
improving that gun's characteristics
considerably, too.

By the time it had celebrated 10 years
in series production, the Minimi had been
adopted by a dozen nations, and had
spawned at least two clones, the South
Korean K3 and the Taiwanese Type 75. It
also had competition, in the shape of the
Ultimax 100 from Singapore, which had
actually appeared on the international
market at around the same time as the
Belgian gun, and the Israeli Negev, the
latter being very similar indeed to the
Minimi in both its basic character and
operating characteristics and in the
extent of its versatility. Elsewhere, a
selection of lighter selective-fire weapons
chambered for the 5.56mm round came
onto the market during the 1980s.

WEIGHT OF FIRE

The main question mark against the new
generation of lightweight GPMGs
concerned their ability to lay down a
sufficient weight of supporting fire at
medium to long range. The maximum
effective range of a 5.56mm weapon is
usually quoted as around 800m (875yds)
certainly, the round – particularly the SS
109 round – is lethal much farther out
than that, but the general consensus was
that at anything much over 805m
(880yds), the all-important beaten zone
fell badly out of shape, and the overall
effect became uncertain. In the event, the
world's armies retained their larger-
calibre weapons – MAGs and M60s, for
example – for use in the fire
support/sustained-fire role, but they also
had a still more powerful card to play in
the shape of the heavy machine gun,
chambered for 12.7mm ammunition or
something very similar. We have touched
briefly already on the genre in its most
effective, and certainly most popular
form, that of the Browning M2, one of the
longest-serving of all the firearms
developed in the twentieth century. The
Browning 'Fifty', in its original, water-
cooled, form, was first fired on 15 October
1918, some four weeks before World War
I came to an end, and an air-cooled
version was tested the day after the
Armistice, on 12 November. Both types
were employed during World War II, but

68,000 units, and the Belgian gun,
manufactured by the company's US
subsidiary, entered the inventory as the
M249 Squad Automatic Weapon; this was
also termed SAW, a new classification
which sat – rather uncomfortably at first
– between the sustained-fire M60 and the
M16, taking over the former's role as
squad fire support weapon. The only
serious problem the American military
encountered involved the continued use

of M109 ammunition instead of the more
powerful Belgian-developed SS 109
round; specifically, there were occasional
problems in pulling the ammunition belt
through into the action, and the cyclic
rate when magazine-fed (when that
problem is naturally eliminated) was
deemed to be too high. Not surprisingly, a
switch to SS 109 ammunition solved the
problems entirely, and a new version of
the M16, the M16A2, was also developed

Stoner M63 A1
(Sustained fire role)

Calibre: 5.56mm NATO
Weight: 5.65kg (12.5lb) (gun only)
Length: 1025mm (40.25in)
Barrel length: 550mm (21.7in)
Effective range: 2000m (6600ft) +

Configuration: belt-fed, gas
**   operated**
Cyclic rate of fire: 700rpm
Muzzle velocity: 990mps (3250fps)
Country of Origin: United States

by 1933, the air-cooled M2, as it was then known, had become the dominant form. When he produced the heavier version, John Browning had seen no reason to change from the simple short recoil system he had devised from his .30in M1917 gun, and the gun has survived to the end of the twentieth century in very much its original form. It went out of production during the 1970s, but returned in original and (several) modified forms when would-be rivals failed to live up to their promise. The .5in round they fired, at a cyclic rate of around 500 rounds per minute (rpm), came in a variety of forms – standard jacketed ball, armour-piercing, incendiary and tracer – and was effective out to 1829m (2000yds), and considerably more when fitted with artillery-type dial sights and used in the indirect-fire role. It was a little heavy for use by foot soldiers – the gun weighed 38kg (84lb) and the essential tripod a further 20kg (44lb) – but it was very easy to mount on even lightweight vehicles.

BROWNING M2 ALTERNATIVES
There was not nearly such urgency to seek replacements for the Browning M2HB heavy machine gun, as there had

been to replace the old, first-generation medium guns, though there were a significant number of improved designs under development by the 1960s. More significant, perhaps, were the new types of ammunition in the familiar 12.7mm-calibre intended to supplement further the jacketed ball round which was most commonly employed. One of them used technology developed for tank main guns, and consisted of a sub-calibre dart mounted in a discardable full-calibre guide which fell away soon after the round left the muzzle. These so-called SLAP (Saboted Light Armour Penetrating) rounds were fully capable of penetrating the protection of armoured personnel carriers out to a range of more than 1km (1094yds). An alternative, developed in Norway, was a remarkable combination of armour piercing, incendiary and fragmentation round.

THE DOVER DEVIL
The adoption of these specialised ammunition types caused an additional problem, however – they were less effective than conventional jacketed rounds against infantry targets, while at the same time being very considerably more expensive. The American AAI

Corporation, working in conjunction with the US Army's Armament Research and Development Command, solved the problems of having the two types of ammunition ready to hand with a gun known generically as the general-purpose heavy machine gun (GPHMG) but usually called the Dover Devil after the town in New Jersey where it was developed. Building on experimental work carried out during and since World War II in calibres heavier than 12.7mm, the Dover Devil incorporated twin ammunition feed-paths, one from each side of the receiver, permitting two quite different types of ammunition to be available, selectable by a simple switch. The Dover Devil was lighter and much simpler in operation than the M2HB it was designed to replace, with fewer moving parts. However, after protracted tests, the US Army decided that it did not offer significant enough advantages over the older gun to warrant the change, and the project was shelved. AAI tried to continue developing the gun on its own, but with no market in sight eventually cancelled the project completely. A gun developed in Singapore by the state-owned Chartered Industries (CIS), which also produced the 5.56mm Ultimax 100, clearly owed a great deal to the GPHMG project. The 50MG, as the gun was called, was a modular design comprising five basic group assemblies and, like the Dover Devil, was capable of taking its ammunition from either side. It went into production, but failed to find export markets.

Such procurement as there was of new 12.7mm HMGs tended to go to traditional sources of Browning M2HB guns: licensees such as Saco and Ramo in the USA and FN in Belgium. Both the American companies developed lightweight versions of the venerable gun – the unloaded weight of their new models was around 26kg (57lb) – but surprisingly enough, not even the added provision in both cases of a quick-change barrel system persuaded customers to switch their allegiance from the original.

The Dover Devil started life in 20mm calibre, and was not the only would-be infantry weapon to deviate from the 12.7mm standard. In Belgium, FN – which showed itself quite prepared to pioneer the development of new ammunition types where necessary – also opted for a bigger, heavier projectile, this time in 15mm x 115 form, but was deterred by excessive barrel wear in the prototypes and subsequently adopted a 15.5mm x 106 round for the gun which was to become the BRG-15. This time, the novel feature of the new projectile was the addition of a plastic driving band, a device common to artillery, but previously unknown in an infantry weapon. A variety of ammunition types including PB-AP (plastic banded – armour piercing), which could penetrate 19mm (.75in) of armour plate at a range of 800m (805yds), and PB-HEPI (plastic banded – high explosive penetrating incendiary) were produced, as were saboted sub-calibre AP rounds. Like the 50MG and the Dover Devil, the BRG-15 was equipped with a dual-feed mechanism to facilitate the changeover from one ammunition type to another. A heavy gun, at 60kg (132lb) unloaded, it was nevertheless capable of deployment from nothing more robust than the tripod and pintle mounts normally employed for the M2, thanks to an internal recoil buffer system.

■RIGHT: The US Army and US Marine Corps adopted the 5.56mm NATO calibre FN Minimi in 1984, in place of the M60, as the Squad Automatic Weapon (SAW) M249.

The development costs for the BRG-15, while they were not a matter of public record, clearly put an intolerable strain on the financing of FN, for mid-way through the project, control of the company passed into foreign hands, and the successor, Fabrique National Nouvelle Herstal (FNNH) became a subsidiary of the French state-controlled arms maker GIAT.

SOVIET HMGS

The projectile weight of the various types of load used in the 15.5mm round varied

considerably but the kinetic energy contained in such a projectile travelling at a velocity in excess of 1000mps (3282fps) is enormous; in the last part of the twentieth century, only one ammunition type in use by machine guns (as opposed to cannon) came even close to

■RIGHT: The FN Minimi didn't offer as much flexibility as the Stoner M63, and was rather more successful as a result. It could be either belt- or magazine-fed, and in the latter configuration used NATO-standard rifle magazines.

it in performance: the 14.5mm x 114 round employed by the Russian KPV (*Krupnokakilbernyi Pulemyot Vladimirovna*), a simple, almost crude weapon devised in the years immediately following World War II. The KPV was widely deployed in both the anti-vehicle and anti-aircraft roles, in the latter in towed or vehicle-borne single-, twin- or quad-mounts styled ZPU (*Zenitnaya Pulemyotanya Ustanovka*). It was

extensively deployed in North Vietnam during the war there. This gun was clearly too heavy for unmounted infantry purposes, and in that role, the ex-Soviet forces replaced the DShK by a 12.7mm gun employing the Kalashnikov rotary-bolt action known, after its designers G.I. Nikitin, J.M. Sokolov and V.I. Volkov, as the NSV. Available in tripod- or vehicle-mounted versions, the NSV was effective out to 2000m (1.25miles), and was

otherwise comparable in every way with the Browning M2HB.

MACHINE GUNS IN THE AIR
Until the machine gun was employed aboard aircraft, aviators had very little to fear from each other; hitting one aircraft in flight from another, even at the slow speeds attainable in 1914, was far from easy with a pistol or rifle, and a single hit was unlikely to do serious damage. As

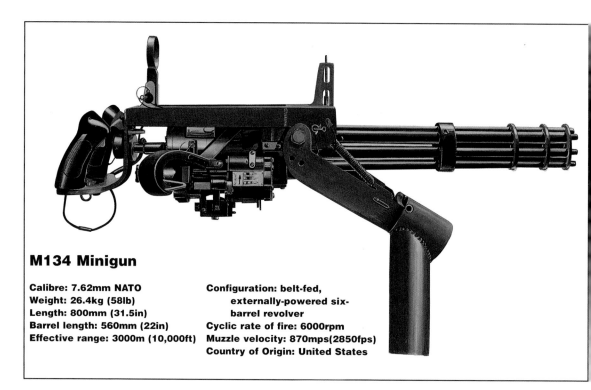

M134 Minigun

Calibre: 7.62mm NATO
Weight: 26.4kg (58lb)
Length: 800mm (31.5in)
Barrel length: 560mm (22in)
Effective range: 3000m (10,000ft)

Configuration: belt-fed,
externally-powered six-
barrel revolver
Cyclic rate of fire: 6000rpm
Muzzle velocity: 870mps(2850fps)
Country of Origin: United States

early as 1912, Isaac Newton Lewis's gun had been fired from an aircraft, and it was to go on to become very popular, particularly as a flexibly mounted gun for use by observers in multi-seat aircraft, but the main problem inherent in fitting automatic weapons to aircraft was how to site them. To be really effective, they had to be parallel to the axis of the fuselage, and in early models, at least, this meant adjacent to the pilot so that he could deal with the inevitable stoppages and that put the the gun behind the propeller. A number of inventors tried to develop interrupter gear to prevent the gun from firing when a propeller blade was actually in line with the barrel, and the best system was devised by Raymond Saulnier in France, though Saulnier was sufficiently unsure of the effectiveness of his system to fit substantial steel deflector plates to the propeller blades, too. The system worked after a fashion, but not well enough to suit the inventor, who had far more pressing demands on his time anyway. A French ace-to-be named Roland Garros was less demanding. He solved the problem temporarily (and it must be said crudely) in March 1915, when he disconnected the interrupter gear and relied on the deflector plates alone to keep him from

shooting his own propeller to pieces, and it worked; in the following three weeks, Garros shot down five German aircraft. However, he was then forced down himself, and though he set fire to his machine, the Germans were still able to deduce the method behind his seeming madness. They were unwilling to adopt such an ugly solution, for they immediately gave the problem to the Dutchman, Anton Fokker, designer of some of the best aircraft of the day. Within two days, Fokker came up with a working interrupter device, based on an invention patented by a Swiss named Schneider, and it was soon in action. Almost incredibly, it took the French and British almost a year to come up with a satisfactory synchronisation gear of their own, and in that period the German Air Force had clear air superiority.

By the start of World War II, fighter aircraft were regularly mounting eight machine guns, and the first heavier cannon had also been employed. By the end of that conflict, the .5in Browning was the airborne machine gun of choice for the Allies, while the *Luftwaffe* relied on MG131s and MG151s, in 13mm and 15mm calibres respectively, from Rheinmetall and Mauser, and both sides employed versions of the Hispano-Suiza

20mm and 30mm cannon. As aircraft got faster, they naturally got harder to hit, and already the search was on for a means of increasing the cyclic rate of fire from the 1200 rounds per minute (rpm) or so which was all that 'conventional' machine guns could reliably maintain, the only means of increasing firepower otherwise available being to mount more and more guns, making the aircraft heavier and heavier and degrading their performance in the process. One of the methods of achieving that higher cyclic rate was to return to the externally powered gun, as first devised by Richard Jordan Gatling a century earlier. By way of experiment, Gatling himself had fitted an electric motor to his guns, and by that means had achieved a cyclic rate of fire of 3000rpm from a gun chambered for the .3in Krag-Jorgensen rifle round.

THE GATLING GUN REINVENTED

With the realisation that any significant improvement on the performance of existing heavy machine guns would require a radical rethink in their design, Gatling's work was reappraised, and as World War II drew to a close, the US Government commissioned Johnson Automatics, Inc., a small private arms manufacturer set up by a retired Marine

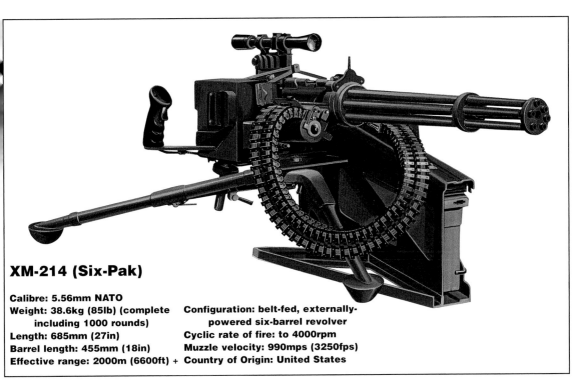

XM-214 (Six-Pak)

Calibre: 5.56mm NATO
Weight: 38.6kg (85lb) (complete including 1000 rounds)
Length: 685mm (27in)
Barrel length: 455mm (18in)
Effective range: 2000m (6600ft) +

Configuration: belt-fed, externally-powered six-barrel revolver
Cyclic rate of fire: to 4000rpm
Muzzle velocity: 990mps (3250fps)
Country of Origin: United States

■ABOVE: The 7.62mm Minigun was readily adopted for use in helicopters, as its inordinately high rate of fire allowed even a rapid pass against enemy positions to be very effective.

Corps colonel, to look into the possibilities of updating Gatling's design. Johnson located a Model 1883 gun in .45in chambering in working order, together with a supply of usable

ammunition. He repeated Gatling's own work almost step for step, but thanks to the improved performance of electric motors, bettered his results considerably: the modified gun fired 50-round bursts at a cyclic rate calculated to be equal to 5800 rounds per minute (rpm).

THE VULCAN CANNON

As a consequence of Johnson's work, the US Army awarded a development contract to the armaments division of the General Electric Corporation in June 1945, and early in the following year, Project Vulcan resulted in a prototype gun known as the T45, which varied hardly at all from the operating principle Gatling had established 80 years earlier. The main distinction was in the firing method; Gatling used percussion caps, while the Vulcan employed electric ignition.

It was to take a further decade to put the gun, now designated the M61 Vulcan, into production, firstly in 20mm calibre. However, it rapidly became the standard by which others were measured, while acquiring its share of imitators, as well as forming the basis for an entire new family of super-fast externally powered machine guns in everything from 5.56mm to 30mm calibre.

The 20mm M61 Vulcan went into service with the US Air Force in 1956 in the Lockheed F-104 Starfighter, and later versions were to become standard equipment for US aircraft. It also won the approval of both the US Army and the US Navy, the Army adopting it as the M168 to form the basis of a towed or vehicle-mounted air defence system. The Navy commissioned GE to build the autonomous Phalanx close-in weapons system around it, to defend ships against missile attack at short range, and also used it in the EX-84 Universal Mount aboard light craft. A lighter, three-barrelled version of the gun, called the M197, was employed by both the US Army and the Marine Corps to arm Cobra attack helicopters, and by the Air Force in fixed-wing gunships.

The essence of the M61 Vulcan cannon was its simplicity. In fact, the most complex feature of the entire gun was the way in which up to 100 rounds per second were presented to its multiple breeches; quite an engineering undertaking in itself. Ammunition was delivered to the gun mount in standard disintegrating-link belts; they passed through a de-linker and into a drum. Individual rounds were then transported from the drum to the gun itself by means of an Archimedes screw. In other applications, 'loose' ammunition was fed directly from a large-capacity drum, once again by means of a helical screw.

THE 7.62MM MINIGUN

With the M61 cannon in series production, development engineers at General Electric began to examine the possibilities of constructing a similar gun in rifle calibre. The US Air Force-funded project got underway in 1960. By late 1962 a prototype was under test, and two years later the GAU-2B Minigun, firing the 7.62mm x 51 NATO round, was adopted. The Miniguns were mounted in SUU-11 pods designed to be slung beneath the wings of aircraft or on the undercarriage of helicopters, but the first combat operations in which they participated saw three of them mounted transversally inside the fuselage of an antiquated C-47 Dakota, firing out through what had originally been the aftermost cabin windows and the cargo door, while the pilot executed a tight

'pylon turn' around a ground target below. Widely known as Spooky or Puff the Magic Dragon, from a song popular at the time, the AC-47s soon proved to be effective ground attack aircraft, and the concept was expanded and extended, firstly into Shadow and Stinger and subsequently into Specter, converted C-130 Hercules, initially armed with four Miniguns, two of which were later removed and replaced by a pair of 40mm Bofors or occasionally, in the Pave Aegis version, by one Bofors and a specially-adapted M102 105mm howitzer.

THE 5.56MM MICROGUN

The next step General Electric took was to reduce the concept still further, and produce a prototype multi-barrelled externally-powered gun in 5.56mm calibre, but this time the US Government proved less than enthusiastic. The Microgun was in fact rather more flexible than its bigger-calibre counterparts, for while they could fire selectively at 1000, 2000, 3000, 4000 or 6000 rounds per minute (rpm), a simple matter of controlling the speed of the drive motor, it was infinitely variable between 400

M61/M 168 Vulcan

Calibre: 20mm
Weight: 136kg (300lb) (gun only)
Length: n/a
Barrel length: n/a
Effective range: 6000m (20,000ft)
Configuration: belt-fed, externally powered six-barrel revolver
Cyclic rate of fire: to 6000rpm
Muzzle velocity: 670mps (2200fps)
Country of Origin: United States

and 10,000 rounds per minute (rpm), the higher maximum figure being due to the reduced revolving weight of the much smaller gun. Ammunition for the Microgun was contained in a pair of factory-packed 500-round cassettes, mounted one each side of the gun. As the last round in a cassette was expended, the feed automatically switched over to the full cassette, while the empty was ejected and replaced. The gun was regularly demonstrated to be able to fire 2500 rounds in a single burst at a rate of 4000rpm. Nevertheless, though it was tested under the designation XM214, the Microgun was never adopted by the US Armed Services, and the project was later suspended. As one commentator put it, the Microgun 'appears to have been an example of a weapon produced to meet a tactical requirement that has yet to emerge', and given the practical limitations on its role imposed by its ammunition, that is scarcely surprising.

THE .50IN GAU-6

There was still a gap to be filled, however – between the 7.62mm Minigun and the 20mm rotary cannon – and GE promptly stepped into it with a rotary multi-barrel gun firing the tried-and-tested 12.7mm round. The original intention was to use 12.7mm-calibre ammunition as a test-bed, and to produce a gun chambered for a new 10mm round to be developed simultaneously, but in the event, the planned new calibre was abandoned, and instead, development of the GECAL 50, as the gun came to be called, went ahead in 12.7mm form. The first prototype, the GAU-6, was a six-barrelled gun, limited to a cyclic rate of 4500 rounds per minute (rpm) by the strength of the individual links in its ammunition belt.

LATER FORMS OF THE GECAL 50

Production-model GECAL 50s later appeared in two forms: a six-barrelled gun firing up to 8000rpm and a lighter, three-barrelled gun capable of half that. Mounts for both helicopters and light vehicles were produced as interest developed in a gun, which combined relatively low weight and the proven hitting-power of the .5in round. There was an even bigger variant, too – the GAU-8A 30mm cannon which formed the basis of the A-10 Thunderbolt ground-attack aircraft. The GAU-8A was a remarkable gun in many ways, and soon passed into the mythology out-of-the-ordinary weapons create for themselves,

■ABOVE: The US Army and US Air Force employ the Vulcan in both six- and three-barrelled forms (like the M197, shown here), mounted on the M113 APC chassis, for mobile air defence.

but there was nothing mythological about its performance. Firing rounds of solid shot composed of tungsten and depleted uranium, which destroyed armoured vehicles by kinetic energy alone, at a cyclic rate of 4200rpm the gun was rumoured to generate more thrust than the A-10's main engines – and since it acted in the opposite direction, pilots were forbidden to fire more than short bursts!

THE HUGHES CHAIN GUN

Richard Gatling's rotating-barrel-and-chamber method was not the only one examined in the course of trying to improve further the performance of the heavy machine gun. A relative newcomer to the world of armaments manufacture, the Hughes Tool Company set out in 1970 to develop a 7.62mm machine gun with the same overall dimensions as the 'conventional' (though very complicated) recoil-operated M79/M219 gun adopted in 1960 as the co-axial gun for the M60 main battle tank. A prototype called the Externally-Powered Armored Vehicle Machine Gun was produced (its name was, thankfully, reduced at once to the rather handier EPAM). Its action was driven and regulated by a gearbox and a series of cams. It worked well enough on test, but was very clearly over-complicated for a weapon which would inevitably have to be field-serviced, and a comprehensive rethink produced a far

simpler action driven by an industrial roller chain such as those used to drive most motorcycles.

An endless loop of chain provides both the motive power for the gun and timed its operation. It passes over four sprockets arranged in a rectangular pattern, one of which drives it while another takes off power to supply the ammunition feed system; the other two are idlers, there to provide the necessary geometry and maintain tension. One link of the chain, known as the master link, contains a cam follower, which is permanently engaged with a slide acting in a transverse slot in the lower surface of the bolt carrier, which carries the bolt itself, (and the integral extractor) backwards and forwards as the chain passes around its sprockets. The resulting gun is much less complex than the rotary cannon, and considerably smaller and lighter (its rate of fire does not approach theirs, but was never meant to), but shares with them the inherent reliability of an externally powered gun – thus the very failing Maxim once used to justify the ascendancy of the automatic, self-powered gun over its manual rivals eventually turned into an asset after all.

■ABOVE: The AH-64 Apache attack helicopter has the Hughes Chain Gun as its main armament, linked to a helmet sighting system, and aimed simply by the gunner moving his head.

By 1972, Hughes Tool was producing a Chain Gun (the term was registered as a trade mark) in 30mm calibre which was adopted by the US Army as the M230 in 1976, and became the main gun armament of the AH-64 Apache attack helicopter, mounted in a chin pod and controlled by a computerised link to the pilot's helmet. A second model, in 25mm calibre, became the M252 Bushmaster cannon mounted on the M2/M3 Bradley AFV and elsewhere, while a 7.62mm version known as the EX-34 was adopted as the co-axial machine gun for the M1 Abrams MBT, the British Challenger II MBT and Warrior AFV.

CASELESS AMMUNITION

A solution to the problem of dealing with spent cartridge cases also harks back to the very earliest days of the machine gun. We noted that in one respect the introduction of the brass cartridge case was a retrograde step, because its predecessor, the paper cartridge, was entirely consumed, and had no need to be ejected when spent.

However, late twentieth century materials technology held out the hope of a return to that state of affairs, the propellent charge itself being formed into a durable, handlable entity, with its projectile encapsulated within it. By the early 1990s, at least one firearms manufacturer had unveiled a design study for a light automatic weapon utilising this ammunition technology in the square-section 4.85mm x 33 caseless format developed to prototype stage by

the Dynamit Nobel company in Germany. Similar research also took place in the United States. Other research topics in ammunition technology in the last decade of the twentieth century included the replacement of conventional projectiles by saboted sub-calibre flechettes or darts, and the emulation of experiments already well advanced in artillery pieces with a view to substituting liquid propellent charges for solid, whether encased in plastic or traditional metal, or caseless. The ubiquitous micro-processor found employment, too, in matching the physical performance of the machine gun with environmental variables such as windage, humidity and temperature, in an effort to ensure that more rounds were first-time hits in the direct-fire role, once again replicating new technology already introduced into the world of heavy artillery.

INDEX